Whose Millennium?
Theirs or Ours?

Publication of this book was assisted by a contribution from
THE JUDY RUBEN OUTREACH FUND

Whose Millennium?
Theirs or Ours?

Daniel Singer

Monthly Review Press
New York

Copyright © 1999 Monthly Review Press
All Rights Reserved

Library of Congress Cataloging-in-Publication Data

Singer, Daniel, 1926-
    Whose millennium? theirs or ours? / Daniel Singer.
        p.   cm.
    Includes bibliographical references and index.
    ISBN 0-85345-946-0 (pbk.) — ISBN 0-85345-943-6 (cloth)
    1. Socialism. 2. Capitalism. 3. Communism. 4. Communism—Soviet
Union. 5. Communism—Poland. I. Title. II. Title: Whose
millennium?
HX73.S557 1999
332.12'2—dc21   98-48885
                                                                    CIP

Monthly Review Press
122 West 27th Street
New York, NY 10001

Manufactured in the United States of America
10 9 8 7 6 5 4 3 2 1

Contents

Acknowledgments

I would like to thank Harry Magdoff, who put at my disposal not only his wisdom but also his deep knowledge of the workings of the capitalist economy, and Paul Sweezy for his warm encouragement. The intellectual influence on my writings of István Mészáros will be perceived by anyone familiar with his seminal *Beyond Capital.* These are debts that cannot be repaid in footnotes. I also want to express my gratitude to Michael Yates who generously helped me, with his great expertise and documentation, in the chapter on labor; to Tom Ferguson, whose sure grasp of issues of international finance was of great assistance for the chapter on globalization; and to Pablo Gonzales Casanova, who, while I was giving lectures in his seminar at Mexico University (UNAM), prompted the idea of developing them into a book. I wish to thank K. S. Karol, Michael Löwy, and John Mage for their stimulating comments on the original manuscript. While all of them, I am sure, share my ideals, naturally none is responsible for the ideas expressed in this book. Similarly, my very gifted editor, Christopher Phelps, can be praised for the clarity and smoothness of the text, but should not be blamed for the literary quirks and predilections of the author.

Finally, I want to pay tribute to Judy Ruben. Collaboration on an earlier book led to a very warm friendship, and we were looking forward to working together again on this one. Alas, Judy is gone. All I can hope for is that this book makes a small contribution to the struggle for a different world, to which Judy devoted her life.

Paris, France
December 1998

Introduction

Their Future or Ours?

THE YEAR 1989, with the East European regimes tumbling in quick succession, could have been greeted as a sign that people do count and that obsolete systems are, ultimately, swept away. Instead it was hailed, illogically, as proof that our system will go on for ever. Naturally, in its extreme form—Francis Fukuyama's pseudo-Hegelian proposition that history has come to an end—such propaganda could not last. But the message which mattered, namely that the reign of capital is eternal, is still triumphant. Do you recall the Reaganite charge describing the Soviet Union—how distant it now seems—as a hell from which there is no exit? The argument has now been cleverly reversed. It is our world—hell, paradise, or purgatory—from which, we are told, there is no possible escape.

You may be repelled by a Western world with its mass unemployment in Europe and its working poor in America, shocked by the contrast between the growing wealth and the spreading poverty, the gap between the have and have-not nations, alarmed by uncontrolled growth clashing with our environment, appalled by open racial discrimination and the more concealed bias against women. You may protest and even try to do something about it. But if you move beyond the symptoms and question the system that is at the root of the trouble, you will get the same answer, like a broken record: there is no alternative. T.I.N.A., *Tina,* was the nickname given to Maggie Thatcher, the British prime minister, who proclaimed more often than anybody and in shriller tones that there was and could be no way out of our predicament. But she was not alone. Broadcast throughout the globe by the huge machines of propaganda, first thunderously, then more surreptitiously, the message has penetrated

1

people's minds, invaded their unconscious. Tina is now the unwritten premise of virtually the whole political debate.

This book is a presumptuous pebble trying to upset the juggernaut. Its writing was inspired by a passionate reaction against the ruling gospel preaching that profit provides the only possible social relationship between human beings and the market the only guarantee for democracy. The need to fight back was thought particularly important because, whatever the objective reasons for its current domination, the power of the establishment and the arrogance of its spokesmen are also due to our weakness, to our acquiescence and our resignation. The ambition of this book is to discard Tina, to start a genuine debate over a possible alternative, and in the search for it—at the risk of being branded dangerously utopian—to venture beyond the capitalist horizon.

The conception of the book dictated its construction. The contention that seeking another world is impossible has been greatly assisted by the clever identification of socialism with the Stalinist experiment and its sequel. Even if one has always been anti-Stalinist, categorically rejecting the confusion between socialism and the crimes of the Georgian tyrant, one must still settle this account with the past.[1] The first part of the book, therefore, deals with "The Heritage." It begins with the Bolshevik Revolution, which happened where it could not accomplish its task, then failed to spread to areas where it could have done so, and it tries to assess the tragic results of that contradiction. But nearly fifteen years have now elapsed since Mikhail Gorbachev embarked on *perestroika* and ten since those heady days when the people of Eastern Europe spectacularly rejected "really existing socialism," enough time, incidentally, for them to discover that "really existing capitalism" was not quite as attractive as it had been painted to be. The second chapter tries to show why Gorbachev's attempt was bound to fail and how bewildered the people of Eastern Europe now are, torn between a rejected past and a disappointing present. The third chapter deals with the impact on an admittedly never quite bipolar world of the sudden disappearance of one of the two superpowers. The consequences

---

1. This note is just for right-wing reviewers who tend to accuse any critic of capitalism of indifference to the fate of the victims of Soviet terror. The author happens to be the son of a *zek*, who barely survived his time in one of the worst labor camps, Vorkuta, in the distant, inhospitable North.

are as complex and ambiguous as Soviet foreign policy was, not in abstract theory but in real practice.

If all these three chapters are logically connected, the fourth, completing Part One and covering the crisis of social democracy, may seem odd. It could have been expected that the official, final collapse of the allegedly revolutionary venture in the eastern half of Europe would be coupled with the glorification of Fabian tactics and the triumph of evolution in the western half. Nothing of the kind happened. It actually coincided with a frontal attack against the social conquests achieved during the past quarter century of exceptionally rapid growth after the last war. Since the expanded welfare state was one of the main attractions of social democracy, now taken to mean the reformist management of existing society, the proposed dismantlement of that state posed a serious challenge to the social demo-cratic leaders, whatever their personal readiness to accept it. The popular resistance against this attempt to impose the American pattern should not be underestimated, and these are only the first skirmishes of a major battle over the social, and hence the political, shape of Europe.

Meanwhile, with the revolutionary project shattered and the reformist strategy bankrupt, the heritage can hardly be described as very valuable. Part Two, concerned with "Changing Europe," is really seeking new sources of hope. For the reader it should provide a bit of a breather: after the mixture of compressed history and speculation, some narrative and three concrete case studies. The purpose is not to ponder how the euro will stand up to the dollar or how dominant a role the unified Germany will play in European integration. It is to discover—east wind, west wind?—where real change will come from.

The first case to be examined is that of Russia, seen through the prism of the miraculous election of Boris Yeltsin as president in 1996, a poll hailed by President Clinton, with unconscious humor, as "a triumph of democracy." In fact it was a striking example of how a free election can be cooked. It showed the corrosiveness of corruption and the power of the profiteers of privatization within the new regime. The conduct of Yelt-sin's henchmen, whom with Orwellian predilection we continue to call "democrats," and the hypocrisy of their Western backers should not lead us to conceal the confusion, lack of new ideas, and jingoism of the other side, that is to say of the Communists and their nationalist allies. Actually,

3

the "miracle" at the polls was in vain. Two years later, Russia's bankruptcy and the fall of the ruble brought the reign of Yeltsin virtually to an end. A postscript on the unmaking of a president tries to assess the seven calamitous years of the Western-sponsored attempt to convert Russia to classical capitalism.

While its plight is in no way comparable, Poland, too, is a sad case. It is the more depressing because of the high hopes it once aroused. Poland, after all, was the only country in Eastern Europe where the change of regime had been prepared by a lengthy struggle and a genuine movement from below. The entry of the Polish workers on the political stage in 1980 precipitated the course of events throughout the area and seemed to open up new historical vistas. The political branch of Solidarnosc is back in office in Warsaw, but it is now clearly a highly reactionary as well as a clerical force. The second chapter traces, and tries to explain, this disenchanting road from Gdansk to the present. The two cases combined, the Russian and the Polish, suggest that for all sorts of understandable reasons—notably the time needed for class interests to crystallize and for the Soviet past to be seen in a certain perspective—in the next few years, the light is most unlikely to come from the East.

More encouraging is the third case, the French winter of discontent, the strikes and mass demonstrations which, in 1995, revealed the potential for resistance in western Europe. Indeed, future historians may treat it as an ideological turning point, the first revolt against Tina. What momentarily caused panic within the establishment was that its usual propaganda—you must accept the world as it is, with Maastricht, the markets, the IMF and all—had no effect whatsoever on the mounting movement. The plain reply of the protesters was: if that is the future you offer us and our children, to hell with your future! The significance of this refusal of permanent blackmail is crucial. We will not be able to achieve anything as long as we accept, even implicitly, that nothing can be done. But the negation is only the first vital step. There is a point in the objection that, if we reject their future, we must provide a vision of our own. This brings us to Part Three, the longest, "In Search of an Alternative," which requires a word of explanation.

Even if I had all the space in the world and the arrogance to pretend that I knew all the answers, the resulting program would be of little use to a genuine popular movement, which must forge its own project. Gone are the days of programs imposed from outside and from above. Later in the book we shall consider the apparent contradiction between this healthy refusal of blueprints handed down by the leadership and the natural desire of the people, if they are to embark on a long-term action, to have a clear vision of where they are going. But the dilemma does not have to bother us here, because I do not have the audacity to present a program. Rather than provide answers, the third part of the book will raise the questions and list the main problems that the left, labor, the progressive movement—call it what you wish—will have to face and solve if it wants to be relevant once again, to mobilize people, and to help them to become, if not yet masters of their fate, at least actors in their own story.

The first series of questions will be concerned with the function work assumes in our fast-changing society, because, if we were really witnessing "the end of work," the labor movement could no longer play a central part in the transformation of that society. What we are actually watching is, probably, the end of the illusion, born during the period of postwar prosperity, that the system, at least in the advanced capitalist countries, can provide steady, fairly decent, and improving employment for all. The problem today, and the task is tremendous, is how to unify a working class that is not vanishing but which has been deeply reshaped in the last half century through the expansion of the service sector, the inflow of women, and, more recently, the re-emergence on a mass scale of precarious, "contingent" employment. Yet even if labor were reunited and forged an alliance with other social movements, could it still play a historical role in a world whose frontiers have been swept aside by the winds of globalization? Since the term is used so obviously as a substitute, or aid, for Tina, it is useful to stress that globalization is not an automatic product of technological progress in the age of the computer. The form economic internationalization has taken is the response of capital to its structural crisis. This having been said, it has changed the rules of the game. The radical transformation of society can still be initiated, say, within a medium-sized European nation state, but it must rapidly move beyond its frontiers. Seen in perspective, internationalism is the reply to globalization.

Looking at the global picture one gets a striking view of inequality. The fact that the combined wealth of the 225 richest people in the world nearly equals the annual income of the poorer half of the earth's population, that is to say more than 2.5 billion human beings, is more arresting than volumes of social criticism.[2] Actually, inequality appears at the very center of the major issues of our time: international exploitation, racism, gender discrimination, and the hierarchical division of labor. And when polarization rhymes with stagnation, it is no longer possible to pretend that, because of the expanding pie, equality is irrelevant. Egalitarianism—not to be confused with levelling and uniformity—must be at the very heart of any progressive project. But, in your quest for equality, will you not be sacrificing freedom? To answer this question, the fourth chapter is devoted to democracy. Democracy is fundamental, and not only because of the horrors committed in the Soviet Union, allegedly in the name of socialism. The Soviet experience has shown how precious the so-called "formal" freedoms—of expression, assembly, election—really are. And yet just to restore them, without filling them with social content, cannot be enough. Democracy has to be reinvented on the shopfloor, in the office, on the campus, at all levels from the local neighborhood to the very top, if Soviet experience is not to be repeated, if power is really to be given to the people and planning turned into the self-organization of society.

Two main lessons are drawn from the chapters devoted to the search for an alternative. The first is that all liberation struggles are closely linked and, however significant each protest movement and however valuable its autonomy, the potential whole is more important than its parts. The capitalist system is an elaborate construction, centuries old, adaptable and invading all walks of life. It will only be thrown off the historical stage by another social order capable of defeating and replacing it on all the fronts. For the second lesson is that all the struggles—for the control over the work process, for greater equality, for real powers to the people—begin within existing society and drive us beyond its borders. This is why the book's conclusion calls for "realistic utopia." *Realistic* since it must be rooted in current conflicts and in the potentialities of existing society. *Utopian*

---

2. In its 1996 edition, the *Human Development Report* stated that the wealth of 358 billionaires (measured in U.S. dollars) exceeded the combined income of 45 percent of the world's population. In its 1998 edition, it puts the wealth of the 225 richest people in 1997 at more than 1 trillion dollars, nearly equalling the annual income of 47 percent of the world's poorest people. *Human Development Report* (New York: Oxford University Press, 1998).

because that is how any attempt to look beyond the confines of capitalism is branded.

Have you not tried to conceal under an initially liberal presentation the real inspirer, the bearded villain, whom so many now present as the begetter of our predicament? There is no reason for hiding. Karl Marx is the great analyst of class society, and the reign of capital, though not eternal, is at present predominant on the bulk of this planet. His inspiration, therefore, is most precious, provided he is not treated, in a most un-Marxist fashion, as an infallible and mummified oracle. Marx did not have the time to complete the analysis of his own society; notably, he did not reach the point where he planned to study the state. For all his extraordinary foresight of the shape of things to come, he could not take into account many features of our society. He probably could not imagine that, with the extraordinary technological progress achieved in the century and a half that followed, the social organization would lag so far behind. The Marxism welcome in this book is not the ritual "Marxism-Leninism," a Holy Scripture serving as a tool and a disguise for Soviet leaders, but a living instrument questioning the fast-changing world and examining its own premises in the process.[3]

Since we are at the confessional stage, let me also admit that this book is not written by an ex- or a post-, but by an unfashionably plain socialist— with hope, however, that it will be read not only by fellow socialists, anarchists, or ecologists. For its aim is very simple, even if in another sense it is quite ambitious. It is to help revive the belief, once quite widespread though now ruthlessly uprooted, that you can change life—yes, your life—by reshaping society through collective political action.

Having explained the construction and purpose of the book, let me now briefly, before the critics do their job, outline some of its limitations. Because it tries in not too many pages to cope with several major issues, the book does not do justice to some of them. Thus, though I hope it is quite obvious that the ecological dimension and women's liberation are for me fundamental elements of any project for the future, these two topics do not figure prominently in these pages. Partly because it was not the purpose of the book, largely because other authors can write about these subjects so

3. For an example of such creative Marxism, see István Mészáros, *Beyond Capital* (New York: Monthly Review Press, 1995).

much better and have done so. This preference for subjects one knows intimately, some will accuse, may explain the emphasis on Poland rather than Hungary or France rather than Italy, though one can plead that the choice is justified on its own. In any case, this argument cannot be used for the admitted Euro-centered bias of the story. This is a question of choice, since the assumption underlying the book is that for all sorts of reasons— the attack on the welfare state, the popular feeling for social conquests and political traditions, weakened but not gone—western Europe is likely to be the terrain of the first big confrontation of the new millennium. I will be delighted to be proved wrong if the limelight is switched to Asia or Latin America, because it is there that the revolt against capital's global offensive has, even earlier, taken the form of a counterattack.

After all, this book wants to be a contribution to a debate which cannot afford to be parochial. It looks forward to publications inspired by the same refusal of resignation, but looking at the system from a different angle because written in Tokyo or Seoul, in Mexico City or Sao Paulo. For the struggle is increasingly and inevitably international. History, far from coming to a stop, has quickened pace. The downturn precipitated by the financial crisis in Asia is no recession, but a slump as we have not seen for years. Its repercussions are unpredictable. There are also signs that France is not the only place where, after a couple of decades of absolute domination, the ruling ideology is starting to be questioned. But together with hope comes danger, its companion. If we do not quickly offer progressive solutions to the growing popular discontent, there are plenty of dark saviors waiting in the wings.

Above all, this is not an essay announcing the impending collapse of capitalism and the advent of a socialist millennium. Too many great expectations have been shattered to revive such exercises. But the certainty of victory is not indispensable for action. Its possibility is a sufficient spur. *Whose Millennium?* is fundamentally a gesture of revolt against Tina, a refusal of the prevailing religion of resignation and of its natural ally, irresponsibility. We are not tied to the system, and nobody can prevent us from looking beyond the capitalist horizon. We cannot just wash our hands and pretend. We are not doomed to impotence and inaction by fate.

Introduction

Men at some time are masters of their fate:
The fault, dear Brutus, is not in our stars,
But in ourselves. . . .[4]

Cassius may have exaggerated.[5] The main fault is not in ourselves. It lies in our unjust and unequal society, in a social system that in no way corresponds to the potentialities of our development, just as our technological sophistication contrasts with the primitiveness of our social organization. But we cannot just plead innocence and irresponsibility. We are not prisoners of this system. Though sobered up by past defeats and burdened by the weight of our environment, we, too, can try to be masters of our fate and fight for a different future.

---

4. Shakespeare, *Julius Caesar* (Act I, Scene 2).

5. So has Shakespeare in leaving women out and putting fate in the hands of men alone. But that was at the end of the sixteenth century. Now even those who think so would not dare to put it in writing.

Part One
The Heritage

Introduction to Part One
1989 and All That

A TURNING POINT in European history, 1989 is clearly one of those dates to remember. In the popular mind it is forever connected with the fall of the Berlin Wall, symbolizing the collapse of the neo-Stalinist empire. But the date stands for much more than that. Geographically, it stretches from Poland, where the first non-Communist government was formed in September, through Germany to Czechoslovakia, where the regime folded in November, to Romania, where the reign of Nicolae Ceausescu came to a close a month later, and finally to the Soviet Union itself. The latter must be included because, chronologically, 1989 extends beyond its own confines to cover its logical climax—the reunification of Germany and the dissolution of the Soviet Union. Thus, in a double sense, it marks the close of an era: a shabby curtain drawn on a drama opened up heroically in 1917 and the end of the years of Yalta, of divided Europe, indeed, of a bipolar world.

The disintegration was predictable. What was suprising was the sweep of the movement and its contagious nature, the speed with which one regime fell after another, once Moscow gave its blessing and people entered the stage. Equally striking was the absence of bloodshed and of real resistance, not only in the outlying empire but also in the Soviet Union itself. The reaction of our establishment, on the other hand, was very much as expected. It hailed the events as the final funeral of socialism and, therefore, proof of capitalist eternity. What is surprising is the tremendous success of this line. Whatever the power of the propaganda machine, I find this coincidence between the fall of the neo-Stalinist empire and the disappearance of the belief in the possibility of building a different society puzzling, because even leftists had, for the most part, long ceased to perceive the Soviet Union as a country providing an alternative solution.

For true believers the shock came in 1956, with Khrushchev's "secret" indictment of Stalin, that is, when the keeper of the shrine told them that their demigod was a sinner. (Collectively it had the same devastating impact as the discovery by Alyosha in *The Brothers Karamazov* that the corpse of Father Zossima, his saintly man, stank.) The most faithful survived this and even the invasion of Hungary the same year, arguing that the system was reforming itself from within. Twelve years later, Soviet tanks entering Prague crushed the remaining illusions. Afterward even the most orthodox Communist Parties, like the French or the Portuguese, did not seriously suggest that the Soviet Union provided socialist answers to our problems or that the future was being forged within its frontiers.

It is, therefore, quite easy to give the gravediggers the reply that you can only bury something that has lived, and that socialism never existed in Eastern Europe. Though the point is perfectly valid, we cannot leave it at that, because for quite a period Stalinism and socialism were identified in many people's minds and, more generally, seventy years of crucial events cannot be dismissed as a mere historical bracket. While Russia should never have been a model, we cannot move forward without settling that account.

This is why the first chapter will address the question: what collapsed and why? It will cope with what I call *the Marxist tragedy,* the contradiction between a vision intended for the advanced countries of Western Europe and the backwardness of Mother Russia, with the cruel result of that contradiction: Stalinism, first conquering the Soviet Union, then invading half of Europe. I will particularly try to determine why optimistic assumptions about economic progress leading to the progressive liberalization of the regime did not come true and to show how Stalin's heirs, a potentially new class clinging to its privileges, managed to preserve an obviously obsolete system.

The resulting stagnation could not go on and so the rulers picked one of their own, both to reform the system and to preserve their power. This brings us to the second chapter, on *perestroika* and its prospects. We shall look at Mikhail Gorbachev's achievements and limitations and try to explain why his revolution from above was bound to end on the road toward capitalism. Yet "really existing capitalism" is not as attractive to the East

Europeans as was its glittering version shown in television soap operas. To understand the unfinished transformation, one must grasp that the struggle for power is linked with the struggle for property. The specificity of this transition is that a class of property owners must take shape in a span of years, not within decades or centuries.

The third chapter will deal with the global foreign policy consequences of 1989. To gather what the disappearance of the Soviet Union means, we must examine the ambiguous role it played during its existence. We shall thus look at the relationship between Moscow and the Communist Parties, which were both puppets and genuine movements with roots in their own country. We shall look at Russia's connection with the movements of national liberation: it crippled them by imposing its own model, but it also protected them as the only brake on America's imperialist expansion. Now, the United States is the only superpower. Capitalism lost its ambiguous opponent. It has no rival. But it has no bogey, no alibi, no excuse, either. It is there in its nakedness.

Finally, there is the question of whether or not the alleged "funeral of socialism" gives a new lease on life to social democracy. Paradoxically, the opposite has happened. The global expansion of capitalism, deregulation, and the lifting of controls over international movements of money have all reduced certain powers of the nation-state and its capacity for Keynesian management. The structural economic crisis became obvious in the mid-seventies, but it is only now that western Europe feels its full political effects with the attack on full employment, the welfare state, and all the conquests made by the labor movement in the unprecedented period of expansion after the Second World War. The left in Western Europe must either reinvent a radical alternative or surrender.

This will be the subject of the fourth chapter, closing this section on our heritage.

1.

A Marxist Tragedy

Under such fatal conditions even the most gigantic idealism and the most storm-tested revolutionary energy are incapable of realizing democracy and socialism but only distorted attempts at either.

Rosa Luxemburg[1]

THE STORY OF SOCIALISM did not begin, nor does it end, with the Soviet experiment, however important, instructive and dramatic that experiment may have been. Rosa Luxemburg's words prove that this is not special pleading after the fact, since they were written not today but back in 1918.

At the beginning of 1914, the Social-Democratic battalions, headed by the Germans, paraded as the army of peace. If the capitalists and their servants in various nations launch a war, the leaders of Social Democracy proclaimed, the proletarians will refuse to fight against their brothers, and if they dare to proceed despite the warning, the workers will aim their weapons against their rulers, turning war into revolution. In August of that momentous year, the same leaders, with a few notable exceptions, climbed on their respective jingoist bandwagons. And their members marched, many of them merrily, into the most horrible slaughter humankind had known until then. Here lie the roots of the glory and of the tragedy of the Bolshevik Revolution.

The enthusiasm which the revolution of 1917 aroused in Europe and the awed admiration with which it was treated for years after was, naturally,

---

1. Rosa Luxemburg, *The Russian Revolution* (Ann Arbor: University of Michigan Press, 1961), 28.

due to a large extent to the pioneering role performed by the Bolsheviks, proving by their action that the working people could not only seize power but also keep it. Yet the original fervor had also a great deal to do with the revulsion against the horrors of the war. The Russians were the only ones true to their promise. The Western social-democratic politicians and union bosses had led their followers astray and were, therefore, responsible for the bloody consequences.

Yet the honor of the Bolsheviks also contributed to their terrible predicament. The fact that they stood on their own meant that something was now put on the historical agenda that up to then no Marxist had seriously envisaged—the building of socialism not in the countries of Europe, with the highest level of development, productivity, culture, and civilization, but in backward, peasant Mother Russia.

What was new was not the idea of a revolution in Russia. With an industrial proletariat relatively small but highly concentrated in huge factories, with a mass of poor, discontented, land-hungry peasants, and with a tottering tsarist administration, Russia was obviously a "weak link" in the chain of European capitalism.[2] An upheaval was, therefore, to be expected. Indeed, some authors even forecast that Russia's revolution might be "permanent" and pass over the bourgeois phase rapidly to a socialist stage.[3] What no Marxist could even conceive at the time was that Russia should achieve this task—the building of a socialist society—in isolation. The idea seemed particularly absurd in 1920, after three years of world conflict followed by three years of civil war, with the country wrecked, its industry in ruins and the workers dispersed (some absorbed by the new administration, others gone back to the countryside), so that one critic could describe the Bolsheviks as "the vanguard of a nonexistent class."[4]

2. The industrial proletariat was less than three million. In 1913, employment in industry, including construction, accounted for 9 percent of the total workforce, while agriculture accounted for 75 percent. Out of a total population of circa 139 million, 18 percent was urban and 82 percent rural. See *Narodnoye Khozaystvo SSR 1958:* 9, 654.

3. The idea of "permanent revolution" was launched by Parvus (the pen name of Alexander Helphand) and developed by Trotsky in an essay called *Results and Prospects*, published in 1906. On Parvus see Z. A. B. Zeman and W. B. Scharlau, *The Merchant of Revolution* (Oxford: Oxford University Press, 1965).

Don't get alarmed. This is not going to be a course of potted Soviet history, from Kerensky to Gorbachev. I shall just try to marshal the facts so as to help the debate on the questions that now spring to mind and that today we can approach with hindsight. Was the attempt to find a historical shortcut, rifle in hand, doomed from the start? What was the right attitude to take when the revolution broke out in 1917? These will lead us to a series of connected issues: if in an isolated Soviet Union, barbarism, as Lenin put it, had to be uprooted by barbarian means, was Stalin the inevitable man for the job? Was there a radical difference between Lenin's regime and that of his successor? Did the former contain the seeds of the latter? Did Stalin produce a specific political regime, one with a life of its own, which even after his death prevented the gradual transformation of the system in a socialist direction, a prospect on which so many hopes, inside and outside Russia, rested?

Among those who welcomed the revolution in Russia when it began in February 1917, one can roughly distinguish three schools of thought. The Russian Mensheviks and their foreign Social-Democratic partners, like Karl Kautsky, argued that since Russia was not ripe for a more radical transformation, the movement should not go any further and socialists should help in the development of a bourgeois republic. The trouble was that the Russian people wanted two things at the time—peace and land—while the provisional government that the Mensheviks were backing offered them neither and was, therefore, doomed.

The Bolsheviks, for their part, thought that power was in the streets and decided, in October, to take it. Then they were to consolidate their hold and wait for the revolution to spread. Once the center of gravity shifted to Berlin, they would stand a chance of building socialism in their own country. The Bolsheviks differed over the wisdom of seizing power, but they were unanimous in their assessment that their only chance of building socialism was connected with the success of the revolution in the advanced capitalist countries.[5]

4. Alexander Shlyapnikov, leader of the Workers' Opposition, to Lenin at 11th Party Congress, March 1922.

5. Lev Kamenev and Grigori Zinoviev were the main leaders opposed to insurrection.

Whose Millennium?

The third position was that of Rosa Luxemburg, who, as the quotation introducing this chapter shows, harbored no illusions. More than anybody, Luxemburg viewed the revolution as a worldwide process covering a whole historical period, as a series of defeats leading to ultimate victory. At the bottom of her analysis was the premise that, sooner or later, the Bolsheviks would be defeated. All the more reason for Lenin, Trotsky, and their comrades to stick to principles, to practice proletarian democracy, so as to prepare the ground for future generations and for future victories both at home and abroad.

Though personally I am in full sympathy with Luxemburg's approach, I must admit that it is easier to accept defeat, for the sake of purity, when one is not concretely in charge. Those who today too easily condemn the Bolshevik leaders for clinging to power rather than to principle should be reminded that, in case of defeat, the movement had to reckon with the rule of ruthless tsarist commanders, not gentle moderate Mensheviks. More generally, to rely on the spread of the movement westward did not seem, at the time, a totally absurd assumption. Who could have then predicted that there would be no revolution in western Europe by the end of the millennium! Just because we now know that the shortcut did lead to a dead end does not mean that the revolution was a blind alley from the start. It is plainly too fatalistic to conclude that what happened had to happen.

Rosa Luxemburg's suggestion that the Bolsheviks, admittedly in a terrible battle and in the most awkward of circumstances, may have forsaken the principles of socialist democracy and forgotten that a viable solution can only be achieved through the "active, untrammeled, energetic political life of the broadest masses of the people," takes us straight to current condemnations of the Russian Revolution as rotten from the very start.[6] It is fashionable now to blacken the early period, to describe the red while ignoring the white terror, to lump Lenin with his successor and Stalin with his many revolutionary Marxist victims, and even to describe Marx as the begetter of the gulag. This new gospel is preached from Russia by people who only yesterday were zealous teachers of a holy scripture known as "Marxism-Leninism," and it is peddled in the

6. Luxemburg, 62.

West with the assistance of ex-rebels who used to chant "Marx, Engels, Lenin, Stalin, Mao, and Lin Piao. . . ."

My obvious contempt for turncoats should not be interpreted as an attempt to whitewash the culprits. Their crimes can be neither forgotten nor forgiven. Their monstrosity is even more terrible for somebody like myself because the crimes were committed allegedly for socialism. Condemnation, however, should not justify multiplying the number of victims, fantastically high as it is, to absurd proportions.[7] There is no need either to paint all periods in equally dark colors as if, after the liberation of millions of prisoners by Khrushchev in the 1950s, things were as bad as they had been in the 1930s, at the height of the Stalinist purges. To be valid and instructive, the judgment, however stern, must be made with historical exactitude and perspective.

Anyone having the slightest acquaintance with the Soviet Union must be struck by the contrast in the political and moral climate between the Lenin period and the Stalin era. During the former the measures of repression, the restrictions on freedom, were being improvised against a background of civil war with foreign intervention. The inspirers of this policy could genuinely believe that the measures were provisional and would be lifted once the revolution spread. Under Stalin, the monolithic party, the mechanism of command from above, the *univers concentration-naire* were all part of an established system of rule which was being presented, with supreme hypocrisy, as an example of socialist democracy and a model for the world at large. The gap was no less in the world of culture. In the early days, modern poets and painters, and innovators in architecture or the theater, competed on the frontiers of the future. In the Stalinist period, artists had to conform, take their orders from Zhdanov, and all writers had to pay their tribute to the genius of the demigod in the Kremlin.[8] It takes sheer ignorance or an extraordinary political bias to blur the line and confuse the two.

And yet, this having been said, the first regime did contain the seeds of the second. When the Bolsheviks grabbed for themselves a political

7. For an attempt to estimate the victims on the basis of the Soviet data see the appendix to Moshe Lewin, *Russia, USSR, Russia* (New York: The New Press, 1995).

8. Andrei Zhdanov was the politbureau member appointed by Stalin after the Second World War to keep strict orthodoxy in literature and the arts.

monopoly, outlawing all other parties, and then in 1921 when they banned factions within their own movement, they were preparing the ground for a monolithic structure and for totalitarian rule. This was not primarily because, brought up in the tsarist underground, their party was unused to democratic niceties. The seeds of Stalinism could grow because of the Marxist tragedy mentioned earlier, because of the conflict between the socialist project and Russia's backwardness. With only abortive revolutions in the West, the Bolsheviks, clinging to power, were left with the immense task of industrializing their country. With no foreign investment, they had to rely on their own resources, carry out their own "primitive accumulation," a historical chapter which in the West, to quote Marx, was "written in the annals of mankind in letters of blood and fire."[9] The working class, as we saw, had dwindled. The country was dominated by a huge peasantry (some twenty-five million households), which had got its land and was no longer frightened that the counter-revolutionaries would take it back. Under these circumstances, it would have been difficult for the Bolsheviks to accomplish their task by democratic means. This is the sense in which Stalinism is the product of that contradiction in terms, "primitive *socialist* accumulation."[10]

Socialism and democracy were out of reach. This does not mean that the future of the regime was predestined. A leader does not shape history on his own. But he leaves a mark, an imprint. The nauseating recantations during the Moscow trials, the hymns and hosannas in an oriental cult of the despot, had something to do with the character of the Georgian tyrant, educated in a seminary of the Orthodox Church. Stalin, however, is responsible for the substance as well as the form of the dictatorship. A master manipulator of the party machine—that is how he defeated his rivals—he, paradoxically, did not take extreme positions at the beginning of a conflict. In 1917, he hesitated before siding with a Lenin determined to seize power. In the mid-twenties, during the crucial controversy over economic policy, he also wavered. Indeed, he started by aligning himself with Nikolai Bukharin, who was telling the peasants to enrich themselves,

9. Karl Marx, *Capital*, vol. 1 (London: Lawrence and Wishart, 1970), 669.

10. On this concept, see E. A. Preobrazhensky, *The New Economics* (Oxford: Oxford University Press, 1965) and Alexander Ehrlich, *The Soviet Industrialisation Debate 1924-28* (Cambridge, MA: Harvard University Press, 1960).

and by attacking Trotsky, branded as the "superindustrializer." What mattered to Stalin was power, not policy. Yet once a line was thrust upon him, he put it into practice with unbelievable ruthlessness, aggravated by the lack of preparedness, the result of improvisation.

This is not the place to debate who was right: Bukharin advocating an advance "at a snail's pace" to placate the peasantry, or Trotsky seeing the only salvation in fairly rapid industrialization. But not even the latter could envisage the liquidation of the rich farmers, the kulaks, as a class and as human beings, *kak klas i kak chelovyek*. This is what Stalin did, when he finally embarked on his collectivization drive in 1929. With not only the rich farmers slaughtering cattle and fighting back in every possible fashion, Stalin had unleashed an upheaval equivalent to a second civil war which, possibly, was even more significant in its influence on the very nature of the regime. Soviet agriculture was to take decades to recover from this calamity. Collective farming, which in the original conception was to attract people voluntarily through higher performance, was discredited for a very long time by this bloody imposition. Since industry was now supposed to break records so as to make up for wasted time, the draftsmen of the Five Year Plan were ordered to set up impossibly high targets and then to ask for their fulfillment ahead of time (in four, or even three, years). Planning, instead of being an instrument of democracy, became a device for administrative coercion and dictation from the top. Above all, society was reshaped by the migration of millions of uprooted, discontented peasants from country to town. They had to be bullied and frightened into accepting the pace of industrial labor and the rhythm of urban life.

Here, I realize, I am almost joining the current fashion of describing only the seamy side of Soviet development. No regime can survive for long propped up only by the power of its police. Russia under Stalin was not just urban overcrowding, the cult of personality, and the gulag. It was also the expansion of health services, mass education in a semiliterate country, and the prospect of social advancement for the children of workers and peasants. While eliminating the critically thinking intellectuals, the regime was mass-producing the professional intelligentsia. The Soviet Union at that time was also the enthusiasm of young *komsomols* building dams on the Dneper and steel mills in Magnitogorsk. It was the breakneck industrialization that, within a dozen years or so, built the factories that provided the tanks and the guns with which the Red Army saved us from the Nazis, and which paradoxically enabled Stalin, the inventor of "socialism in one country," to extend his brand of "socialism" up to the Elbe.

So as not to be carried away now in the opposite direction, let me make three crucial points. Whatever the achievement, it was accomplished at an economic, political, and human cost that was prohibitive. Secondly, even when it worked, that is to say when the planners could control a limited number of big plants and projects, the system had little to do with socialism, if that word means for us mastery by the people over their work and their fate. Last but not least, the system was self-destructive. Designed to rule over an army of uprooted, uneducated *muzhiks* driven to town, it could not function properly once the economy, and the population, got more sophisticated. By the time of Stalin's death, it was already obsolete.

This, incidentally, is something to keep in mind when looking at Eastern Europe. It was this obsolete system that the Red Army brought up to the Elbe as it both liberated and occupied Romania, Hungary, Bulgaria, Czechoslovakia, and Poland. Eliminating capitalists and big landowners, the Soviet troops were not quite as unwelcome as it is now being suggested. But once Europe was split by the Cold War, the very idea of "independent roads to socialism" was condemned as a heresy and the Soviet model was imposed throughout the area. Politically this meant, under the ironic name of "people's democracy," ruthless Stalinist rule from above. Economically, it meant that all these countries were cut off from the international division of labor. This might have been more than offset if they had been joining at the same time an alternative system, with its own dynamism and drive. But the Soviet system was by then obsolete. Here you have the seeds of 1989. The regimes of Eastern Europe were not only introduced from outside and from above. They also proved hypocritical and, increasingly, inefficient.

Let us not run ahead. After this digression we must still look at the complex relationship between Stalin and the ruling bureaucracy. Master of the party machine, he rose to power on the backs of the apparatchiks, of the pushing newcomers who had joined the party during and after the civil war. Contrary to legend, he was no leveller. He was the enemy of egalitarianism, of *uravnilovka*. He favored Stakhanovism, big wage differentials, privileges for the few. As such, he was the champion and spokesman of the bureaucracy. But he was also its scourge. His absolutist rule had no room for the sharing of power. His ghastly periodic purges were not only designed to frighten the peasants into obedience and instill labor discipline among the new workers. They were also aimed at preventing the privileged elite from crystallizing its interests as a class. Mighty and faithful Stalinists did not know how long their luck would last.[11] Stalin thus created a system run by the privileged, but he prevented that elite from consolidating its position. His successors wanted to preserve the system, while getting rid of the blind purge. They strove for a Stalinism that would not devour its children.

At the time of Stalin's death in 1953, about 57 percent of the Soviet population was still living in the countryside. Or should we say: the rural population now accounted for only 57 percent, because more people were by then working in industry, building, and transportation than in agriculture. Society was changing and changing very fast. The methods of management, political as well as economic, had to be revised. It was indispensable to provide some housing to the millions of newcomers crowded in the towns, to give a new deal to the badly neglected consumer, and to find new inducements for the more educated population.

Nikita Khrushchev, half-peasant and half-townsman, Stalin's faithful servant who then toppled the statue from its pedestal, was a symptomatic leader of this Soviet Union in transition. He was aware of the need for change. He offered the Russians goulash communism. In a confident mood, helped by the launching of Sputnik in 1957, he projected production curves into the future and promised to overtake America by 1980. His idea was that increasingly skilled producers would enable the Soviet Union to preserve a rapid rate of growth, while higher living standards would allow him, gradually, to liberalize the regime.

In practice, Khrushchev proved a man of half measures. He revealed some of Stalin's crimes, then refused further investigation, fearing the charge of complicity. Instead of a radical managerial reform, he produced a series of schemes: the planting of maize, the conquest of virgin lands in

11. Out of the 1,966 delegates to the 17th Party Congress—that of the "victors"—1,108 were executed. So were 98 out of 139 of the Central Committee elected at that congress. These figures were confirmed by Khrushchev in his "secret" speech delivered on February 24, 1956. The English text was released that June by the State Department. See *Anti-Stalinist Campaign and International Communism* (New York: Columbia University Press, 1956).

Kazakhstan and Siberia, the reshuffling of various administrative institutions. Why could he not go any further? Having picked as the main instrument of his action the party—in which the apparatchiks still dominated the managers—he could not proceed very far in the direction of the market. Yet could he not move in the opposite way? Was it not the last chance for the Soviet Union to seek a socialist solution?

To do so, its leaders would have had to wrestle with all sorts of difficult questions that we ourselves have not answered so far. How do you make people work if you don't want to replace the Stalinist way of coercion through the gulag by our own method of compulsion, fear of unemployment? What institutions do you have to invent to turn planning—indispensable if only to eliminate inequalities between groups, classes, regions—into the democratic self-organization of society? The Soviet leaders could have begun by putting some substance into their mythology, by giving enough say in running their own affairs to workers and collective farmers so as to make them really feel that they were, at least to some extent, the owners of their factories or their *kolkhozy*. Just to suggest this is to show the quixotic nature of such an idea. The workers were not yet sufficiently conscious to press for such a program, while the haves—apparatchiks, managers, and the privileged sections of the intelligentsia, which we shall call the *priviligentsia*—were violently opposed to such a heresy. They wanted to preserve their privileged position. They were in favor of Stalinism plus security of tenure. They were against repression only so far as it affected the faithful upholders of the regime.

Indeed, for them even Khrushchev's half measures proved too much, for when these seemed to threaten the stability of the system, they got rid of him, in 1964. They put in his place Leonid Brezhnev, whose rule of conduct was the opposite—to take no measure that might antagonize any section of the establishment—and who, acting on this principle, stayed in office for eighteen years. Since the brief interlude of the ailing Yuri Andropov was followed by the election of the decrepit Konstantin Chernenko, whose main claim to fame, remarked the witty writer Ales Adamovich, was that "he sharpened Brezhnev's pencils," it is fair to say that Brezhnevism, this strange rule of conservative compromise, lasted twenty-one years and filled the gap between the fall of Khrushchev and the rise of Mikhail Gorbachev. It shattered not only Khrushchev's boastful predictions, but also the hopes prevailing on the left in the West, despite the invasion of Hungary in 1956, that, driven by economic expansion, a reforming Russia would have to move in a progressive direction.

This optimism was based on the belief that, increasingly more urban, more industrialized, and more educated, the Soviet Union would have to adapt itself to its new structure. The leaders would make some concessions, the people would ask for more, and under the combined effect of reform from above and pressure from below, the country would move forward. It would put some substance into its phony institutions, some social content into the public ownership of the means of production, and some democracy into the soviets. In other words, it would narrow the yawning gap between the bright promise and the horrible fulfillment. Underlying this optimism was the belief that the foundations of Soviet society were somehow sound and potentially socialist. There was also a second postulate, namely that Stalin had it right in a sense: that with the Western labor movement failing in its historical mission, it was nevertheless possible to build socialism, if not in a single country then in a single area the size of Eastern Europe.

We now know that the theories were wrong, and not only because these assumptions were unwarranted. The authors missed the deep connection between ends and means. They did not allow enough for the weight of political inertia, for the ability of a regime in control of all levers of power—not to avoid the inevitable, but to put it off for quite a time. Stalin had forged a political system. His successors, once they had consolidated their position, proved able, in the defense of their vested interests, in the attempt to preserve an unchanged structure of power, to resist indispensable reforms even at a very high, indeed prohibitive, economic cost. They could not do it forever. They did it long enough to change the course of history. Indeed, when they were finally forced to yield, it was not, like the optimistic theories had forecast, because of the developing productive forces under the impact of expansion. On the contrary, it was because economic stagnation had reached a point which was politically intolerable, potentially explosive.

Brezhnevism, this interlude of successful resistance to change, can be described as the highest and last stage of party rule. The secret of this long reign lay in Brezhnev's capacity to reach compromises between the various factions of the Soviet establishment. Particularly since 1973, when the ministers of defense, internal affairs, and foreign affairs were included in the highest organ of the party, the politburo, that body became the place where the deals were made. Later on, Brezhnev was also forced to strike a bargain with the workers, a tacit truce based on the principle that you let us govern as we please and we shall not speed up the pace of assembly lines too fast, allowing you some energy for moonlighting. (Incidentally, the so-called second economy, illegal and therefore unaccounted for in official statistics, was gaining a lot of ground at the time.)

Let us not conclude that it was a gentle regime. When their own interests seemed at stake, Brezhnev and his henchmen could be ruthless, as the Czechs experienced in 1968 and the brave Russian dissidents, faced with the camp or the *psykhushka*, the psychiatric ward, could feel throughout their reign. It was simply a conservative, aging, tired regime, capable of grabbing whatever could be taken without risks, yet unable to embark on any bold, imaginative venture. Incidentally, the gerontocracy, the presence around Brezhnev of tottering cronies, was not due to any absence of change at the top. On the contrary, the reshuffles were many. Only with the Stalinist mincer no longer cutting off heads, in a highly hierarchical society, the political ladder was tall and those who climbed to the top, to the politburo, were no longer youngsters.

The real price paid for the apparent political stability was the absence of reforms, stagnation, the dangerously slackening pace of growth. The leaders were actually unlucky. Earlier, when everything else failed, it was possible to boost production by importing additional labor from the countryside. Now this source was rapidly declining and was expected to dry up by the mid-1980s. Simultaneously, the cost of investment was rising. Soviet finances and foreign trade were saved for a time by increased supplies of oil and natural gas from Siberia. The exploitation of these new sources of raw materials in distant and difficult surroundings, however, was getting more and more expensive. With reduced sources of labor, a declining return on investment, and a slowing rate of growth, the economy was clearly heading for trouble.

To speak of stagnation is not quite accurate, because while the political structure was frozen and the economy half-paralyzed, society kept on changing. People still migrated from the countryside, shifting further the balance in favor of the towns. The number graduating from both high school and university kept rising fast. In the Khrushchevian version, here were the ingredients of the Soviet miracle: bigger output, higher living standards, and relaxation of tensions, paving the way for a freer society. In the stagnating Brezhnevian economy, this dream was turned into a nightmare. The scope for social advancement was dwindling, the prospect for professional promotion was declining, and factories and offices were filled with young people who felt they were getting jobs below their capacities and beneath their expectations.

In addition, the arms race was forcing the Soviet leaders to match the American effort out of a much smaller national product. The burden was, therefore, considerably greater and with their economy of scarcity the Russians did not require a big defense budget to spur production. This external factor, however, was additional. The main reasons for radical change were domestic. The regime was at the end of its road. It was no longer possible to just make minor changes within the system. New methods of management were required, new ways for extracting the surplus, new forms for running the country. How reluctant the party leadership was to take the plunge had been shown when the politburo picked the hapless Chernenko, obviously with the sole purpose of postponing the decision. But in May 1985, it opted for a younger leader, Mikhail Gorbachev, and for the unknown.

It is worth repeating that this big transformation was not dictated by the development of the productive forces and, with the people awakened by this process, by pressure from below. Once again the change was going to be determined by decisions and rivalries at the top. In the third of a century since Stalin's death, things had both altered greatly and remained the same. The industrial workers were now incomparably more numerous, less frightened, and better educated.[12] Yet without tradition, without memory, without a political practice, they were to be onlookers in this battle. Within the ruling establishment, the Brezhnevian interlude had shifted the balance of power in favor of the managerial wing and away from the apparatchiks.

---

12. In 1987, the Soviet Union had 80.4 million workers, of whom 38.4 million were employed in industry and construction.

What, for lack of a better term, we can call Russia's budding ruling class had greatly gained in confidence since Stalin's death. At the time all it wanted was to enjoy its privileges in peace, to have assurance, metaphorically speaking, that the five o'clock knock was the milkman, rather than the secret police. But the years in office and the relaxation had increased their ambition. By now the rulers wanted to consolidate their power, put it on solid foundations, be able to transfer it to the next generation. Beyond power, they began to perceive property. The Soviet Union, or rather Russia, was ready to embark on the road to capitalism. Mikhail Gorbachev was to be, unwittingly, the main actor in this new drama.

2.

The Road To Capitalism

Society waits unformed, and is for a while between things ended and things begun.

Walt Whitman, *Thoughts I*

AS A RULE, fifteen years is a short period in historical terms, but the nearly fifteen years that have elapsed since the beginning of perestroika have been packed with momentous events, major shifts, and deep changes in the mood of the population. It all began gloriously, with glasnost, as Mikhail Gorbachev moved boldly where Nikita Khrushchev had failed to tread. We could see the frontiers of freedom being extended as we watched. The Soviet Union was awakening from its crippling collective amnesia. The people were recovering their memory. They were also discovering the pleasure of reading a free press and the excitement of the vote with a choice. The transformation had repercussions beyond Soviet frontiers. It became increasingly obvious that the countries of Eastern Europe would be allowed to choose their own future. Above all, Gorbachev's daring initiatives in foreign policy revealed the dangerous absurdity of the Cold War, with its piling up of weapons of total destruction. No wonder that some leftish people in the West jumped to the conclusion that the Soviet Union had finally resumed its journey toward democracy and socialism (or should I say, unkindly, toward the promised land).

Once again, it proved an illusion. The end of the Cold War, it turned out, was not the result of a stalemate but of a surrender, with one of the superpowers accepting subservience. Gorbachev, still a hero in the West, was fast losing his popularity at home, in a country where discontent was rising together with economic failure and where the leadership, after a period of uncertainty, was clearly searching not for socialism but for some form of capitalist solution. Indeed, for the priviligentsia Gorbachev was not moving fast enough in that direction. It therefore dropped him, climbing on the bandwagon of his bitter rival, Boris Yeltsin, who was heading for capitalism without hesitation. The parody of a putsch by the conservative diehards, in August 1991, served as a pretext. Yeltsin, the hero of the resistance, managed by the end of that year to deprive Gorbachev of his last key position, the Soviet presidency, caring not that in his bid for power he was speeding up the break-up of the Soviet Union.

It was now the turn of Yeltsin to drop in the popularity ratings, and he did it faster than his predecessor. Understandably so. The dissolution of the Soviet Union, a highly integrated unit, damaged the economy of all the member republics. In Russia itself the economy was damaged even more by the policy of Yeltsin's young advisers, seeking a short cut towards capitalism. Here, as elsewhere throughout Eastern Europe, shock therapy, so-called, had the great merit of being approved by the international financial establishment and the minor inconvenience of antagonizing the bulk of the native population. In 1991, Yeltsin stood on a tank urging Moscovites to defend the White House, seat of their parliament, against the army. Two years later, he was sending tanks to shell the same building, and he did so with the blessing of the Western powers, presumably having discovered a new form of parliamentary democracy, one resting on the firing power of a tank.

This is only one of the many paradoxes of this period of transition. Looking at Eastern Europe as a whole, who could have guessed in 1989, as the regimes were tumbling, rejected by their people, that three or four years later the same people would be, if not hankering after the old regimes, at least rejecting the new ones they had welcomed with such enthusiasm? Or that, in another four years, in Poland or Hungary, they would kick out the re-elected former Communists, by then completely converted to running a capitalist economy? In trying to answer these questions, we are less concerned with the provisional leaders—Gorbachev, the reformer who lost his way, and Yeltsin, who seemed not to care where he was going as long as he stayed at the top—than with the social forces that are shaping their policies. The problem is that in this period of transition, classes are still in the process of formation, their interests are not clearly crystallized, and a multiplicity of shifting political parties is groping for positions to represent those interests. (For example, no fewer than forty-three parties put up candidates for national office in Russia's 1995 parliamentary elections.)

We are faced with something historically unprecedented. In Western Europe, it took centuries for capitalism to emerge from the feudal womb, for a new class to take shape and then to take over. In Eastern Europe today, a class of property owners—I mean tycoons, and not just shopkeepers or craftsmen—is coming into being after only a few years (and it already has power, at least by proxy). There is another important novelty. The budding capitalists of yesteryear were forging things as part of their bid for power. Even the robber barons built railroads or steel mills as they robbed. Our East European newcomers take over what has already been built. They steal or, if you prefer, take part in the biggest swindle, the daylight robbery, of our time—the privatization of property in Eastern Europe.

Let me make it quite clear that I am not a victim of old legends. To say that capitalism is being built, or rebuilt, in Eastern Europe does not mean that these regimes were previously socialist.[1] They were nothing of the sort. Similarly, the slogan about the workers being the owners or masters of their factories was pure fiction. It is this theoretical claim to property that the workers were now giving up in exchange for a bribe. On the other hand, the real rulers, who had run the factories, exploited the workers, and lived on the surplus, formerly could not dispose of that property at will or hand it over to their children. Now they were to be able to do so. Throughout Eastern Europe, whatever the bribe (vouchers, free shares, a number of shares at a cheaper price), the workers were not asked to take over on their own. The search was really for major shareholders. In this still unfinished competition, the question is who will come out as the master: the managers, the mafia, the black marketeers with foreign backing? It is a skin game, a bitter conflict in the Kremlin and beyond. Control of power today determines the ownership of property which, in turn, shapes the balance of power for tomorrow.

Mikhail Gorbachev was very much a pure product of the Soviet establishment. Born in 1931, he climbed to be the party boss of the southern region of Stavropol. By 1978, he was already in Moscow, one of the party

1. The end of classical capitalism should not be confused with the reign of capital. I have borrowed this concept, beginning some time ago, from István Mészáros. For his latest and full development of this idea, see *Beyond Capital* (New York: Monthly Review Press, 1995).

secretaries. The following year, he was a candidate and, by 1980, a full member of the politburo. Thus, still in his forties, he belonged to the very top leadership, a youngster among the gerontocrats. But whatever his background, he was keenly conscious that things could not go on as they had. It is very doubtful that, when he started, he knew where he would lead his country. He sensed, however, that this time the changes would have to be fundamental.

To begin with, he felt that the country must be awakened from its slumber and freed from its superfluous political straitjacket. He deserves a place in history books if only for the exhilarating campaign of liberalization that took place under the name of glasnost. On the economic front, Gorbachev started in a more routine fashion. It was only by 1987 that he realized that the whole system of management would have to be over-hauled. Wiser than most of his advisers, he grasped that since the reform giving more power to the managers would hurt the workers, the latter must be won over. He tried for a time to woo them, notably with a proposal that managers be elected by their staff. But he did not proceed very far, or for very long, with that line. To say that he gave up because he was not getting much response is insufficient. We must examine two deeper reasons which will help us, more generally, to understand why Gorbachev did not move in a socialist direction.

While a pragmatist, Gorbachev is not, like Yeltsin, a pure opportunist. When he proclaims, as he did shortly before his fall when it was hardly popular, that all his life he has been a socialist, one must take his word. All that this tells us, however, is what happened to the socialist idea under Stalin and his successors, when socialism was no more than a religion for Sunday preaching and Marxism-Leninism the gospel, with useful quotations to justify whatever the rulers were doing. The attack on the social division of labor, the elimination of classes and of inequalities based upon them, leading to the gradual withering away of the state—all this was Greek to Gorbachev, whose vision of a socialist society boiled down to a prosperous capitalist one, with a welfare state and a decent minimum wage. Toward the end of his reign, he was pleading for the "organic inclusion of the Soviet Union into the world economy" and the convertibility of the ruble.[2] Because of the different levels of productivity between the two systems, a full

2. See, for instance, his speech on 2 July 1990 at the 27th Congress of the CPSU.

convertibility of the ruble, giving up the monopoly of foreign trade, could have only one result. Gorbachev's conversion to capitalism was thus undeniable.

The second reason why Gorbachev did not move in a socialist direction is that for the workers he was one of the rulers, one of "them." He may have been chosen to reform the system and was ready, in the process, to give up the party's monopoly of power. But he was expected, while making concessions, to defend the interests of the privileged. Who were the rulers and the privileged elite while Gorbachev was in office? Clearly not all the nineteen million or so members of the Communist Party. Since a university degree plus the party card were a passport to success, we must look for them among the *sluzhashchyie*, the employees, some forty million people with more than secondary education who accounted for nearly one third of the Soviet labor force. We must at once eliminate from that figure the majority—the twenty-three million or so with merely a junior technical college degree—who were the non-commissioned officers of the army of labor. Of the remaining seventeen million with a full graduate diploma we must count out production engineers (quite close to technicians) and the many teachers (predominantly poorly paid and female)—all those who enjoyed neither privilege nor power.

We are thus left, depending on the definition and the authors, with some six million or so, accounting at the time for roughly 5 percent of the active population.[3] This privileged elite, naturally, included the apparatchiks, the key party supervisors from the politburo down to the local level. It also included the nomenklatura, that is to say, people with jobs sufficiently crucial to officially require the party's approval. It extended to the mass of managers, to the senior figures in the state and local administration, to the apparatus of coercion (the officers' corps in the army or the police), and to the propagandists (the scribblers and providers of quotations). The real rulers were thus statistically hidden within what I have called the priviligentsia. In the ongoing struggle, both were divided between the apparatchiks, those backing the existing system of party supervision and state control from the center, and what one might call a reformist or managerial wing, favoring the abolition of that system. The intelligentsia was more

3. See Daniel Singer, *The Road to Gdansk: Poland and the USSR* (New York: Monthly Review Press, 1981), 102-16, and the footnotes giving Soviet sources.

prominent in the second group, that of a self-appointed meritocracy. In the first phase, that of glasnost, the intelligentsia did play a progressive role, pushing for the extension of freedoms. When it came to economic per-estroika, it fought for its own interests. In material terms, it had done well under the previous regime, but it hoped to do even better—to get bigger privileges and a share of power—under the new. This desire led it to drop Gorbachev and his Fabian road to capitalism for Yeltsin and his shock tactics.

Gorbachev was thus left without a constituency. He, the New Dealer, could not lean on the conservative diehards in the apparatus of the party, the army, and the police. Indeed, they were soon to stage their ridiculous putsch and precipitate his fall. Unwittingly, Gorbachev had paved the way for Yeltsin, the man whom he had once picked, then dropped, and who became his most bitter rival. The apparatchik turned reformer was being replaced in the Kremlin by the apparatchik adventurer.

Like Gorbachev, Yeltsin was a tough operator who had fought his way to be party boss of a region, in his case the industrially more important area of Sverdlovsk. Actually, in his memoirs, you can detect a note of resentment that the leader of a less important region should be above him.[4] Still, it was Gorbachev who brought battling Boris to Moscow as part of his perestroika team. The newcomer showed too much zeal in fighting bureaucracy and attacking privileges. Gorbachev removed the pushy upstart in a rather Stalinist fashion but did not finish him off politically in the good old way. Yeltsin was thus down but not out, and he staged a spectacular comeback on a populist platform, getting brilliantly elected in Moscow to the Soviet Congress of Deputies in March 1989 and then voted Russia's first president chosen by universal suffrage in June 1991. If I called him an adventurer—one who sticks to shifting principles might be a kinder defi-nition—it is because this man, whose original claim to fame was that he was the scourge of the privileged, was now victorious with the backing of Russia's yuppies, preaching that for the successful the sky should be the limit.

He took this line to win the support of the priviligentsia and defeat Gorbachev. He did it also to get Western backing. Gorbachev, it should be remembered, was not only enthusiastically greeted by people all over the

4. Boris Yeltsin, *Against the Grain* (New York: Summit Books, 1990), 92.

world, he was also treated rather warmly by the Western powers, for good reason. After all, he was handing them a victory in the Cold War and a gradual conversion of the Soviet bloc to classical capitalism. To outdo him, Yeltsin had to promise that he would do the same thing, only much faster and much more thoroughly. A born-again capitalist who saw the light when he visited a supermarket packed with goods on his American journey, this is what he dangled in front of the West, and it worked.[5] For Western governments and for the bulk of the Western press, whatever he did, however preposterously he behaved, his enemies would be the apparatchiks and he the democrat, our man in Moscow.

The change at the very top from Gorbachev to Yeltsin did not put an end to the tense struggle for power and property. It only changed the alignments. The advocates of party rule and the old system of exploitation had been defeated earlier. The question was no longer whether Russia was going to move towards capitalism, but how fast and who would be the main beneficiaries. Who would inherit the vast property that, in practice, had been run by the nomenklatura and, in theory, belonged to the people?

It was not a battle between the enemies and defenders of socialism. It was a conflict between two loose gangs within the ruling establishment over who would loot and how. To describe, as it was done in the West, those who tried to preserve state property temporarily as party apparatchiks and the privatizers siding with Yeltsin as "democrats" was plainly absurd. The early leader of the latter, of the so-called "shock therapists," Yegor Gaidar, was, if one may say so, a third-generation Communist aristocrat. The therapists, in a sense, represented speculative money, and their opponents rallied around managers retrenched in their factories. The conflict was between those wanting to take over and those holding on to what they had.

To describe the factory managers as defenders of state property is an exaggeration; caretakers would be more accurate. Their ambition was to run as capitalists the factories they had managed as representatives of the party, if necessary after a transitional period of state capitalism. For this very reason, however, they did not want the property to be broken up and sold on the cheap to outsiders. The therapists relied on the financial squeeze to grab this property with the help of foreign speculators and domestic

5. Ibid., 255.

swindlers. (In fairness, it must be added that the Russian mafia, of which more later, was to be found on both sides.)

Yeltsin was surrounded always by a camarilla, nicknamed wittily the collective Rasputin (headed first by Gennadi Burbulis, a teacher of Marxism-Leninism converted to Von Hayek, then by Major General Alexander Korzhakov, his bodyguard as well as tennis partner, and subsequently by the more complicated Anatoli Chubais, the privatizer, whom we shall see time and again). He chose to back the shock therapists who, for obvious reasons, were also the darlings of the International Monetary Fund (IMF). The trouble was that their therapy was fast rendering the ailing nation terribly sick. With galloping inflation, real income drastically reduced, and small savings wiped out, the poor were getting much poorer and the rich ostentatiously richer. The mood of the country was such that even the Russian parliament, originally Yeltsinite, voted against the government. Yeltsin reacted typically: he half-yielded and prepared his revenge. In December 1992, he agreed to sacrifice Gaidar as acting prime minister and to accept as his replacement one of the people put forward by parliament: Victor Chernomyrdin, a man whom he could trust but who, as the former boss of Gazprom, the giant natural gas conglomerate, was clearly connected with the industrial lobby.

Chernomyrdin, however, was surrounded by orthodox monetarists in financial ministries and was forced, in a way, to stick to the same line. Simultaneously, Yeltsin prepared his coup. He got a new constitution made to measure for him with vast presidential powers and was determined to impose it on parliament by hook or by crook. If this could not be done legally, then so much the worse for the law. This led to the bloody confrontation of October 1993, the shelling and the storming of the White House. We can limit ourselves here to two brief remarks. Though Yeltsin's conduct was entirely based on the principle that might is right, this does not turn all the defenders of parliament into figures of virtue; some of them were dangerous jingoists, not worth touching with a barge-pole. On the other hand, the way in which Western governments and the press endorsed and justified this blatant act of bloody coercion should open the eyes of those who genuinely believed that what the Western powers were interested in throughout Eastern Europe was democracy and not profits.

The Road to Capitalism

Even the bloody coup was not enough. In the referendum that followed, some "miracles" apparently had to be performed so that the constitution was approved by the required proportion of voters. The real shock, however, came with the results of the vote for the new parliament. Angry and bewildered, 23 percent of the voters cast their ballots for the ultra-jingoist party of Vladimir Zhirinovsky, deceptively called Liberal-Democratic. The reformed Communists got 12 percent and their rural allies, the Agrarian Party, 8 percent. Russia's Choice, the semiofficial party headed by Gaidar, was approved by only 15 percent of the voters. Two years later, in the new parliamentary poll, it was even worse for Yeltsin. Zyuganov's Communist Party of the Russian Federation (CPRF) got on its own more than 22 percent and, adding the more orthodox CP, over a quarter of the vote. True, Zhirinovsky's share, at 11 percent, was halved; but this time the official party, Chernomyrdin's Our Home Is Russia, got less than 10 percent.

In any case, Yeltsin had already gotten the message in 1993. He could no longer stick to his golden boys. To save his skin he had to work out a compromise. Chernomyrdin was given a freer hand in forming his new government. The practitioners, the tycoons, led by first deputy premier Oleg Soskovets, gained ground. The most prominent therapists—Gaidar himself, the finance minister Boris Fedorov—left. But the monetarist lobby and the international financial establishment kept a guarantee. The other first deputy premiership was given to Chubais who, as minister in charge, had been the architect and supervisor of Russia's privatization.

In Eastern Europe privatization was not, as in the Western world, the transfer of some enterprises to a dominant private sector. It was the creation of that sector almost from scratch. In Russia, as elsewhere, this proved easiest in retail trade and the services, where little capital was required. But a striking feature was the refusal of farmers to give up collective ownership and working of the land. Yet the key problem was how to privatize the means of production, the medium-sized and big plants. Of the various methods of mass privatization, the Russian government picked the voucher scheme. In 1992, as payment for her or his Soviet birthright, each Russian was given a voucher worth ten thousand rubles, about a couple of weeks' wages at the time. Their value did not keep up with the rapid rise in prices. Poor Russians sold vouchers to live, while speculative investment funds bought up vouchers judiciously to grab the state enterprises in auctions.

The draftsmen of the privatization scheme had to reckon with the prevailing feeling that factories should, in some undefined way, belong to their employees. As a compromise, they therefore offered the workers the possibility of getting 20 percent of the shares in their enterprise free, but without voting rights, or else to buy, together with the management, 51 percent. In the firms that were not too expensive, the latter mechanism prevailed. The managers made deals with their staff to keep outsiders out, rightly convinced that they would rapidly boost their original 5 percent into a controlling interest.

Mafia   The auctions varied from place to place. Wherever the mafia picked a factory, it was unwise to outbid its representatives. Altogether, Russian enterprises have not been sold at bargain basement prices. They have been dumped at prices bearing no relation to their value. An OECD study of voucher auctions noted that "US manufacturing companies have market value of about US $100,000 per employee. Russian manufacturing companies, in contrast have market value of about US $100 per employee. The difference is 1000 fold!"[6]

The voucher scheme ended in 1994. Since then the state enterprises, turned into joint stock companies, were supposed to be sold for cash to the highest bidder. By that time, the juiciest plums, notably in oil and other raw materials, were involved, and the bidding proved highly restrictive. The full story of the hidden connection between Chubais, who supervised the whole process either directly or through members of his team, and the main beneficiaries of this robbery may never be told; we got glimpses of the bribes and the ties when the partners quarreled, particularly in 1997. But the privileged position of a few money moguls was plain to see. Even the Western admirers of Chubais were slightly ill at ease over the operation known as "shares for loans," carried out in the second half of 1995. To get $2 billion into its coffers, the Russian state "auctioned" among highly selected banks the shares in some of its most valuable possessions. It actually got $1 billion, and, according to most accounts, this was really its own money (the government, while borrowing, was also depositing in favored private banks funds that could have been held in the central bank). In exchange, the privileged financiers got, at ridiculous prices, the control,

6. OECD, *Mass Privatization: An Initial Assessment* (Paris: OECD, 1995), 171.

and an option for the future possession, of some of the world's biggest oil and other companies.[7]

You may know the main profiteers of privatization under the name of the Magnificent or the Sinister Seven, depending on your own opinion. How much of the country's wealth did they really grab? The most conspicuous among them, Boris Berezovsky, who started as a mathematician and made his first big money selling cars, claims that he and his six fellow tycoons, all heads of big conglomerates, own half of Russia.[8] The man may be boasting. His once-partner and now chief rival, Potanin, may be closer to the truth when he suggests that ten to fifteen big businesses account for about half of the country's riches.[9] One must add groups in which the state still has a controlling interest. This includes, in the first place, the giant Gazprom, producing more tons of petroleum equivalent than any of the Seven Sisters, and now headed by Rem Vyakhirev but still closely connected with the former prime minister, Chernomyrdin. It is also necessary to include the economic empire of Yuri Luzhkov, the ambitious mayor of Moscow, who succeeded in keeping the privatizers of Chubais out of the Russian capital. Finally, there are the big enterprises of the partially privatized industrial-military sector, squeezed at the moment, but which cannot be discounted.

Despite the progress of privatization and the high degree of capitalist concentration, there is something fragile, uncertain, unfinished about the whole setup. One reason is that the sale is not yet over. Shares in Gazprom, in the oil companies, and in communications and electricity are still to be

7. One shocking example was the $170 million paid by Oneksimbank, owned by Vladimir Potanin, the closest associate of Chubais, for a 38 percent share of Norilsk Nickel, producer of 20 percent of the world's nickel or cobalt and 42 percent of its platinum, with earnings of nearly $700 million in the year preceding the transaction. See *Business Central Europe,* February 1996.

8. See his famous interview in the *Financial Times,* 9 November 1996. The other six are V. Potanin, head of Oneksimbank, with interests particularly in oil and communications; Gusinsky, boss of Most Bank, with interests concentrated in the media; Mikhail Khodorkovsky, presiding over the Menatep financial and oil empire; Alexander Smolensky of the SBS-Agro Bank; and Mikhail Fridman as well as Petr Aven of the Alfa financial group. Aven is often replaced as the seventh figure by Vladimir Vinogradov of Inkombank. All of them have interests in the media. For a succint summary in English of those interests, see Anne Nivat, "His Master's Voice," *Transitions* 5 (1998).

9. See interview in *Moskovskoye Novosti,* 5-12 July 1998.

sold to domestic and foreign buyers; the operation was slowed down in 1998 by the slump in petroleum prices, then stopped by the financial crisis. The uncertainty may have something to do with the fears of the profiteers that their swindles are sufficiently recent to be undone. They have had to fight the Communists to preserve their newly gained property and are looking suspiciously at Luzhkov who, though no nationalizer, might redistribute the spoils if he were elected president. The misgivings may also be due to the extent to which the level of taxation, the waivers, the exonerations are dependent on the decision of the tsar and the actions of his servants. But the principal reason is the provisional nature of the whole economic structure, which seems to stand only because nobody shakes it seriously. The state does not quite pay salaries but neither does it fully collect taxes. Workers don't get proper wages but are not really kicked out of their jobs. Barter accounts for at least one-half of economic transactions.[10] So far, much more has been done in terms of transferring property rights than in terms of capitalist restructuring. The financial squeeze, the bankruptcies, and the firing of surplus labor are still spelled in future tense. When Yeltsin assured the Russians that the worst was behind them, he was not telling them the truth. Worse unemployment is certainly still to come, with its unpredictable political consequences.

Is Victor Chernomyrdin, as whispered, one of the richest men in Russia? In how many privatized pies did Chubais, the minister in charge, have his finger? Such Moscow rumors and suspicions convey the prevailing feeling that corruption has invaded the entire economy, penetrated the whole body politic, and is spreading from the very top. In a country where old laws and customs have been relaxed and the new ones are either unwritten or unapplied, the whim of the prince, the signature of his servant on an export license, turn the favored subject into a millionaire (measured in dollars) overnight. Graft and corruption are to be found at all levels, and the desire to be master in one's own kingdom, capable of determining the redistribution of wealth, may partly explain the breakup of the Soviet Union and the struggle to create fiefdoms within Russia today. The opportunities to grant

10. This is the most common estimate. Grigori Yavlinsky, speaking on NTV (19 July 1998) claimed that "75 percent of the economic turnover is barter, surrogate money, and promissory notes."

advantages are being used to the maximum, and their beneficiaries flaunt their affluence with unrestrained arrogance.

The Soviet Union, it will be objected, also had its opulent elite. But its privileges came with the function and were lost together with the office. Now privileges are personal and for keeps. The profiteers are also more numerous and more ostentatious. In the Soviet Union, despite years of preaching against egalitarianism, huge discrepancies between haves and have-nots went against the grain, against the inherited ideology. The wealthy had to enjoy their lucre with curtains drawn. Today the beautiful people who emerge from Moscow's gourmet restaurants and nightclubs into chauffeur-driven limousines or rush to the airport for a trip to the French Riviera do not conceal their luxury—they parade it. What they have, they believe, they deserve. And the half-starving pensioners, the poorly paid workers, and the public employees have only themselves to blame for their fate. Neo-Stalinist hypocrisy has been replaced by the law of the capitalist jungle.

In this climate, the mafia is bound to prosper. Once again, let it be clear that organized crime was not invented by the new regime. In the Soviet economy, where supply and demand never matched and the managers had to operate most of the time on the wrong side of the law, there was plenty of scope for shady intermediaries and, behind them, for the mafia outfits. The phenomenon, however, was then marginal. Now it is central. In a society where the frontier between legal and illegal, between successful and criminal, is blurred, the mafia, like corruption, pervades all. The mafia has faster cars and better communications than the police and, if needed, can afford to bribe the policemen.[11] It can buy property on the cheap for its clients or for itself. It can rob bankers or set up banks. When the president shells a parliament that stands in his way, why should the mafia not "remove" people who hinder its purpose?

This makes the problem of Russia's masters sound too moral. After all, the Rockefellers and Carnegies were no angels, either. The trouble with

11. For a description, see Stephen Handelman, *Comrade Criminal* (New Haven: Yale University Press, 1995). According to a spokesman of the Ministry of the Interior, "organized crime controlled 550 banks, or nearly half of Russia's financial institutions, and more than 40,000 businesses." These include "over 500 big state-owned enterprises, 4000 joint-stock companies, 500 joint ventures and 700 wholesale and retail firms." (*Interfax*, Moscow, 26 November 1997.)

Russia's new rulers is that they do not give the impression of knowing where they are heading. They have the arrogance of the nouveaux riches, not the self-confidence of a class conscious that it is forging a new order. To paraphrase Marx, they are still at the stage of the accumulation of joys, not at that of the joy of accumulation. Their distinctive features are conspicuous consumption and flight of capital. They find it safer to put their money in foreign accounts rather than in productive investment in Russia. And, purely in terms of security, who could blame them? As the Russians watch the real-life remakes of Murder Inc. in Moscow, those among them who can recollect the holy scriptures learned at school must be reminded of Marx's description of primitive accumulation: "Capital comes [into the world] dripping from head to foot, from every pore, with blood and dirt."[12]

You can accuse me, with justification, of having dealt all this time with politicians and profiteers rather than with the people. But I have done so because perestroika so far has been carried out from above. To say that the people were mere onlookers, however, would be too much. The collective farmers, as we just saw, refused to play the part appointed to them by the privatizers. The industrial workers, particularly the miners, come out on strike and into the streets from time to time, notably to recover wages unpaid for months. So do the teachers and members of other professions. They defend their narrow stakes, but, so far, do not yet try to impose their broader interests as the superior interests of society as a whole. Up to now, the people have been the object of this transformation and not main subjects in their own story.

One of the terrible heritages of Stalinism is the confusion it has left in people's minds. Take the Russian working class. Its revolutionary ancestor had been bled by the civil war and absorbed into the new administration. The next generation was that of uprooted muzhiks. It took some time for the workers to become essentially town dwellers, accustomed to the rhythm of industrial life. Yet even this new working class was never allowed to organize on its own, to test its strength, to ponder its role in society. It knew it was not the "ruling class," but it did not know what it was. When the tacit truce reached under Brezhnev came to an end, the working class was

12. Karl Marx, *Capital,* vol. 1 (London: Lawrence and Wishart, 1970), 760.

bewildered and torn by contradictions. It was against the CP, because the party was the boss. It was vaguely in favor of the market, which meant the collapse of the existing system. But it was against everything that privatization involved—job insecurity, big pay differentials, growing power for the boss. And now Russian workers spend most of their energy simply trying to survive, doing odd jobs, selling the goods they get in place of wages.

A genuine socialist opposition could help the working class in its search for an identity and the intelligentsia could in the process recover their traditional role in Russia as dissidents, reformers pushing society in a progressive direction. After all, the priviligentsia does not account for all the educated. Besides, the technical and professional intelligentsia is now too large to be bribed by the promise of a privileged position. It can be won over if it gets concrete proof, not just the feeling, that it has a serious say in shaping its destiny, both in its place of work—the factory, the office, the laboratory—and in the larger society. This is also the potential ambition of the working class, and the technicians, growing in numbers and social importance, could act as a link between the two.

To separate socialism from Stalinist crimes and post-Stalinist distortions, to propose a pattern for running society distant from both Soviet command from above and from capitalist exploitation, to invent forms of democracy which will make such a system workable: this is already a tall order. If you add that Russia needs an ecological upheaval and that women's liberation has miles to travel there, the task becomes gigantic. Moreover, to say that the socialist opposition is, for the moment, still in its infancy is an optimistic exaggeration. Will it grow fast as eyes open during the current phase of redistribution of wealth, or will it have to wait for the full effects of privatization to be felt?

A gigantic task for a socialist party

The factor of time is complex. On one hand, the imposition of capitalism is a much harder exercise than our pundits and their Russian favorites have proclaimed and even assumed. Yeltsin's regime may have proven insufficiently arbitrary and authoritarian for the job. In case of complete social stalemate, a candidate in military boots could step forward (and get Western blessing?). This is the reason to hurry. On the other hand, time is needed for some things to be forgotten and others to be learned anew so that socialism can finally be put on Russia's agenda. Such are the clocks against which history races.

3.

The World After the Fall

A curse may be a blessing in disguise.

Folk wisdom

WHEN AN EDIFICE RESTS on two pillars and one of them goes, the building should collapse. The dissolution of the Soviet Union did not prove quite as dramatic as the architectural metaphor suggests, because the world had ceased to be entirely bipolar for some time, and eager efforts were being made for the main pillar, the American one, to do the job of two. Thus, it was not the end of the world, but it was the end of *a* world. Gone was a world in which many people had believed, admittedly lately in dwindling numbers, that an alternative to capitalism was being forged in the East. Gone, too, was the world fashioned at Yalta, in which the two global policemen, soon to be nuclear superpowers, both rivals and partners, were somehow shaping fate together. The collapse of the Soviet Union left a big gap, with international consequences.

We could measure the consequences geographically, starting close to home with the disintegration of the USSR, the Union of so-called Soviet and Socialist Republics, the former tsarist empire, first shaken by the revolution, then consolidated, particularly during Stalin's reign. One could only welcome the end of the bureaucratic rule from the center over the periphery, of the heavy hand of Moscow, of the domination of Russian nationalism. Alas, one system of corrupt rule from above was replaced by a series of such systems. The artificial erection of frontiers, tariffs, and customs within an economy that had been conceived as a highly integrated unit depressed still further the already low living standards. Popular discontent spurred local nationalisms hitherto repressed and fermenting below

44

the surface. Atavistic hatreds reappeared with a vengeance. The bloody conflicts between Armenians and Azeris, between Abkhasians and Georgians, or between the different tribes of Tadjikistan were a reminder that decentralization is a means to an end, not a virtue in itself. The absurd war in Chechnya, where the Russian army got bogged down between 1995 and 1997, showed the catastrophe that nationalist resurgence could produce.

Or we could move back further still, to the empire conquered when the Red Army drove the Nazis back to the Elbe. Actually, the dissolution began earlier here, in those heady days of 1989 as the people of Eastern Europe climbed spectacularly onto the political stage. Unfortunately, they did not stay on it for very long. The problems facing the countries of Eastern Europe—the drive towards capitalism, the search for property owners, the disappointment with new doctors, and the return of the old-timers, the converted Communists—are similar to those affecting Russia, only the crisis is much less acute, because the former regime did not linger so long in the outlying area and had always been a foreign imposition. Naturally, each country has its specificity—Poland has its labor movement, Hungary its longer period of reforms, the Czech Republic its industrial tradition—yet the only real exception, and one which teaches us a great deal about the rule, is that of the DDR, the former East Germany.

Capital, when it invades new territory, tries to destroy as much as it can in order to be able to build anew. (This, incidentally, may explain something about the state of the economies of the former Soviet bloc after 1989. They had been in a pretty bad state before, and they were clearly heading for a dead end. Yet they appeared in an even worse condition once they were submitted to the shattering wind of foreign competition.) In East Germany the invading capital could wreck innumerable enterprises and deprive nearly half the population of employment. While the economy was being restructured, the victims were getting their unemployment benefits. This takeover by West German business was being subsidized by the country as a whole and, indeed, by the European Union, which had to put up with the financial policy dictated by the Bundesbank. However unpleasant, the operation was bearable. A Marshall Plan of impossible proportions would have been required to extend such a scheme to Eastern Europe as a whole, including the ex-Soviet Union. This subsidized takeover of the DDR by the

ıl Republic gives an idea of what the unsubsidized colonization of
n Europe by Western capital is likely to be.

All these are interesting issues. Yet I want to concentrate here on
something else. The 1917 revolution was originally conceived by its actors
and sympathizers as the first concrete movement in humankind's great leap
from the kingdom of necessity to the realm of freedom. Then the movement
was isolated, frozen, and it degenerated. So far we have looked at the
domestic aspects of that tragedy and that degeneration. But it also had a
tremendous impact on the outside world. The Soviet Union inspired millions to radical action and repelled others, turning them against socialism.
It helped countries of the third world to liberate themselves, then paralyzed
them by its own model. It simultaneously prevented the further expansion
of American imperialism and contributed to its domination. What does its
disappearance mean? Concretely, does the left, labor, the progressive
movement—call it what you like—in the advanced capitalist countries find
it easier or harder, as a result, to perform its task? Are the countries of Latin
America, Africa, and Asia in a better or worse position to seek their own
ways out of exploitation? In this new global world does it herald "the end
of history," the fashionable name for the eternal reign of capital or, on the
contrary, the beginning of the end of that reign?

One's judgment of the significance of the disappearance of the Soviet
Union naturally depends on one's assessment of the part it performed
during its existence. The answers are difficult to give, because the subject
itself did change over nearly three quarters of a century, and so did its
influence. They are complex, because the role played by the Soviet Union
was more complicated and ambiguous than it now appears in the
Manichean funeral orations.

The Communist parties are children of the Russian Revolution. Amid
retrospective reassessments, it is too often forgotten that in the days of 1919
the best and most radical people in the labor movement accepted the
twenty-one conditions required to join the new International in order to be
linked with the Revolution and dissociated from the Second International,
which had betrayed its members and its principles at the outbreak of the
First World War. For the Bolsheviks, the building of socialism in their own
country depended on the spread of the movement, so it was natural that the

Third International, the Comintern, centered in Moscow, should be the headquarters of world revolution. Things began to go wrong when, the revolution failing to expand, a clear distinction appeared within the organization between the successful Russians and the unsuccessful outsiders. The Russians, turning necessity into virtue, were tempted to present their example, their solution, as a model for the world at large. What was still a minor failing under Lenin and Trotsky became the dominant feature of Stalin's Comintern.

The Georgian dictator's only contribution to revolutionary thought was that Marxist contradiction in terms—"socialism in a single country." That idea had not been invented in 1924 to convince Stalin's rivals that something had to be done to defend and consolidate the regime in the Soviet Union. Everybody agreed on that. It was a doctrine of consolation for the tired, isolated Soviet people, and one which had extraordinary implications for the international Communist movement. If one could go the whole way, build full-fledged socialism in the Soviet Union, then that became the supreme goal to which everything else was to be sacrificed. The Communist movement was thus conceived as a great revolutionary army fighting on many fronts, with one of them, however, decisive—the Russian front, where the future was being forged. This is how the interests of world revolution were subordinated to those of the Kremlin and the Comintern became a mere instrument of Soviet diplomacy.

This conviction was not only imposed from above. It was internalized and accepted by the rank and file. Otherwise one cannot explain their relative fidelity as the Comintern switched its line in sudden turns on orders from Moscow.[1] In the 1930s, the sectarian class line of the so-called Third Period, which unwittingly helped the rise of Hitler, was followed by the search for the broadest alliances under the banner of Popular Fronts. This honeymoon with liberalism against fascism was interrupted by the Nazi-Soviet Pact. Then, once again, the line reversed when the USSR was invaded in 1941. Indeed, to please the bourgeois wartime allies, the Comintern was dissolved in May 1943, and at the end of the war the Western CPs, though greatly strengthened by the part they had played in

---

1. Relative, because one of the features of the Western Communist Parties was a quick turnover in membership. The biggest political party in France, wits used to say, was that of the ex-members of the Communist Party.

the resistance, did nothing to turn the liberation into a crisis of the system. Actually, they propped up capitalist regimes until after the Marshall Plan, the full freeze of the Cold War, and the setting up of the Cominform in September 1947. And throughout these turns and twists, they followed Soviet strategy with the discipline of military battalions.

And yet this is only half the story. True, even major parties, like the Italian or the French, echoed Moscow like ventriloquist's dummies. But they were at the same time genuine political forces, expressing the interests of the downtrodden in their own countries. The now fashionable books, condemning the Western left and particularly the intellectuals for their infatuation with the Soviet Union, read like mystery stories.[2] Because these authors minimize the evils of capitalism, because they put little stress on the Great Depression with its mass unemployment, on social conflicts, on Algeria or Vietnam or the anticolonial struggles afterward, it is difficult to understand from their accounts why intelligent people sided with Russia and turned a blind eye on crimes committed in the name of socialism. Those who lived through that period can assure the reader that it was not easy to condemn both sides, because the Communists were at the time the main force in many vital battles.

In any case, the time of the believers, the simultaneously heroic and horrible period of international Communism, came to a close shortly after Khrushchev's "secret" indictment of Stalin in 1956. Something snapped with that revelation. That year, all Communist parties still approved the invasion of Hungary. Twelve years later, the Soviet tanks in Prague could not claim the same unanimity. Italian Communists, for instance, disapproved of the Soviet action, though they did not yet draw conclusions about the nature of the Soviet regime. By the time of the invasion of Afghanistan, condemnation was the rule. It may seem unfair that the decline of the international movement coincides with a certain liberalization of the regime at home and of its treatment of foreign parties. But the resurrection having failed domestically, the failure had repercussions abroad. From Togliatti's polycentrism through Eurocommunism, the Communist parties found their way leading away from Moscow. The irony is that most of them finally opted for capitalism just as capitalism was entering into crisis.

2. See, for instance, Tony Judt, *Past Imperfect* (Berkeley: University of California Press, 1992) and François Furet, *The History of an Illusion* (New York: The Free Press, 1997).

Here I just want to stress a puzzling development. Though by 1989 the link with Moscow had long been broken and hardly anyone on the left seriously maintained that the Soviet Union offered a socialist alternative, the fall of the Berlin Wall has been taken by the general public as a setback for the left, for radical action, for socialism. Since this sweeping reaction, coming a third of a century after Khrushchev's speech, took me aback, I must confess, I will only dare to offer a series of suggestions rather than an explanation. People crave for concrete illustrations and, by conditioned reflex, the Soviet model may have survived in the popular mind more than one thought. Gorbachev's success certainly revived illusions about the possibility of reform from within and from above. The state of the economy in "socialist" countries, once the frontiers were opened, shocked outsiders. Last but not least, the mighty Western propaganda machine, working full steam, has succeeded in convincing the public that Soviet equals socialist and that the collapse of the former means, therefore, the funeral of the latter.

The immediate effect is clearly negative. The mood is even more pessimistic than before and, whatever the discontent, the belief in an alternative has been still further reduced. Yet the setback may be temporary. The Soviet Union had nothing to offer, and now the radical opposition in the West is free to face up to its own problems and invent its own solutions. When it does so, it will no longer be handicapped by a cumbersome model and guilt by association—provided, of course, that it manages to convince people once again that life can be changed through collective political action.

For attempts of the underdeveloped world to get out of the capitalist orbit, the prospects look gloomier, because here the Soviet Union, with its nuclear weapons, did set a limit on American intervention. How serious a limit? Before embarking on a discussion of the vexing problem of the Soviet Union as a factor of world revolution, I would like to make a preliminary remark.

In a nutshell, my argument so far has been that since the revolution happened in a backward country, where by Marxist definition there was no scope for a socialist society, and since that revolution failed to spread, the tragic, abortive attempt proves nothing about the impossibility, or the possibility for that matter, of building socialism. On the other hand, the fundamentals of Marxism are called into question by the failure of the revolution to happen where it was supposed to happen, that is to say in the advanced capitalist West. Is it because capitalism, contrary to forecasts, still had a lot of room for development, for real or artificial growth? And how much did the Soviet Union contribute, through its policies and its image, to render, say, West Europeans allergic to radical transformation? I will not pretend to have the answers. What is important to remember here is that after the initial Bolshevik period, the USSR no longer relied on revolution in the Western world. Stalin's remark that "communism fitted Germany as a saddle fitted a cow" was a good example of that contempt.[3]

Moscow, actually, neither relied on revolution nor hoped for it. Since the ultimate victory of "socialism"—too distant to bother the pragmatic men in the Kremlin—was really to be the extension of the Soviet model on the world scale, spontaneous upheavals, movements from below, systems more attractive because built in a more advanced environment, all were potential nuisances, undermining the model and Moscow's mastery. Stalin was only in favor of revolutions, or rather acquisitions, that he could keep under strict control. His successors were instinctively even more conservative. To imagine that Brezhnev or Chernenko spent sleepless nights bothering about the progress of Marxism on our planet required the chutzpah, or the sense of humor, of Western propaganda services.

The movements of national liberation were somewhat different. From the beginning the Bolsheviks grasped that anti-imperialist struggles, say, in China or India could greatly weaken the capitalist states and back in 1920 they called from Baku for the oppressed people of the East to rise. Once the hope of revolution in Western Europe was given up, this became not the supplementary but the main foreign front. But here, too, the condition was total subservience to Russia's interests, as the Chinese Communists discovered in 1926-1927, when their lives were sacrificed for the sake of good relations with the Kuomintang. In fact, the greatest Communist victory in Asia, that of the Chinese Revolution in 1949, was achieved by Mao against Moscow's advice.[4] The other Communist victory, in Vietnam, was the product of a more balanced situation. It is true that in 1972 the Russians, with their emphasis on an understanding with Washington,

3. Stalin made the comment to the Polish prime minister in exile, Stanislaw Mikolajczyk.

4. History, incidentally, was to explain Stalin's reluctance, as China proved too mighty to be treated as a satellite.

greeted Nixon warmly in Moscow—a Nixon who had just bombed North Vietnam. It is also true that the heroic struggle of the Vietnamese people was greatly helped by Russian arms and by the very existence of the Soviet Union. Yet successful insurrections in Cuba and Vietnam got from Moscow, along with weapons and economic aid, the Soviet model. The kiss of life, if one may say so, was infected.

In addition to the few countries which went the whole way and joined the Communist bloc, you had the more numerous, nonaligned states with different regimes, which could keep Communists in their jails and, nevertheless, to avoid Western domination, chose the Soviet Union as trading partner, supplier of military aid, and to some extent protector. Moscow did not do it out of love or revolutionary fervor. In its trial of strength with the United States, it found it convenient to extend its influence, say, in the Middle East thanks to Egypt. Khrushchev even tried to rationalize the mechanism. Under the rules of peaceful coexistence, he argued, the nuclear balance will act as an umbrella under which the movements of national liberation should be allowed to prosper. Washington never quite accepted this doctrine and tried to impose its laws outside the strict frontiers of the Soviet bloc. Since Russia was reluctant to face a direct confrontation with the United States, an American client was probably better shielded than a Soviet protégé. Nevertheless, the balance offered scope for neutrals, for outsiders, that is now bound to be drastically narrowed.

To sum it up, countries joining the Communist bloc were getting an obsolete economic organization and a political straitjacket. Once their victory had been achieved, they would be better without it. But the road to victory will now be incomparably tougher. People ready, like the Vietnamese were, for heroic sacrifices should still be able to make it, though the fate of Vietnam today raises the question of what they would do with their victory. But it must be reckoned that any country trying now to break the capitalist rules of the game is bound to face economic strangulation and, if it survives, may well be threatened with invasion.

This prospect throws the main burden on the progressive forces in the advanced capitalist countries. Imagine for instance the rise of a socialist Western Europe. It would preach by example (not to be confused with the imposition of a model). It would have to establish entirely new relations with the exploited countries and thus challenge the dictatorship of capital throughout the globe. But such a prospect is still a figment of our imagination, and meanwhile the progressive forces in the West, greatly weakened, are reduced to propaganda designed to put pressure on their governments. They must rely on movements of public opinion and exploit inner conflicts between capitalist blocs and the complicated mechanisms of international institutions.

We are living a terribly difficult period of transition. The reign of classical capitalism now stretches throughout the planet, and the world, so unified, cries for an international democratic order. Instead, it gets capitalist disorder producing monstrosities from Bosnia to Rwanda, with ensuing mandates to remove them. The dilemma is obvious: to institutionalize international organs of repression is, in present circumstances, to consolidate and codify the world disorder supervised by the American sheriff, yet to do nothing is to tolerate human slaughter, rape, and ethnic cleansing. We are reduced to ad hoc decisions, lesser evils, calculations in each case whether the remedy is not worse than the disease. We must improvise until the socialist movement reappears on the international scene as an autonomous political force.

This was no digression. We are now getting to the heart of the matter, to the world we have lived in and the one we are inheriting, to what once looked like the great contest between two systems, between Western capitalism and the Soviet bloc, between Nato and the Warsaw Pact, between America and Russia. In its last phase, the conflict became complicated. It looked, we mentioned, like one between rivals and partners, enemies and accomplices, two boxers in a clinch, about whom it is difficult to say whether they are exchanging punches or propping each other up.

The deep division was undeniable. Russia may not have escaped the reign of capital. It was clearly outside the kingdom where classical capitalism held sway. The Soviet Union, in fact, presided over a gigantic portion of the world that capital could not easily penetrate in search of profits. It was actually a potential protector for those who wanted to leave the classical capitalist orbit. No wonder that our propagandists were regularly repeating a modern version of *Delenda est Carthago*.[5] The reverse was also

5. "Carthage must be destroyed," the cry with which Cato "the Elder" ended all speeches, exemplary of a crusading campaign against "the enemy."

true. For the men in the Kremlin, America was a permanent danger. Its high productivity was a threat to the economy, its high living standards were a perilous attraction for the people throughout its empire, and its high expenditure on arms, boosted as if on purpose, imposed a burden reaching unbearable proportions.

Nevertheless, the two protagonists were also accomplices. Moscow was particularly keen on reaching an agreement with the other nuclear giant and establishing together the rules of coexistence.[6] But they needed one another on a more practical level. For most of the period, the "red peril" enabled Western governments to get out of their legislatures the high military expenditure which fueled their economies and produced profits. The need for unity, faced with that threat, kept capitalist rivals together and allowed the United States to preserve the undisputed leadership of the alliance. Critics of the evils of our society could be dismissed and ostracized as "agents of Moscow" and, more recently, the prospect of the gulag was brandished to discredit those who dared to preach the need for radical change.

Within the Soviet bloc, dissidents during that time were sentenced and silenced as "imperialist agents." The low living standards were explained away by the imperative needs of defense. The preservation of stupid political controls, of a clumsy economic mechanism, of an altogether obsolete regime was being justified by the necessity to resist capitalist encirclement. It is now obvious that the anti-Soviet crusade, the all-out offensive, had postponed, not precipitated, perestroika. On the other hand, to say that the development of the welfare state and the progress achieved by the working people in Western Europe during the years of prosperity after 1945 were a by-product of Western policy in the Cold War is an exaggeration. Big business made concessions because it could afford them, and the unions made conquests because they were strong enough to exercise pressure. The October Revolution and the existence of the Soviet Union were, naturally, not unconnected with the strength of the labor movement or the readiness of employers to make concessions.

The relationship between the protagonists in the Cold War contest was not always so ambiguous. It started as a mortal combat. The Bolsheviks

---

6. It was that search, with its implication that on each side there should be only one finger on the nuclear trigger, incidentally, which precipitated the Sino-Soviet break.

saw themselves as a vanguard in an international struggle that could only be won by attacking the main fortresses of capitalism, the advanced Western countries. The latter saw the Soviet Union in the same light. Foreign intervention in Russia's civil war was an attempt to nip the danger in the bud. In recent years, passion was only to be found, on both sides, in propaganda. The nature of the conflict altered gradually as the Soviet Union ceased to provide the image of the radical alternative.

The USSR differed fundamentally from the capitalist states in property relations and forms of exploitation. The means of production were not in private hands, and the surplus was being extracted by essentially political methods rather than the forces of the market. Yet, except in its early aspirations, this society had nothing to do with socialism. Collective ownership of the means of production is not an end in itself. At no level, from the shop floor to the country at large, did Marx's "associated producers" run their affairs, determine their work and their fate. Planning took the form of dictation. The state, far from withering away, towered over society. Instead of providing, as expected, new freedoms, new ways of living and loving and creating, it invented new, terrible ways of coercion, and, after a spell, restored old values.

Dagnat i peregnat Ameriku: to catch up with and overtake America. When this slogan was first invented in the early days of the new regime, the assumption was that once Russia reached the same level of productivity, it would invent a bright future, an entirely different society. The expansion of mass education and health services, as well as the effervescence in the arts stimulated originally by the Revolution, gave credibility to the idea and the illusion then persisted for a long time, sustained by conditioned reflexes and wishful thinking. But for quite some time now, radicals in the Western world understood that the Soviet model offered no solutions, except negative ones, to the major problems they were facing. Back in the 1960s, the young rebels who took to the streets in Paris or Rome may have sung "The Internationale," but they were not looking to Moscow for inspiration.

The attraction lasted longer in the third world, where Russia appeared as a model for rapid industrialization defying the orders of international capital. This appeal also declined and then disappeared during the Brezhnev stagnation. The last to go over, understandably, were the main beneficiaries, the Soviet elite, including the country's rulers. Until the very end, they paid lip service to Marxism-Leninism, which had lost all critical capacity when it became a state religion. They obviously did not believe their Sunday prayers, but power was worth a mass. *Dagnat i peregnat*. . . . When the lag, instead of narrowing, began to widen, it was not worth it any longer. If you can't beat 'em, join 'em. They then embarked on their conversion, with scruples in the case of Gorbachev, without them in the case of Yeltsin. And this is how a whole historical period, which had begun with a defiance of fate, with a bold challenge to the capitalist order, ended in humble surrender, with the people of Eastern Europe joyfully celebrating their recovery of freedom and the people of the Soviet Union not quite knowing what there was to celebrate.

Our establishment, on the other hand, knew perfectly well what should be celebrated. With the help of its pundits and its preachers, its press and its television, it has been drumming, ever since, the same overwhelming message: the Soviet Union was socialism and this is the final funeral for socialism; history has come to an end; capitalism will now rule forever; rebels of all lands, get it into your heads: there is and there can be no alternative. That the victors should thus seize the opportunity to gain political advantage out of the celebrations is only natural. What is perturbing is the ease with which the general public, including large sections of the left, has swallowed this message, not so much about the end of history as about the vanity of even searching for an alternative.

And if the repetitive stridency of that machine concealed fears rather than self-confidence? Maybe our propagandists are less fools than knaves. Maybe, while proclaiming capitalist eternity, they know perfectly well that the lesson of 1989 is quite different, namely, that when a system is obsolete, sooner or later it will have to yield, and when people inspired by an idea enter the stage as actors in their own drama, they can shape history.[7] Maybe our persuaders are stressing the permanence of the established order they are paid to praise because they are aware that it is now its turn to face the verdict of history, and they hope in this way to postpone the day of judgment.

7. To be sure, that second aspect was less striking than it appeared on the spur of the moment; the people did enter the stage, but left it almost at once.

Whose Millennium?

Capitalism has clearly gained a new lease on life. It is by its nature an expanding social formation, one that feeds on territories that it conquers. The collapse of the Soviet competitor enables it to consolidate its rule in Asia, Latin America, and Africa, while also invading lands from the Elbe up to Vladivostok, hitherto uncharted on the capitalist map. Whatever its current difficulties, and they are very serious, the extension of capitalism should normally strengthen it. The question arises, however, whether capital did not have to stretch across the globe to reach the end of its tether. There are seeds of defeat in this victory.

To begin with, there is no common enemy to unite the capitalist rivals. Before, the leader of each alliance was imposing some discipline. Now, with relaxation, local wars, fueled by ethnic strife, multiply from Bosnia to Tadjikistan. It is not certain what will happen within the various blocs into which the Western alliance is splitting. Thus, in Western Europe it is far from clear whether the united Germany will play the role of Prussia in the Zollverein, that of the unifier, and then use the European Union under its auspices for an economic *drang nach osten*. And will the United States be able to play sheriff to the world at large, impose its law on Japan and western Europe, despite obvious and growing conflicts of interest?

Secondly, it is no longer possible to use the Soviet bogey to explain our predicaments. If expenditure on arms remains horrendously high, it is not to match the Russians, but because it is an intrinsic element of our society. If Indian peasants rise in Chiapas, it is not because their leaders were bought with Moscow's gold. It will be increasingly difficult to brand as agents of the evil empire those who proclaim that the kingdom is rotten and must be entirely rebuilt. The venom with which all those who suggest that it is possible to look for a different society are attacked as dangerous utopians is, probably, explained by the knowledge of our preachers that soon they will not be able to get away from it all with repeated warnings about the gulag.

The third and essential point is that, in its hour of triumph, capitalism appears in its nakedness, without frills. Gone is the talk about capitalism with a human face.[8] It is back to the old jungle. The gap is growing not only

8. It did not last very much longer than that other seven days' wonder—"the socialist market."

56

between the have and have-not nations. It is widening between rich and poor in both the oppressed and the advanced capitalist countries. The latest technological discoveries are being used to impose cultural conformity throughout the globe. Our old friend, mass unemployment, which was supposed to have vanished forever, is back with a vengeance, rising together with productivity. All that it proves is that even when our economy grows, it does not do so for the benefit of the majority of the people, that there is a striking contrast between our technical inventiveness and our total lack of a social imagination—or, if you prefer the old Marxist terms, a conflict between productive forces and social relations.

No serious effort is really made to pretend that we are all social democrats now using Keynesian tools. On the contrary, we in Europe are told that in the new, deregulated world we can no longer afford a welfare state, a national health service, a reasonable pension scheme, a not-too-indecent minimum wage. In other words, the labor movement is told to give up all its postwar conquests. What the world is being offered today is not the American dream but the American nightmare.

In Western Europe—it is not as paradoxical as it sounds—the collapse of neo-Stalinism coincides with the crisis of social democracy.

4.

Requiem for Social Democracy

When sorrows come, they come not single spies
But in battalions. . . .

Shakespeare, *Hamlet*

THE FALL OF THE SOVIET EMPIRE was greeted not only as the funeral of socialism but as the final dead end for all revolutionary roads. The practitioners of revolution, Maximilien Robespierre and Oliver Cromwell, as well as its theoreticians, Rosa Luxemburg and Karl Marx, were lumped together in retrospective condemnation. Logically, such an offensive against the very idea of radical transformation should have been coupled with praise for gradualism, for Fabian tactics, for progressive change. To use two clichés at once, the "collapse of communism" could have been combined with the "triumph of social democracy." Actually, nothing of the kind happened. On the contrary, the disintegration of the neo-Stalinist system has been followed by a major crisis of social democracy, taken here in its very narrow current definition—the reformist management of capitalist society.

The actual meaning of words is not unimportant. We saw the damage done by the identification of communism or socialism with Stalinism and its sequels. Let us be more precise about the term *social democracy.* Originally it was a synonym for the socialist movement. Lenin and Martov, the Bolsheviks and the Mensheviks, were all members of the Second, that is to say the social-democratic, International. So were the "evolutionary" socialist Eduard Bernstein and his arch critic, Rosa Luxemburg. In theory, at least, reformers and revolutionaries agreed on the final objective: a classless society, with the means of production socialized and inequalities uprooted. In principle, they were not even fundamentally divided over the use of violence, since its degree depended on the resistance provided by the privileged minority. Where they really differed was over the continuity of the movement. The reformers argued that you get to that different society gradually, progressively, within existing institutions. The revolutionaries replied that you cannot get there without a break and a radical reshaping of the institutional framework.

On paper, the unity of purpose survived the interwar period even if in fact, while the Communist parties aligned themselves with Moscow, the Socialist parties became increasingly the upholders of the established order. Even after the last war, however, it took the Socialist parties quite a lot of time to square their official proclamations with their practice. The German Social Democrats revised their statutes at Bad Godesberg in 1958, and it was only in 1995 that the British Labour Party got rid of the reference to "the common ownership of the means of production, distribution and exchange" in the famous Clause Four of its charter. But these were clearly shibboleths, relics from the past. The French Socialists were probably the last ones, until 1981, to still pay lip service to the alleged "break with capitalism," and we know what happened to that after Mitterrand's two years in office. Today there is no possible misunderstanding. Social democracy no longer claims that its purpose is to get rid of capitalist society. Its only aim is to make improvements within the framework of that society.

But now, apparently, there is no scope any longer in Western Europe for such a reformist management of capitalism, and this is why the current crisis of social democracy is so serious. To grasp its importance, we shall look at the quarter century of unprecedented growth after the war, when there was room for improvement; at the ideological consequences of that prosperity, including the reincarnation of Communist parties; at the historical irony that this reorientation coincided with the beginning of the economic crisis; at the quarter of a century of restructuring that followed; and finally at the dilemma facing the West European left as a result.

The twenty-five years after the Second World War were for Western Europe a period of exceptionally fast economic growth and deep social transformation. A combination of factors contributed to this unprecedented change. There was the need for reconstruction after the war and the opportunity to absorb the progress achieved by U.S. industry during the conflict. There was American investment and aid, more generous than it would have been otherwise because of the confrontation with Russia. Western Europe could also use on a wider scale the American methods of mass production when Europe's inner market expanded after the mid-fifties as a result of the successive stages of economic integration. Finally, there was the second phase of the industrial revolution, particularly striking in countries like France and Italy, where concentration had not gone as far as in Britain or Germany during the nineteenth century.

The clearest sign of the changing social landscape was the disappearance of the peasant in the western half of continental Europe. At the end of the Second World War, close to a third of the labor force was working on the land in France and more than that in Italy; a quarter of a century later, the proportion was approaching Anglo-Saxon levels.[1] This mass migration from country to town, rendered possible by a very fast rise of productivity in agriculture, was insufficient to satisfy the urban demand for labor. Foreign workers were imported, first from southern Europe, then from overseas. And women entered the labor market in increasing numbers to fill jobs in health and education, in shops and offices. If you take the quarter century as a whole, you see a dramatic reduction in farm labor, rough stability among blue collar employment, and fast expansion among white collar workers.

A rapid growth of the national product, however, is the main feature of the period. If you except Britain, the national product was growing, year in, year out, by an average of 5 percent. Such a pace, maintained over a long stretch, made it possible and worthwhile to pass on part of the increment to working people. Those nearly thirty years thus witnessed an exceptional rise in living standards and a deep change in the patterns of consumption. The car, the washing machine, the refrigerator, the television, those luxuries connected with the American dream, became within a generation quite common, and this mass diffusion of durable consumer goods was accompanied in Europe—this is a big difference from the United States—by collective conquests. The national health scheme was gradually extended to the entire population throughout the area. Some limits were put

---

1. By 1996, the share of agriculture in the labor force was down to 4.6 percent in France and 7 percent in Italy. See *OECD in Figures* (Paris: OECD, 1998).

on the employers' power to hire and fire. A minimum wage, not decent but significant, was introduced. Sickness and unemployment benefits as well as old age pensions were raised. Social-democratic ideas prospered as capitalist Europe was building its version of the welfare state.

We should not idealize what the French nostalgically call *les trente glorieuses*, the thirty glorious years. They had their seamy side: the oppression of immigrant workers, the double exploitation of women at work and at home, the distress of uprooted peasants, the tensions and insecurity of the overcrowded towns, particularly in their suburbs, and we could go on. The amount of pent-up discontent below the glittering surface of our smug consumer society was revealed spectacularly in 1968-1969 by the students and young workers in France and Italy who seized their campuses, paralyzed factories, and took to the streets raising questions still unanswered today, though more topical than ever. Growth for what purpose? For whose profit? For what kind of society and what sort of life?

Yet capitalism, still growing fast at the time, managed to resist that wave of protest, and it is amusing to see today on what grounds capitalism was defended. Not just negatively, with the claim that the gulag is the only possible alternative: capitalism was advocated then because of its own virtues, on the basis that the system had found the secret of eternal youth, permanent growth. The curse of unemployment had been lifted as economic crisis vanished, replaced by minor variations in the trade cycle. Why abolish a society which has managed to get rid of its worst calamities, in which the harsh laws of the market have been replaced by Keynesian fine-tuning, in which the long lines for the dole have been replaced by the social protection of the state? The climate was social-democratic even in countries where the Socialists were not in office. And the mood was contagious.

By the mid-1970s, the Communist orphans, long deprived of their Soviet model and unable to replace it with a project of their own, were also converted. Even their long-term ambition was no longer to change society, only to make changes within that society. Historians may one day report with amusement that the Communist conversion to the *compromesso storico,* to give the historical compromise its original Italian title, occurred just when the period which gave birth to this strategic change came to an end. One may argue whether the Western structural crisis began with the fall of the rate of profit or with the boom in oil prices, but it is around the mid-1970s that the big break in postwar history takes place. Almost thirty years of unprecedented growth and social-democratic climate came to an end. Nearly twenty-five years of ideological and political swing to the right, against the background of economic restructuring, began.

Paris was a good vantage point from which to observe the extraordinary ideological somersault. It was in France, after the student and workers' rising of 1968, that the cultural and ideological pillars of our society looked most shaken. The edifice still stood because the various protest movements were unable to combine in a joint offensive. The economic crisis now threatened to provide the unifying element. For those in power it was vital to persuade the young that, while to rebel might be just, to move from there to collective action on a wider scale was both dangerous and potentially criminal. The message had to be delivered by relatively young apostles vaguely connected with the May movement of '68. The *nouveaux philosophes* offered their services. Their fare, as is well known, was neither new nor profound. It was old and imported: a slice of Popper, a piece of von Hayek, and a big cut of Solzhenitsyn. The young French cooks added only the commercial gravy. Intellectually, the product was nonexistent. As an exercise in propaganda, it proved very successful. With the help of the media the message was passed on that a revolution could only lead to the gulag and that *totality* was tantamount to *totalitarian.* From "any break is dangerous," it was easy to shift to "there is no alternative" and, finally, to "history has come to an end."

Having learned from Marx that the ruling ideology is the ideology of the ruling class, we should not really be surprised. After all, the movement had failed, the regime survived, and it preserved its hegemony. But in fact the ideological metamorphosis has been so striking that it cannot be explained just by the clever campaign of the establishment and of its servants. To understand it, we must now look at the last twenty-five years or so, at the offensive of capital, the retreat of labor, and the present dilemma of the defeated left.

To see how far we have traveled in less than a quarter of a century, it is enough to listen to the new message. Gone are the social-democratic tales about capitalism with a human face. It is the old capitalist dogma, at its toughest, that is once again being preached. Profit is the Almighty and everything must be subordinated to its cult. Private is beautiful and public, by definition, wasteful. The role of the state should always be reduced, except—and it is an enormous exception—where it helps business to make a profit. We can no longer afford to pamper and cuddle the idle, the misfits, the dissolute. And if capitalism happens to favor the rich and impoverish the poor, it can't be helped, it's part of its principle: "For unto everyone that hath shall be given."[2] While what the French used to call *la gauche respectueuse,* the respectable left (more literally, the left respectful of the established order), was reluctant to accept the end of its illusion, the right was boldly on the attack.[3]

The trade unions were in a weak position to defend the interests of their members. Not only were they mentally unprepared for the offensive. They had not used the earlier period to adapt themselves to the deep changes in the structure of the labor force: they did not recruit on a mass scale among immigrant or female workers. And now the restructuring struck at their strongholds—the mines, the steel works, the shipyards, the auto industry—all places where they had their big battalions. True, we were told that this was transitional trouble, that only old industries were affected and the loss of jobs there would be offset by expansion in the services. Indeed, it happened that way for a time. Then came the computer. Automation invaded banks, insurance, and distribution, cutting jobs there in the same fashion. Mass unemployment is now at the heart of the European crisis, and we shall return to it, having looked first at the environment in which the crisis occurs, an environment that has not been thrust upon us accidentally, but is a product of conscious policies designed to strengthen the power of capital.

Trade barriers having been lowered earlier, the emphasis in the last twenty years was put on the almost total lifting of restrictions on the international movement of capital. Computers and modems have quickened the pace of communication, facilitated around-the-clock operations, and made possible the invention of all sorts of hedging systems, but the decision to let money travel freely was political. As a result, daily

2. Matt. 25:29.

3. The term itself was not very respectful, as it was coined on the basis of Sartre's well-known play *La Putain Respectueuse,* or *The Respectful Whore.*

international transactions now exceed on an average the astronomical figure of more than $1.5 trillion, more than the total gold and foreign currency reserves of all the members of the International Monetary Fund.[4] Even allowing for double accounting, this gives an idea of the relative weakness of individual governments. Financial capital now reigns supreme, and central banks are its subordinates. Each state knows that its monetary and fiscal policies are constrained by the threat of capital flight. The bargaining power of labor unions is also weakened by this possibility given to capital to move freely in search of cheaper workforces.

Western Europe was very far from an exception to this trend. As the European Economic Community, now known as the European Union, moved first towards a single market and is now, painfully, in transition to a single currency, the euro, the individual nation-states have lost many of their powers to protect their territory, to control flows of capital, to influence the management of their economy. Yet the powers were not transferred to a larger European state wielding them from Brussels but to a regime of free trade, that is to say, the rule of capital. In the Maastricht Treaty, allegedly the guide to European unity, a social chapter was introduced with some minimum guarantees for the working people, only so that it could be claimed that labor was not entirely forgotten.[5]

Within this free trade framework, Europe rediscovered the curse of mass unemployment. It was no longer possible to pretend that the phenomenon was transient or due to the vagaries of the cycle. Naturally the number of the jobless was smaller in boom phases than in slumps, but it was higher at

4. The latest figures of the Bank of England, quoted by *The Economist,* 3 October 1998, put the daily transaction of the United States, Britain, France, Germany, Switzerland, Japan, Singapore, and Hong Kong at slightly more than $1.6 trillion.

5. This "agreement on social policy" increased the number of issues on which the rule of unanimity was no longer required. Altogether, the social legislation of the European Union has some relevance on matters of health and labor safety as well as the coordination between the security systems of various countries. Otherwise, even when common regulations do exist—for example, the limitation of the working week to forty-eight hours—there are so many waivers as to render them irrelevant. The contrast between the huge economic legislation and the very limited social legislation is striking. The so-called Social Charter of 1989 was a list of pious hopes, not of binding rules, that is to say a piece of propaganda. Even that proved too much for the British Tory government, but the Labour government of Tony Blair did accept it, while showing, like its predecessor, very little enthusiasm for measures limiting the powers of the employers. For a well-documented critical analysis see Y. Salesse, *Propositions pour une autre Europe* (Paris: Editions du Felin, 1997).

the end of each cycle than it had been at the corresponding stage of its predecessor, and the share of the unemployed in the labor force reached double digits even in the official data, always crooked on the subject. This was the end of the fairy tale about capitalism without crises. We were back in familiar Marxist territory with dead labor replacing the living and creating a reserve army of the unemployed in the process.

Things seem more complicated with the second half of the familiar story, with the need for capital simultaneously to create other jobs, allowing it to extract more surplus value. There are signs that it is losing its capacity for doing it. We may be getting close to the era described by Marx in the *Grundrisse* when "the theft of alien labor time, on which the present wealth is based, appears a miserable foundation in face of this new one, created by large-scale industry itself."[6] This is what I had in mind earlier when I contrasted our technical progress with our social backwardness. If we limit ourselves to the advanced capitalist countries, simply for the sake of argument, we could already today approach the frontier between labor and leisure in an entirely different way, though to address the problem of unemployment, like all other key issues, including those connected with our environment, we need both a completely different social organization and its democratic application on a world scale.

Forgive me for this digression. This is not the message on unemployment the governments and the people of Europe received from the IMF, the World Bank, or the OECD. Their joint recommendation was much simpler: follow the American example. Not the magic vision of America that impoverished Europeans imagined after the war: the real United States of today, with its growing gap between haves and have-nots, with its ridiculous minimum wage, with its "working poor" and its millions without health insurance.

Not the most splendid of models? If you don't like it, you'll have to take it. You have no choice. In the deregulated world we have built together—and of which we, the international institutions, are the watchdogs—you can no longer afford a livable minimum wage, some degree of job security, fairly decent unemployment benefits, or old-age pensions. You have no longer the means to pay for a national health service. You will have to rely

6. Karl Marx, *Grundrisse* (New York: Vintage, 1973), 705.

increasingly on private insurance and private schools, on two-tier health and two-tier education. To cut a long message short: you will have to speed up the dismantling of your welfare state. And since the welfare state was social democracy's main claim to gratitude and success, its crisis is, this time, in earnest.

The progress of social democracy is not just the result of betrayal by ambitious politicians and union bosses. It is a question of general mood, conditioned notably by the scope for meeting popular demands within existing society. During the postwar quarter century of unprecedented prosperity, the climate was particularly propitious for social democracy to prosper. During the following twenty-five years, on the contrary, conditions have become more and more unfavorable. Yet it is only now that the crisis is coming to a head.

It will be objected that the leaders of the respectable left have already put a great deal of water into their *vin rosé*. The Socialists who were in office at the time—in France under François Mitterrand or in Spain under Felipe Gonzales—took an active part in deregulation, in the reduction of state power, in the preparation of the ground for their current dilemma. And those who were then in opposition in Britain, Italy, Germany, and the like, were no better. A weekly that is the mouthpiece of the international financial establishment noticed how the British Labour Party has discovered "social-Thatcherism" and how Italy's former Communists "have found free-market economics."[7]

The objection, however, is off the mark. I never suggested that Europe's Socialist leaders were great radicals eager to reshape society. Very far from it. They have swallowed a lot, and are probably ready for more. But what they are being asked now is not to be the reformist managers of capitalist society, not even to manage that society as it is, without further reforms. They are told to get rid of the conquests achieved by the labor movement in the postwar period, on which their reputation was built and their attraction rested. What is at stake is their own fate, the very survival of a kind of left that hitherto existed in Europe, though not in the United States.

Here again it may be said that the leaders of the European left are ready to accept the political consequences of Americanization. After his first electoral victory, President Clinton was the toast of the town amid the

7. *The Economist,* 2 September 1995.

respectable left in London, Paris, and Rome. Then—nothing failing like failure—his attraction diminished. The second electoral success, despite the compromising concessions made to achieve it, restored him as a model. His silly sex scandal did not enhance his political reputation as a "winner." Nevertheless, British Prime Minister Tony Blair (smooth leader of the Labour Party), Lionel Jospin (Mitterrand's reluctant heir, who holds the same position in France), Massimo d'Alema (the first converted Communist to become Italy's prime minister), and Gerhard Schroeder (Germany's new Social-Democratic chancellor) are all more or less eager to turn their movements into an equivalent of the American Democratic Party.[8]

The problem is that even today such a move still involves important modifications: a break of organic links with labor unions; a transformation of parties that were once built on militants into pure electoral machines; and a very serious retreat on the front of social provision. Though the rank and file are bewildered and in total disarray, they are the products of a certain political tradition. They are deeply attached to their social conquests, even if they have quite natural misgivings about the structure and the functioning of their welfare state. They will not give up this heritage without a fight. In other words, the question is not whether Tony, Lionel, Massimo, and Gerhard are willing to oblige. It is whether they can deliver.

In fairness, it must be added that the choice is not between surrendering or carrying on as before. The main argument here has been that it is impossible simply to go on. The Socialist leaders may have contributed, wittingly or unwittingly, to the transformation of the terrain on which the confrontation takes place. But neither the game nor its rules are any longer the same. And I am not referring here to any revolutionary activity. That is not on the immediate timetable. Simply to preserve the paychecks and the

---

8. D'Alema is less keen on such a transformation than his party colleague, Walter Veltroni, and Jospin is less enthusiastic than Blair for this further move to the right. But the tendency is across the board. For a vacuous glorification, see the book *The Third Way* (London: Polity Press, 1998) by Blair's guru, Anthony Giddens. For a devastating description of Labour's ideological and political descent, see Leo Panitch and Colin Leys, *The End of Parliamentary Socialism* (New York: Verso, 1997). To elucidate one minor feature of this, in their zeal for change, Italy's former Communists keep altering their name. They were known as the PDS, Italian initials for Democratic Party of the Left. But, having admitted ex-Socialists and former Christian Democrats into their ranks, they dropped the *Partito* and are now called DS, Left Democrats.

employment of their members, to maintain their social gains, the trade unions and the left in general would have to fight to reduce drastically the hours worked and move that struggle rapidly from the national level to that of the European Union. In other words, for merely defensive action the left would have to mobilize on a mass scale and to think internationally, something it has not done for many, many years.

Will the left in Western Europe now follow its leaders down the American way, forsaking its inheritance and committing, in fact, political suicide? Or will it rebel, use its imagination, discard Stalinist crimes and social-democratic impotence, and, in trying to protect its immediate interests, reinvent a socialist project for our times? This choice will have to be faced all over, sooner or later. What I am simply claiming is that Western Europe, because of the contrast between its traditions and the American pattern now being imposed, is the forerunner—that in Europe the choice will have to be made, the battle fought, at the turn of this millennium. The demonstrations staged in Italy at the close of 1994, when Silvio Berlusconi attacked Italy's old age pensions, the 1995 strikes which paralyzed Paris and precipitated the biggest demonstrations ever in the French provinces when Jacques Chirac, likewise, tried to carry out the instructions of the financial establishment: these were only the first skirmishes of this great battle.

It would be nice to be able to assert that imagination is going to seize power and socialism will be revived in Western Europe on the ruins of shattered models, particularly because it would mean history coming full circle. It was our fault, the failure of the socialists in the advanced capitalist countries to carry out a radical transformation of society when we were expected to do so, which led to the Marxist tragedy in Eastern Europe. And now, at the end of that tragedy, it would be the Western left, finally beginning to perform its task, which would give an example and revive hope throughout the world. What is desirable, however, is not necessarily inevitable. There is no guarantee that the story of the socialist struggle in Europe, which neither started nor ended in 1917, is inevitably a story with a happy ending.

Part Two

Changing Europe

Introduction to Part Two
Ex Occidente Lux?

WESTERN EUROPE is in the throes of a big transformation. Since January 1, 1999, eleven of the fifteen members of the European Union have had a common currency. Early in the year 2002, the process will be completed, with marks, francs, gulden, and liras physically replaced by the euro. Handing over monetary policy to a European Central Bank, the various governments will also lose some control over their budgets and, in case of major difficulties, will no longer be able to extricate themselves through devaluation. Big business makes no secret that it will use the new framework for an offensive against wages and working conditions under the banner of "labor flexibility." And the unions, if they do not learn quickly how to unite across frontiers, might as well surrender, especially since the beginning of the new millennium should also witness the eastward extension of the European Union, with the Czech Republic, Hungary, Poland, Slovenia, and Estonia already knocking at the door.

One major question lies behind all these developments and behind the speculation over the euro's rivalry with the dollar: can a European Union, which is itself increasingly Americanized, form a new entity and stand up to the United States? I have my doubts, but they are irrelevant, because what interests me more is the other side of the same question: can Europe build a society in which property relations, social organization, and political perspectives are radically different from those prevailing in the United States? In this section we are surveying Europe to see where a break may occur in a not-too-distant future and we are starting this search in the East, in the land of the aborted revolution.

For Russia, one episode, the making of the President in 1996, is a perfect illustration of the epoch of Tsar Boris, with its rule of the moneybags, corrupt scramble for profits, collapse of production, and the terrible plight of the bulk of the population. By now, despite repeated Western efforts to paint our "democrats" in the best possible light, it can no longer be concealed that the Yeltsin regime is bankrupt and that it is leaving a very explosive heritage. The gloomy reality is that, should an explosion occur at this stage, it is difficult to perceive the prospect of a progressive solution.

In the case of Poland, we shall look at the situation in a more historical perspective because today's disappointment is a measure of yesterday's expectations. Poland was the only country in the Soviet bloc where the workers fought successfully for their rights, their struggle climaxing triumphantly in 1980 with the setting up of an autonomous, independent union, Solidarity. Here we try to retrace that union's defeat in victory after 1989, and to explain why it happened and why the resurrection of the movement is not to be expected in the near future.

In the last example, we move again from the particular to the general. The French upheaval of 1995 has been the biggest revolt so far against the capitalist drive designed to destroy the postwar conquests of the labor movement, an offensive that is not limited to French borders. It concerns the whole of Western Europe and, having started as an attack on the welfare state, it now expands into a more general assault on workers' rights. The counteroffensive cannot be purely national, either. Something flickers in Western Europe today because after years of passive acceptance the French protesters have shown their colleagues that one can resist, that resignation is not the only possible reaction. But one will be able to talk of a light only when protesters throughout the European Union move beyond this defensive victory and start struggling together in search of a different future.

5.

Russia's Miracle at the Polls

That the rules were obviously stacked in Mr. Yeltsin's favor does not change the fact that at least the game was played to the final whistle.

Lee Hockstader, *Washington Post,*
4 July 1996

A triumph of democracy.

President Clinton on Yeltsin's victory

REALLY, A MIRACLE. At the opening of 1996, Boris Yeltsin's chances did not seem worth a kopeck. The ruling party—Our Home is Russia, led by the prime minister, Victor Chernomyrdin—got only 10.1 percent of the vote in the Duma elections the previous December, and even adding other groups favoring the administration the total came up to less than 18 percent. Yeltsin himself, an obvious wreck, was not reaching double digits in opinion polls. The army was bogged down in Chechnya. In Russia, exhausted and angered by poverty, shocked by corruption and crime, some eight people out of ten, when asked by pollsters, replied that they were better off under the previous regime. No wonder that Yeltsin's closest associates, like Alexander Korzhakov, head of the presidential guard, were pondering how to put off the vote. Indeed, the war in Chechnya may well have been launched in December 1994 with the idea of introducing martial law and thus dispensing with such democratic niceties as elections for quite a time.

A successful recovery was difficult to imagine, even if one knew about Yeltsin's resilience, his appetite for power, the backing of the bankers, domestic and foreign, and the bias of the media.[1] Imagination actually paled compared to reality. Naturally, it would be foolish to talk of Goebbels or make comparisons with Stalinist precedents. Gennady Zyuganov, the Communist candidate, did not suffer what Bernard Shaw called the extreme form of censorship: execution. None of Yeltsin's other rivals were deported to Siberia. Yet this miracle at the polls is worth studying to see how one can have the letter of democracy without its spirit, how power and money combined can sway the verdict of the people in what, on the surface, looks like a real election with a choice between various candidates. It is also worth taking a look at how Western governments and their servants, when their interests are at stake, are ready to hail such a parody of a poll as a "triumph of democracy." At the same time, the election shows the limits and ambiguities of the opposition, the utter confusion in people's minds, the absence, as a result, of a coherent pressure from below; in other words, the extent to which political life in Russia is still a struggle for power among the privileged, a confrontation of the self-appointed "elites."

For the sellers of the president the task was tremendous. First they had to put their contender into shape. On February 1, 1996, he was to be sixty-five. He was not in the best of health. In the previous year he had gone through two serious, though unspecified, bouts of heart trouble. He also appeared on several public occasions in a state, to put it politely, of not total sobriety. The immediate duty of his handlers was to put their champion on the wagon. The next one was to get him fit for a long and grueling campaign. Even in an Olympic year, when doctors show what they can do for athletes, their achievement was impressive. True, by the end of June, Yeltsin looked once again like a zombie, with a wooden face, an artificial gait, one arm glued to the body, and it was up to the propaganda machine to conceal this image from the public. But up to then, for over four months, starting on February 15, when his campaign was officially launched in Sverdlovsk, his former fief now rechristened Yekaterinburg, he travelled across the huge country speaking, shaking hands, distributing gifts, and making promises. He was twisting in Ufa and competing with rockers in Rostov-on-the-Don not merely to woo the youthful voters but to convey to the vast Russian

---

1. "His friend, his concubine, his lover, his passion, is power," said Vyacheslav Kostikov, his former press secretary, about Yeltsin in a TV interview on 4 February 1996.

public, with the obedient assistance of television, that he was back alive and kicking, once again able to cope.

The second stage was to render their candidate presentable. If Chernomyrdin did badly in the parliamentary election, it was because of the economic and social record, their common record. Yeltsin had to brush up his past, and he did it with his usual dose of chutzpah. He thus claimed credit for Gorbachev's glasnost, that is to say, the spectacular extension of freedoms. Since the Communists did well in the parliamentary election, he did not hesitate to steal their garb. The emphasis in official propaganda would now be shifted to Russia's grandeur, its independence, and, since this was the Communist trump, to the need for social justice. To render justice "first and foremost to the weak and the unprivileged—this is our main objective for the next five years," Yeltsin proclaimed.[2] The unkind echoed: for the next five months, until the election is over.

While unable to disclaim all responsibility for the horrible sequels of shock therapy, the president did his best to shift it to other shoulders. He put the blame on the government "which has failed to carry out the tasks in the sphere of social policy" and on the rather undefined "reformers." But Yeltsin also confirmed his readiness to drop allies in order to lighten his load. Two substitutions at the turn of the year illustrate this trend. At the Foreign Office, Yevgeni Primakov, the crafty survivor, replaced Andrei Kozyrev, known in his country as the Western stooge. More significantly still, Anatoli Chubais, the darling of the international financial establishment but a symbol of privatization scandals to Russians, was removed from his job as first deputy prime minister and financial overlord of the economy; his post was taken over by an earthy manager, Vladimir Kadannikov, the boss of AvtoVaz, Russia's biggest car producer. But you don't dispense so easily with the services of a man backed by foreign financiers and domestic speculators. Ousted through the front door on January 16, Chubais was smuggled a few weeks later through the back into Yeltsin's electoral headquarters.

The third task was to present their man as the most efficient fighter in the struggle against communism and thus ensure his presence in the decisive second round. The president is elected in Russia in two ballots. In

2. Boris Yeltsin, speech at Yekaterinburg, 15 February 1996.

the first you need an absolute majority of the votes cast to get elected. If nobody gets it, the two top contenders fight it out in a second contest. Zyuganov, relying on the support of his own party and its allies, could hope to get about a third of the total vote and was thus certain to survive.[3] Yeltsin was not. Indeed, in the early polls he was trailing not only behind Zyuganov but also behind economist Grigori Yavlinsky, an advocate of the market but critic of the regime, behind ex-general Alexander Lebed, the deep-voiced champion of law and order, behind the villain Vladimir Zhiri-novsky, the wolf undisguised in "liberal-democratic" clothing. If the first two had combined their efforts and, possibly with a third candidate, the eye surgeon Svyatyslav Fedorov, had formed a "third force" joint ticket, Yeltsin would have lagged so far behind at the beginning of the race as to be practically out of it.[4]

It was, therefore, imperative to gain time so as to reduce the whole show to Yeltsin versus the red peril, and his backers used both their financial power and the mastery of the media for this purpose. It was useful to sponsor some phony opinion polls showing Yeltsin ahead of the pack, running neck-and-neck with Zyuganov; it was the Russian version of the self-fulfilling prophecy. Television was used to focus the limelight on the president and keep it off his competitors. And it was jolly useful to have the rivals divided. With hindsight, knowing the Yeltsin-Lebed pact re-vealed immediately after the first ballot, it is tempting to conclude that Lebed was already earlier serving his new master. Actually, some com-mentators do claim that the deal was struck back in January. So far this is just guesswork. It was only around May that Lebed got a more favorable treatment in the media, a clear hint of an arrangement with the authorities.[5] Thus, it is impossible to say with certainty whether the failure of a "third force" to emerge was the result of conspiracy or merely the clash of mighty

3. In the parliamentary election the CPRF got 22.3 percent of the vote, the Communists—Working Russia 4.5 percent, the Agrarians 3.8 percent, and Ryzhkov's Power to the People 1.6 percent. If you add the Derzhava of former Vice President Rutskoy and the bloc of Govorukhin, you get 24.8 million votes or 35.8 percent of the total. This was Zyuganov's potential base, to be compared with his first and second ballot results in the presidential election.

4. The determination of Gorbachev to run showed how difficult it is for a once-prominent actor to leave the stage. He was finally to get 386,000 votes out of 75.6 million votes cast.

5. Boris Berezovsky now admits that he had talks with Lebed before the first ballot.

egos. Whatever the reason, division among his opponents saved Yeltsin's political life.

His backers could exploit the situation because they enjoyed what Western correspondents described euphemistically as the "benefits of incumbency." Put more crudely, this meant an almost unlimited purse and a control over the media unique in a non-totalitarian state. Zyuganov had the backing of a couple of national dailies with small circulation and of a few provincial papers. Yeltsin could rely on the rest. The difference was most striking in broadcasting and, above all, in television. The two public television channels were obedient tools of presidential propaganda. The third channel, the private NTV, followed their example, its chief executive, Igor Malashenko, actually joining Yeltsin's electoral staff. That staff, naturally, used the instrument at its disposal. Television, we saw, helped Yeltsin to outdistance his rivals. It then conveyed the impression that men like Yavlinsky were eager to serve under his leadership. And throughout, but particularly in the second round, TV was a weapon aimed at Zyuganov.

There were no pretences of neutrality. When Zyuganov was shown on public television, for instance, the interviewer accused him of "primitive populist pre-election agitation."[6] When Yavlinsky appeared on the tube after the first ballot, the interviewer proved to be a preacher: "Maybe the most moral thing for you to do now would be to offer your services to the government. Since they find themselves in this difficult situation, you should help them to extricate themselves from it somehow."[7] The worst thing was not that Yeltsin appeared more often than Zyuganov on the little screen. It was that Zyuganov was always shown as the villain to be branded and Yeltsin as the hero to be praised and protected. Russia's television, on this occasion, was unashamedly its master's image and voice.

But did not Russia have a central electoral commission whose function was to prevent even much milder biases? It did. Only, under the leadership of Nikolay Ryabov, it could easily be confused with an annex of Yeltsin's campaign headquarters. One of its decisions, taken at random, should give you a flavor: "Photo albums devoted to Boris Yeltsin do not represent campaign material in the opinion of the commission's legal experts, and

6. Nikolai Svanidze on Russia TV Channel, 12 May 1996.

7. Interviewer Pavel Lobkov on NTV "Hero of the Day," 21 June 1996.

therefore giving them away does not amount to a breach of the electoral law."[8] Actually, that law contained so many loopholes that the alleged principle of equality between contenders was a sinister joke. In theory, none of the candidates was allowed to spend more than 14.5 billion rubles, circa $3 million, on his campaign (individual contributions were limited to about $600 and institutional ones to $60,000). Yet, since propaganda could be financed through other channels, all these provisions were farcical. Yeltsin's expenditure on the campaign was estimated by his sympathizers at around $100 million and by his opponents at five times that figure.

And this was only on such expenses as propaganda material, the cost of canvassers and supervisors, the fees of rock stars and bands at electoral concerts. The bill is incomparably higher if you include the gifts and pledges distributed by the bountiful tsar on his travels. Wherever he went, Yeltsin had something for the local population. Signing decrees by the handful, he gave presents, or rather compensations, to all sorts of social categories: to miners or teachers who had not seen a salary for months; to old-age pensioners whose savings had been wiped out; to farmers and workers, to tinkers and tailors. The billion dollars that a reluctant Bank of Russia was forced to withdraw from its reserves and hand over to the executive does not measure the full cost. To estimate it, one would have to take into account the sharp drop in taxes paid during the period, the widening of the budgetary deficit, and additional billions of dollars, not rubles. Clearly, for the men clinging to power and privilege victory was worth any price.

Keeping this in mind, we may return to the electoral campaign, starting with the question necessary to assess the democratic nature of this exercise, though literally unanswerable: did Yeltsin and his henchmen even contemplate abandoning power should the verdict of the people turn against them? The answer of the ordinary Russians was obvious, summed up in a witticism fashionable at the time: "Zyuganov can win, but Yeltsin cannot lose." As a matter of fact, neither Yeltsin nor any of his key associates, as far as I know, ever proclaimed that if Zyuganov were elected, they would simply leave. On the contrary, they always stressed—and this was the

8. *Itar-Tass,* 7 June 1996.

refrain of official propaganda—that Zyuganov's victory would spell civil war. On reflection, this really meant that if you dare to elect this Communist, we, the incumbents, the beneficiaries of the regime or what not, shall take up arms to thwart your will—and this clearly was not very democratic. It was the propagandists' duty to simplify this argument and limit it to the plain conclusion: a vote for Zyuganov is a vote for bloodshed, for civil war, for disaster.

The best guess is that Yeltsin had two irons in the fire or, if you prefer, two policies and two teams to carry them out. The first was headed by Yeltsin's old crony, Korzhakov, his bodyguard, by the latter's associate, Mikhail Barsukov, director of the Federal Security Service, heir to the KGB, and by their ally, Oleg Soskovets, first deputy prime minister in charge of industry, an engineer by training, a former manager of a big metallurgical plant, with the reputation of representing the military-industrial complex. For this team, what mattered was that Yeltsin, and therefore they themselves, should stay in power. Since the election threatened this state of things, it had better be postponed by agreement, even with the Communists, if possible. If not, then by any means, a coup, the introduction of martial law, whatever brought the right result.

The opposite team, in which the reinstated Chubais was going to play an increasingly important role as spokesman for the profiteers of privatization, also wanted to cling to power, yet argued that this could be achieved without resorting to force. With our money and your prerogatives, they pleaded with Yeltsin, we can bribe and twist our way to an electoral victory. We are able to perform the miracle at the polls and to preserve appearances. Chernomyrdin, the prime minister, leaned towards this second approach. Yeltsin, most of the time, wavered between the two.

Korzhakov and company may have missed their opportunity in mid-March. On the fifteenth, the Duma passed a resolution renouncing the Belovyezhskaya Pushcha agreements of 1991, which had put an end to the Soviet Union. For the Communists, dominant in the Duma and feeling that the Russians were hankering after their past grandeur, this was pure electioneering. Then hell broke loose. The move was hailed as unconstitutional and dangerous, a proof that if they won the Communists would reimpose the empire by force. It was even hinted that the resulting constitutional void threatened the presidential elections. Something bizarre happened on the evening of the seventeenth. That night and the morning after, the deputies could not enter the Duma, occupied by Special Service squads. The explanations varied: the search for a bomb, a threat from Chechen terrorists, a high level of radioactivity inside the building. The Communists said at once that this was a dress rehearsal and their version gradually gained ground. Yeltsin's inner circle had apparently met to prepare a coup involving the dissolution of the Duma, the banning of the Communist Party, and the postponement of elections. The project was allegedly given up when the men who were to carry it out, notably the ministers of defense and interior, said it would not work.

This was roughly the time of a shift in the balance within Yeltsin's band. Originally, Soskovets was to preside over his electoral headquarters; by February 20, he was no longer sure whether he would head the president's campaign. Two days later, Yeltsin mentioned that Chubais would join his electoral team (the man, while too unpopular to be displayed in public, had enough administrative skills and financial contacts to be useful working behind the scenes). Early in April, Yeltsin announced that he himself was "the leader of the whole campaign." By then, though it was clear that the outgoing president was to be the top anti-Communist candidate, the shadow of Zyuganov remained impressive, and the temptation to somehow avoid the contest was still considerable. Toward the end of that month, a strange manifesto was published in Moscow.[9] In it, thirteen of the country's top tycoons (four bankers, two chairmen of oil companies, several heads of conglomerates) urged the politicians to get off "the path that leads to civil war and the break-up of Russia" and instructed them "to make very significant mutual concessions, to come to strategic political accords and consolidate them in law." What is so strange about big business interfering in politics? It does so all the time in the Western world. Yet it does so more discreetly. One can't imagine the presidents of Chase, General Motors, Exxon, and Microsoft getting together with a few fellow CEOs to produce a text to be published in the *New York Times* telling the presidential candidates to reach a compromise, ending with a warning like this: "Russian business people have the necessary resources and will to influence politicians who are too unprincipled and those who are too

9. See *Izvestia,* "We must break the deadlock," 27 April 1996.

uncompromising." In Russia, at this stage, things are less smooth and more naked. The interference provoked no protests. All of the candidates, including Zyuganov, answered politely that they were sweet reasonableness personified but, alas, the other side. . . .

It was Korzhakov who climbed on the financiers' bandwagon. In an interview granted to a London Sunday paper, he pushed the argument to its logical conclusion, namely that the vote should be postponed, since Russia needs stability and this election stands for struggle.[10] Such plain talk by his closest servant created quite a stir, and it forced Yeltsin to proclaim that the election would take place and Russians would make the right choice. Korzhakov, he said, should stay out of politics, though he did not really disavow his faithful crony, adding that many people in Russia shared his opinion. After all, if Russians dared to make the wrong choice! The ambiguity and suspense would last at least till the first ballot. But there was no ambiguity about the attitude of Russia's moneymakers. We now know that in February seven of the most powerful tycoons got together, appropriately in Davos, the meeting place of Europe's moneybags. There they decided that it was urgent to come to Yeltsin's rescue. They provided millions of dollars for campaign propaganda. They provided the media under their control: commercial TV, radio, and most of the country's publications. Acting as their agent, Chubais returned to the headquarters as the mastermind of the electoral campaign. Desperately defending their own interests, the Sinister Seven made an essential contribution to Boris Yeltsin's survival.

Two points must still be made to complete the story of Boris the resurrected. The first concerns the enthusiastic Western backing for our tsar in Moscow. It did suffer a brief lapse, at least on the level of the press, after the dismissal of Anatoli Chubais. The storming of Russia's parliament was a defense of democracy, the war in Chechnya a regrettable, though forgivable, mistake, but the removal of the last "shock therapist" from the government—that was ethically unacceptable. Such establishment publications as the *New York Times* and *The Economist* argued for a time that Moscow should be told who paid the piper and who called the tune in economic as well as in foreign policy. The spell did not last and never

10. *The Observer,* 5 May 1996.

reached the level of the chanceries. Whether the Western governments knew from the start that the eclipse of the unpresentable Chubais was just an electioneering device to fool the natives or whether they thought, rightly or wrongly, that Yeltsin was in any case our best bet for keeping Russia safe for capitalism, they backed him to the hilt throughout the period.

President Clinton from the start urged international institutions to come to Russia's rescue. Chancellor Kohl rushed to Moscow to show his country's backing for Boris. The Council of Europe, supposed to have standards for membership, admitted Russia into its ranks as if the bloody war in Chechnya were a crusade for human rights. Michel Camdessus, managing director of the International Monetary Fund, answered Clinton's prayer, and he himself brought to Moscow an exceptionally large loan ($10.2 billion over three years, with $4 billion in the first). This, God forbid, was no political interference, even if the lender duly insisted that should Russia change policy—by changing its president?—the aid would be suspended. The so-called Paris Club, regrouping state as opposed to private creditors, rescheduled Russia's $40 billion debt for an unprecedented twenty-five-year period. The Big Seven, or rather the Big Eight since Russia was included, staged a meeting in Moscow in April and invited Yeltsin for another in Lyon, timed for the eve of the second ballot.[11] To sum up all these efforts, if the electorate for Russia's presidency had been limited to Western foreign ministries and financial institutions, Yeltsin would have been chosen unanimously.

The impact of this preference on the Russian electorate is another matter. It is far from certain that the resulting feeling of reassurance and security outweighed the resentment felt by millions of Russians, convinced that all their vicissitudes in recent years were part and parcel of a premeditated Western plot. On the other hand, the second point to be mentioned, the cease-fire in Chechnya, was pure benefit for Yeltsin, an almost unexpected last-minute electoral gift. Here, too, the West made its small contribution since it was the head of the Organization for the Security and Cooperation in Europe (OSCE) mission in Chechnya: the Swiss Tim Guldimann, who performed a key function as middleman between the two sides.

---

11. Actually, the trick proved a boomerang, as Chernomyrdin had to replace the ailing president.

The war in Chechnya, started with a queer mixture of arrogance and miscalculation, was the symbolic horror story of the regime, illustrating its corruption and incompetence, its blindness and bloodymindedness.[12] The fact that the heirs to the once-dreaded Soviet army could not cope with the volunteer fighters of a tiny republic was for nostalgic Russians a reminder of their decadence. The organizers of this expedition had hoped to revive the jingoism of the Russian people; they provoked their revulsion instead. This was Afghanistan all over again, only much more so, because it was closer to home and shown on the little screen. Day in and day out, the Russians could see the absurdity and cruelty of this conflict, the civilian victims, the misery of their "boys," with no prospect of a solution.

The killing of the Chechen leader, Dzhokhar Dudayev, by a Russian missile on April 22 did not seem to provide new openings. Still, by mid-May, Guldimann was negotiating with his successor, Zelimkhan Yandarbiyev, and on May 27 the latter was in Moscow signing a cease-fire. The talks on its implementation then moved closer to Chechnya, to Nazran in neighboring Ingushetia, where a tentative agreement on the pullout of troops and the release of prisoners was signed on June 10. The truce was fragile and broken frequently but, while it lasted, was most precious for Yeltsin the candidate. Did the Swiss intermediary offer some serious promises to the Chechens, or did they themselves conclude that the presidential election was the most propitious moment to get concessions from Moscow and extricate their country from the bloody mess? For the Russians, this was clearly an electoral operation, since a few days after the second ballot they were shelling again all over Chechnya, their attack provoking a spectacular counteroffensive on the capital, Grozny, which spoiled Boris Yeltsin's inauguration.

But let us not anticipate. The cease-fire was still on as the Russians went to vote on June 16 in a climate the outgoing president could hardly have dreamed of at the beginning of the campaign. They did so after four months of relentless propaganda designed to convince the electorate that Zyuganov stood for past evils and a future civil war, that Battling Boris was the only one capable of defeating him, and that any other vote, therefore, was

---

12. The minister of defense, Pavel Grachev, allegedly claimed he could crush the rebels in a few hours with a paratroop brigade.

wasted. And they went to the polls in great numbers, nearly seven out of ten, more than 75 million out of an electorate of over 108 million. Yeltsin did manage to come out on top, with 27.7 million votes or 35.3 percent of all the valid ballots and particularly good scores in Moscow and St. Petersburg. But he was followed closely by Zyuganov, with 24.2 million votes (more than 32 percent), strong not just, as it was said, in rural areas, but also in Russia's devastated industrial belt. Thanks to a final spurt, Lebed left the pack and came in third, with nearly 11 million votes (14.5 percent). Yavlinsky, possibly because of what was presented as his "voluptuous dance" with Yeltsin, a sort of hesitation waltz, came in fourth with only 5.6 million votes (7.5 percent), while Zhirinovsky, no longer a novelty and suffering from nationalist competition, was reduced to 4.3 million (5.8 percent). Each of the remaining five candidates got less than 1 percent, and 1.5 million Russians bothered to vote simply to say that they liked none of the candidates.

Nothing was really over. Yeltsin, while performing much better than he could have expected at the start, did much worse than in the presidential poll of 1991 when, with propaganda much more balanced, he won easily in the first ballot, with 57 percent of the vote, and with the candidate following him, the Communist Nikolai Ryzhkov, capturing less than 17 percent of the vote. This time the gap was narrow and the victory uncertain. The electorate of Yavlinsky, fundamentally favorable to the new system, though not to the manner in which it was being introduced, was likely to vote for Yeltsin or to abstain. Those who had voted for Lebed, on the other hand, did so because the general was the scourge of criminals, the enemy of corruption, and, like themselves, a resenter of Russia's humiliation. They would be much more difficult to persuade. So would the discontented electorate of Vladimir Zhirinovsky. For a while, it was really touch-and-go.

Then the Yeltsinites produced their trump card, the sudden, or really not-so-sudden, conversion of Alexander Lebed. On Monday, everybody was still counting and drawing conclusions from the Sunday ballot. On Tuesday, it was announced that General Lebed was to be Yeltsin's aide on issues of national security and was appointed secretary of the president's security council, an important body, whose powers were to be restructured and widened to give him even greater scope. The newcomer was joining the presidential team as a major figure, almost the heir-apparent and in the following fortnight (the second ballot was scheduled for July 3, a weekday, so that the better-off people, favoring Yeltsin, would not vanish to their country dachas), he was to play a key role in the campaign.

Lebed was fitted for the part. Handsome in a sort of tough way, with the build of a boxer and the booming voice of a sergeant-major, he easily filled the screen. He had spent twenty-six of his forty-six years in the armed forces. He won his reputation as a paratroop commander in Afghanistan and gained popularity as the head of the Fourteenth Army in Moldova, where he bullied the contesting parties into a settlement. He increased his prestige through blunt criticism of the military establishment, notably on the war in Chechnya. Forced to leave the army the previous year, he then had a checkered political career: the small party he had joined did not reach 5 percent in the December 1995 parliamentary poll, but he himself was elected to the Duma. Modesty is clearly not one of his handicaps. Asked by *Der Spiegel* whether he saw himself as president in the year 2000, he replied, "Maybe earlier." The man is ambitious, and in a hurry. No stickler for legal procedures, he has a populist contempt for wealthy scoundrels, though not for their money. While obviously no intellectual, he has a blunt common sense and, valuable in our age, a knack for tossing around one-liners: "He who shoots first, laughs last. . . . God created big and small people and Colonel Colt created his revolver to make them even. . . . A democratic general is (as rare as) a Jewish reindeer breeder."

He needed all his talents to convince his own electorate of the rectitude of his conversion. After all, he had campaigned against "nomenklatura capitalism," against the profiteers he was now to join in office. Lebed's argument was crudely simple. He had to make a choice. Communism was splendid in theory and tragically inapplicable in practice. Yeltsin stood for the "new idea" to which the future belonged but which, up to now, had been very badly implemented in Russia. The obvious conclusion was that it would soon be applied very differently now that he, Lebed, was going to be in charge. He could nevertheless be asked how he intended to fulfill his main pledge—to fight against corruption—while collaborating at the top with Prime Minister Chernomyrdin, the wealthy former boss of Gazprom, and the privatizer Chubais, soon to be appointed Yeltsin's chief of staff.

(In view of his tarnished reputation, they did not dare to announce it before the second ballot.)

Since Lebed was not going to be made the overlord of the economy, for him to appear credible it was important to show that he was somehow in control of all the armed forces, including the security police, and presumably, by the same token, in charge of Chechnya. Lebed's appointment, quite logically, was coupled on the very same day with the dismissal of his enemy, general Pavel Grachev, the minister of defense, known as Pasha Mercedes because of his fondness for foreign luxury cars. Since the new man was unlikely to tolerate any empires within his fiefdom, the position of Yeltsin's closest servant, Korzhakov, and his associates also looked threatened. The paradox is that in the battle between the president's two teams, Lebed may have unwittingly contributed to the victory of Chubais, for whom he clearly had no sympathy whatsoever. Actually, the political fall of Alexander Korzhakov was one of those Kremlin melodramas that tell a great deal about the climate of the regime.[13] On June 19, or rather the next day, since it was already one in the morning, NTV interrupted its late-night program to announce dramatically that "two key figures in President Yeltsin's election campaign" had been arrested that afternoon "on instructions" from security chiefs Barsukov and Korzhakov, and that this was part of a plot "aimed at cancelling the second round of the presidential election." The security services subsequently produced a very different story. Both agreed only on the names of the "two key figures." One was Sergey Lisovsky, a rather shady character prominent in Moscow showbiz and advertising circles; he had mobilized Russian pop stars for the "Vote or Lose" concerts to back Yeltsin throughout the country. The other was Arkady Yevstafyev who, having earlier worked with Chubais on privatization, had now joined him on the electoral staff. In the police version, the two men were detained because they were leaving the White House with "an office copier packing box" filled with foreign currency and no document to justify it. Half a million dollars was apparently involved.[14] By

---

13. For his own version of the events and an unflattering portrait of his former idol, see A. Korzhakov, *Boris Yeltsin: Ot rassveta do zakata* (From Dawn to Dusk) (Moscow: Interbook Publishers, 1997).

14. According to Viktor Ilyukhin, the Communist chair of the Duma security committee, the origin of that money could be traced to the Ministry of Finance.

lunchtime on June 20, an excited Chubais was giving a contrasting interpretation in a triumphant press conference. His was the TV version rendered still more sensational. The money was a plant and a provocation. The
plot was part of a larger scenario. Korzhakov and company, the strong-arm
wing of the Yeltsin administration, wanted to crush the "liberal" wing and
usurp power without elections. In its efforts, it would stop at nothing, not
even murder; he specifically referred to the attempted assassination, two
days earlier, of Boris Fedorov, former head of the National Sports Foundation.[15] Chubais could gloat because a presidential decree had just announced the dismissal of Soskovets, Barsukov, and Korzhakov. It was
the removal of the faithful Korzhakov, his old companion, that was particularly painful for Yeltsin, as we know from the testimony of his wife,
Naina: "It feels as if a part of your body has been cut off . . . as if a member
of the family has gone. . . ."[16] But power was dearer to Yeltsin than
friendship. This was probably also the moment when he finally decided
he could keep that power by purely electoral means, by crook rather than
hook.

There were still thirteen days to go till July 3, and three features were to
mark this last phase. The first and dominant one was the relentless drum of
propaganda reaching its paroxysm: posters and pamphlets, whispering
campaigns, articles in all sorts of publications, and, above all, the insinu-
ating refrains of radio and television. All now could be concentrated on a
single target. Thus, Gennady Zyuganov's electoral broadcasts, imposed by
law and free of charge, were followed by paid spots showing, in black and
white, pictures of labor camps, of famine in the early days of the Soviet
regime, or relatively more recent long lines and empty shelves. And these
were accompanied by repetitive comments: "nobody in 1917 imagined that
there could be famine," "nobody in 1917 imagined that brother could fight
brother," "it is still not too late to prevent civil war and famine," and so on

---

15. In one of the typical Yeltsinite arrangements, the National Sports Foundation had special
customs concessions on the import of alcohol and tobacco. Not all the resulting profits were
used to foster sport; some of the money went to party or private pockets. Fedorov allegedly
got into trouble because he changed sides and clashed with his protector, Shamil Tarpishchev,
sports minister, a member of Korzhakov's band and one of Yeltsin's tennis partners. The
bloody settlement of this affair is a confirmation of the small distance separating the Kremlin
from the gutter. Incidentally, this Boris Fedorov should not be confused with the financier.

16. Interview on NTV, 4 July 1996.

and so on. In a report published immediately after the second ballot, the European Media Institute, sponsored by the European Union and well-disposed towards Yeltsin, deplored that in terms of media coverage the 1996 Russian election marked a step backwards compared with 1991; that the electoral commission was not impartial; that except for Yeltsin (and Lebed during the last ten days before the first ballot) no candidate was shown in a positive way on the three TV channels; and that despite complaints, things got much worse in the second round, when Yeltsin was mentioned 247 times favourably and Zyuganov 240 times in negative fashion.[17] With so much at stake, the authorities did not even bother to conceal the bias.

By contrast with the aggressive tactics of the Yeltsinites, the Communist campaign in the second ballot seemed moderate and even halfhearted. It is not just that the Communists did not have the money and the prerogatives of power at the disposal of their opponent. In the first round, the candidate Zyuganov traveled and canvassed throughout the country. In the second, he limited himself to daily press conferences in Moscow, a strange choice knowing that the media were not inclined to echo faithfully his arguments. Stranger still was the new Communist predilection for match-making with the other side, Zyuganov's proposal to set up a Council of National Accord including all of Russia's key politicians—who promptly turned down his offer—and under the auspices of that council to form a government made up of three blocs: one third of the ministers to be proposed by his own "popular-patriotic front," one third by other parties in the Duma, and a final third suggested by the team now in office. The obvious purpose of the Communists, painted as bloodthirsty, was to show their moderation. But it was too obvious. Either it was a gimmick and would fool nobody, or the proposal was serious and it did not make much sense.

It was odd to hear Zyuganov in an electoral broadcast delivering a scathing indictment of Yeltsin, who deprived Russians of "everything, including their burial savings," describing Russia as "a beggar sitting in the G-7's waiting room" having lost "its dignity as nation and as state," only to propose that they should form a government together.[18] One could

17. See *Le Monde,* 7-8 July 1996.
18. Electoral broadcast, 1 July 1996.

not resist a sneaking suspicion that the man might not want to be elected president. A case could actually be made for such reluctance. With the economy in a catastrophic state, the West ready to squeeze, the armed forces in the hands of opponents determined to cling to power, was it not too risky, or too soon, to take over? Was it not preferable to wait a bit longer, as a strong opposition backed by millions, while the regime disintegrated further still, so as to pick the fruit when it was all but ready to fall from the tree?

When all thus seemed settled, with one side desperately clinging to power and the other apparently not too eager to succeed, the scenario got out of hand in the very last week. Suddenly it was the Russian version of Hamlet without the Prince of Denmark, with Boris Yeltsin vanishing from the stage. The first signs that something was wrong came with rumors that all his trips to the provinces were cancelled. By June 28, a Friday, when Yeltsin had to be replaced by Chernomyrdin at an agricultural conference held in Moscow, the trouble could no longer be concealed. "A sore throat" was a rather unconvincing explanation. And the same Chernomyrdin had to replace him at the G-8 meeting in Lyon. When on the following Sunday Yeltsin did not turn up for the *Moskovsky Komsomolets* festival, the alleged reason for his staying in Moscow, and then, on Monday, had to cancel appointments with the presidents of Ukraine and Moldavia, the cat was out of the bag. Western correspondents, the scent of scoop provisionally overcoming the political preferences of their employers, went after the sensational story. Was it his heart again or a depression aggravated by the Korzhakov affair? Was it sheer exhaustion, or had the doctors abused their "magic" in boosting the candidate? Where Western newsmen were seeking a story, their Russian equivalents, helped by Western diplomats, had to conceal and deny it. Here the control of the Russian media was most important. You could publish long interviews of the president in the papers or revive pictures from the archives. The stage managers even succeeded, on July 1, the last day of the campaign, in producing a film of the president addressing the nation. The performance was that of an automaton, but this was almost unnoticed amid the noise of propaganda. Zyuganov's suggestion that Russia was a strange place in which you had to pass stiff health and alcohol tests for being a bus driver, though not for being a president, was drowned by the chorus of time-servers singing the Russian version of *tout va très bien Madame la Marquise.* For the Russians their president's illness was an Orwellian unfact. Even on July 3, the day of the election, they were urged—by the mayor of Moscow or the patriarch of Russia—to do their duty, and they went to the polls, almost as numerous as in the first ballot. Yeltsin won comfortably with more than 40 million votes (53.8 percent). Zyuganov got more than 30 million (40.3 percent). Five percent of the voters expressed their rejection of both candidates.

The kingmakers sighed with relief and got busy preparing a great celebration, the inauguration of Boris, scheduled for August 9, which was to be worthy of a tsar and indeed modelled on tsarist coronations. But it wasn't to be. Six days before the chosen date, the Chechen fighters launched their counteroffensive, gaining control of Grozny and the two other main towns. With soldiers massacred, the troops besieged, and the army humiliated, this was hardly the time for rejoicing in Moscow. The ceremonies were reduced in rank and scope. Actually, there was nothing to celebrate and nobody to do so. An obviously ailing Yeltsin barely managed to swear the oath. The apotheosis turned into a flop and the symbolism was, for once, appropriate. This was not the triumphant start of the rule of Boris the Second. It was the twilight of Yeltsin's reign, and the struggle for succession had already begun with Lebed the bold, Luzhkov the ambitious, Chernomyrdin the stubborn, and Chubais the sly openly fighting for the spoils, while Zyuganov regrouped to do better next time. It had really been a Pyrrhic victory, a miracle at the polls, but a miracle for nothing.

I have devoted so much space to this parody because it tells us something not only about Russia but about our own methods of government. It is clear that, had the conditions been equal, Yeltsin could not have defeated Zyuganov. Indeed, he was not best suited for the task and, assuming no bias, would not have been picked in the first round to fight in the second. If this is democracy triumphant, then the substance of the process is irrelevant as long as certain formal rules are preserved. If the American president really believes what he says, then the Russian caricature and our more sophisticated exercises in the West, far from being fundamentally different, have a great deal in common. What really matters is the preservation of a society resting on profit. In both cases, the name of the game is the same: how to fool most of the people all of the time.

To leave it at that would be to leave the picture incomplete. We have no need to invert the example of those Western commentators who, having equated Zyuganov's victory with the return of the "red peril," were ready to forget or forgive all the crimes committed by his opponents. The fact that Yeltsin was surrounded by scoundrels and speculators trying to consolidate the new rule of money does not turn their opponents into angels. Within the "popular-patriotic" coalition there were Stalinist diehards and reactionary jingoists with whom any alliance is immoral.

Whether in the biased circumstances of Russia it was at all possible for a candidate of the opposition to win the election or, to broaden the question, whether the West can now prevent anywhere the formation of a government not openly committed to capitalism is debatable. What is unquestionable is that the campaign could have been run very differently, guided by the idea—victory or no victory—of mobilizing a movement from below around the vision of an alternative society. Thus, to complete the picture, we must look at Zuyganov's coalition, at its nationalist connections, at its program (or rather the lack of a real program), for the future, and, finally, at the risks involved when an explosive social situation is combined with such an absense of a genuine alternative.

We are faced in Russia with a dual contradiction. We have been dealing so far with the first aspect: how could a man who had presided over the economic collapse and the pauperization of his country be re-elected through universal suffrage? The second is how, merely ten years after the beginning of perestroika and five years after the collapse of the Soviet Union, can a party claiming the heritage of the notorious CPSU be the main political force in Russia? The two are deeply interconnected. The Russians, having rejected their neo-Stalinist heritage, were then given a very rapid "short course" on the nature of "really existing capitalism."[19] They had no time for a critical examination of their own history, for searching the reasons of the gap between the socialist promise and the Stalinist fulfillment. They were quickly brought to a mood of nostalgia for their own past. Naturally, no one hankered after the gulag or the long lines. Still, after a few years of shock therapy, the job security and welfare services of

19. An allusion to the classic of the Stalinist period, *History of the Communist Party of the Soviet Union (Bolsheviks), Short Course* (New York: International Publishers, 1939).

Brezhnevian stagnation, however drab that period was, acquired for millions of Russians a retrospective glow. The success of the Communist Party of the Russian Federation owes more to Jeffrey Sachs or the International Monetary Fund than to Marx or Lenin.

Stocky and solid, shrewd if uncharismatic, Gennady Zyuganov is an appropriate leader for this provisional-looking party of a society in transition. Born towards the end of the war, in 1944, he followed the example of his parents, both schoolteachers, and became a mathematics master. He simultaneously climbed the *Komsomol* ladder, winding up in the ideological section of the Party's central committee in Moscow. However, he can in no way be described as one of the princes of the former regime like Yeltsin, admittedly thirteen years his senior. Zyuganov was never an enthusiast of perestroika, and in July 1991 he signed the manifesto, most of whose signatories were prominent in the putsch of the following month.[20] But, mysteriously, he refrained from taking part in that coup. Similarly, during the storming of the Duma in October 1993, while naturally on the side of its defenders, he was not among them. The man seems to have a talent for compromise, for stopping just before the brink. He also has skills as an organizer since he played an important part in turning the CPRF into Russia's only mass party, with a claimed membership of just over half a million. Zyuganov can appeal to its various sections. Ready to describe "our Orthodox Church and the army" as the country's "two most important institutions," having himself worked on the jingoist daily *Dyen,* he can attract traditionalists. Cleverly balancing expressions of regret for Soviet-era repressions with the assertion that "it was not easy to imagine our victory without Stalin," he tries to reconcile the ancients and the moderns, the nostalgics and the advocates of change.

Such flexibility was of even greater use for the presidential candidate of the populist-patriotic coalition and for the leader of the unity coalition bearing the same name formed immediately after the presidential election. After all, this wider coalition included the smaller and more orthodox CPs, notably the biggest among them, the Russian Communist Workers' Party, but also Ryzhkov's Power to the People, the nearest thing to social democracy in the present Russian context, and the Agrarians, with their own

20. "Appeal to the People," 23 July 1991, first published in *Sovietskaya Rossiya.*

specific interests. It also had room for all sorts of nationalists, from Sergey Baburin of the Russian National Union and the former Vice President Alexander Rutskoy (who shortly after would make his peace with Yeltsin's regime) to much more disreputable xenophobes. It is not, incidentally, as difficult as it would seem to keep together unreconstructed Stalinists and reactionary jingoists. They sometimes co-exist in one and the same person. Viktor Anpilov, former leader of the above-mentioned Communist Workers' Party, can in the same breath express his proletarian internationalism and say that he is sick of seeing Jewish faces and hearing Jewish voices on Russian television.

And so we have reached the sore spot. Actually, there is nothing wrong in admitting the existence of scum in Russian politics. What is wrong is to recognize that stench only when it comes from one direction. The term "red-brown," with its national-socialist connotation, has been used and abused to justify the worst turpitude of the Yeltsin regime on the grounds that anything was better than such a prospect. Let there be no mistake. Correspondents were doing their duty reporting racist comments or innuendos by so-called Communists and their allies, for instance, when the editorialist of *Pravda* in his obituary of the Nobel laureate poet Joseph Brodsky insisted heavily that he was a Jewish not a Russian writer. Alas, they did not show the same zeal to report and illustrate when the "national Bolshevik" Eduard Limonov or the ultra-reactionary Alexander Barkachov expressed their preference for Yeltsin. One example sums up the whole lack of balance perfectly. If there was a party, as opposed to a small sect, which symbolized the rotten side of Russian politics, it was that misnomer, the Liberal-Democratic Party of Vladimir Zhirinovsky. Indeed, you may have read quite often that we had to put up with Yeltsin because he was the rampart against both the Communists and Zhirinovsky. Yet when it came to the second ballot of the presidential election and he had to make a choice, Zhirinovsky said that he himself would vote for neither, but the categorical imperative for his electorate was "don't vote for Zyuganov." Had Zhirinovsky said the opposite, giving implicit backing to Zyuganov, you can imagine the moral indignation of the editorials and the size of the headlines in the Western press. As he came to Yeltsin's rescue, the event was worth no more than a snippet, and the fact is probably unknown to the vast Western public. Incidentally, since then Zhirinovsky's parliamentary troops have time and again come to Yeltsin's assistance in the Duma.

The hypocrisy, however, is much less important than the reasons why, at this stage, xenophobia, the mistrust of the alien and particularly of the Westerner, is prevalent among large sections of the Russian population. The division into Slavophiles, for whom salvation can only be found within native, Slavonic traditions, and the Westernizers, for whom progress—cultural and social as well as economic—was bound to come from the advanced Western countries, has roots going back to the last century. To suggest that it was then a conflict between reactionaries and progressives would be an exaggeration since the Slavophiles included the *narodniks* and Social Revolutionaries, who searched for social justice via peasant traditionalism, while among the Westernizers were also people mainly interested in spreading capitalist exploitation to Russia. And yet in rough terms the definition was true. The West for the Russians was associated with progress, not only because it was substituting machinery for hard human labor (a popular folk song contrasted the clever Englishman who ties engine to engine with the muzhik who can only rely on his wooden stick, his *dubinushka*), but also because it symbolized social advancement. By the end of the nineteenth century, a good portion of the Russian intelligentsia assumed that it was importing from the West, together with its methods of production, the most progressive idea of social organization, namely socialism.

A century later, things are very different. The West still stands for up-to-date technological invention, but for very many Russians it now also stands for social regression. Its victory, the triumph of its system in their country, coincides not only with a sharp drop in living standards, but with an attack on their social services, a widening gap in incomes, and growing inequality in health, housing, and education. No wonder that, shocked and humiliated by the arrogant power of money, many Russians have concluded that all this had been plotted by outsiders and some that the plot was perpetrated by foreign unbelievers against Holy, Orthodox Mother Russia. At home, anything different—non-Slavonic, unorthodox—became, therefore, suspicious. Anti-Semitism, said August Bebel, the German Social Democrat, is the socialism of fools. His shrewd definition can equally be applied to jingoism and other forms of xenophobia. When frustrated people see no progressive solution and have no rational explanations for their fate, they opt for irrationality and the search for scapegoats.

This argument implies that the popular-patriotic coalition and the CPRF, whatever its name may suggest, did not offer the Russians a genuine alternative, and certainly not one that could be called socialist. This line is reinforced by the study of Zyuganov's "social-economic program," produced rather late in the electoral campaign.[21] The document is at its best, understandably, in the indictment of the five-year record of Yeltsin's rule. Behind the 40 percent drop in the national product, it shows the reduction of investments to a third of their former level, the fall in the output of light and textile industry to a fifth, and an even more dramatic collapse in the technologically most advanced branches. Relying increasingly on its base of raw materials, the Russian economy is falling more and more into the classical pattern of the third world. On finance, the document contrasted the savings of the poor, wiped out by galloping inflation, with those of the very rich, finding a profitable haven abroad. Yeltsin and his government, it argues, are intrinsically unable to alter this policy, since doing so would require "violating the main interests of the super-rich comprador elite and their powerful foreign patrons."

The draftsmen of this Zyuganov document were much less precise about the kind of system of production and social organization they intended to substitute for the primitive capitalism sponsored by their opponents, and I do not think this haziness was essentially due to a desire to conceal their designs from foreign lenders or to a need to reconcile conflicting sections within their own electorate, made up mostly of the victims of the new regime yet including a managerial wing that could prosper under a state-sponsored capitalism. It would seem that, products of the ideologically vacuous post-Stalinist regime and stunned by its bankruptcy, they are genuinely at a loss, not knowing where they are going. They have not yet accomplished the full conversion to classical capitalism like their now "social-democratic" comrades in Eastern Europe, and hence the Western veto against their coming to office, but they give the impression of moving in that direction.

21. For full text, see *Sovyetskaya Rossiya,* 28 May 1996; for an interesting previous draft, see *Nezavissimaya Gazeta,* 25 May 1996.

Russia's Miracle at the Polls

The stage they are at is probably best defined as that of state capitalism and this may explain the praise for Chinese success in the earlier draft of the program. A strong case can actually be made that to consolidate capitalism in Russia, Friedrich List is of greater help than Adam Smith. For the key industries to survive and develop, they need to be sheltered from foreign competition, with the state aiding and directing investment. A recipe of this kind is to be found in Zyuganov's program. What is totally missing is a discussion of matters that a socialist opposition must analyze if it wants to be credible once again, especially in a country with Russia's past. There is nothing about power relations in the factory and in the office, about division of labor and the hierarchical structures, nothing either about creating new forms of democracy at all levels of society to prevent planning from being what it used to be, sheer dictation from the top. There is nothing about the common concepts and interests in the name of which the technicians and the professional intelligentsia should ally themselves with the workers. Having failed to settle accounts with their past, the so-called Communists proved unable to offer a serious project for the future and the absense of such a credible alternative is another reason—in addition to the exorbitant biases in favor of Yeltsin—why Zyuganov did not sweep the country.

In its initial draft, Zyuganov's program ended with a plea that, since the Yeltsin team had lost the confidence of the people, "the ruling elite must be changed." This revealingly got to the heart of the matter: the election was but a struggle between "elites." Not that working people were uninvolved or did not count. We saw how Yeltsin had to travel around the country promising that after months of delay, back wages would finally be paid. But they were involved as electoral fodder, not as main actors. Feeling betrayed by the former regime, in which they were the alleged masters, and bewildered by the new, which destroyed their feeling of security, forced to fight to get their pay and scrambling to make ends meet, the working people of Russia have not been able so far to rise above the immediate struggle for survival, to elaborate their broader interests, and to seek allies with whom to reshape society so that those interests could be satisfied. How long will it take them to develop their consciousness and rediscover their strength? For the moment no party, no movement appears on the horizon looking able to help them in this immense task of self-education. All that can be said is that time is running out. Here is a country in deep and worsening economic crisis, where crime is rampant and corruption is invading every walk of life, but capitalism still finds it difficult to establish its reign. The sword is often used in such situations to break the stalemate, and the shadow of Bonapartism is lengthening over Russia. It is small consolation to know that if a socialist solution does not emerge rapidly and if the other side is convinced that ruthless authoritarian rule is the only way to consolidate capitalism in Russia, a Western president will be found to proclaim that, after all, dictatorship is also a form of democracy, though possibly not the most triumphant.

A POSTSCRIPT, on the unmaking of a president: On August 17, 1998, Russia, if it did not quite shake the world, certainly took it by surprise. Considering the length and gravity of its economic crisis, the devaluation of the ruble could not be ruled out. But the default, the moratorium, the decision to suspend some foreign payments for ninety days and to renegotiate the reimbursement of treasury bills, provoked panic among speculators and shock in Washington, at the headquarters of the IMF. This bankruptcy marked the end of an epoch. True, Boris Yeltsin did not actually resign. Clinging to his throne, he even tried for a time to impose the return of Viktor Chernomyrdin as prime minister. But by now, parliament was no longer playing. Whatever the constitutional texts, Yeltsin's days of absolute power were over. He had to appoint as prime minister a man welcomed by the Duma, and the choice of Yevgeni Primakov was significant.

A clever jack-of-all-trades—a journalist, a fully qualified economist, the chair of an academic institute, the boss of the secret services, and then head of Russian diplomacy—and a man of many masters, including Brezhnev and Gorbachev before Yeltsin, Primakov was clearly an able survivor. All his talents and diplomatic skill were required for the task with which he was entrusted, that of Russia's transition. Hitherto the Russians had capitalism pushed down their throat through "shock therapy"; they proved totally allergic, and the treatment a disaster. The new government—curiously reconciling the Communist opposition and the party of the ruling establishment, Our Home is Russia—was supposed to offer to the Russian people something different, namely a capitalism that was bearable. Whether it could provide this capitalism with a human face is another matter. What the very attempt did confirm, however, was the utter failure of the entire Yeltsin era. I shall first try to sum up briefly the twilight of this reign and then, before successful efforts are made to brush up and distort this history, put on record the names of the really guilty men, responsible for these seven Western-sponsored and Russian-performed years of calamity.

The presidential election of 1996 changed nothing or, to put it more accurately, changed nothing for the better. Boris Yeltsin, having survived a quintuple bypass in November 1996, soldiered on, if one may say so, a sort of semi-absentee lord, relying on the exorbitant powers of the made-to-measure constitution. Having neither the strength nor the imagination to inspire truly new initiatives, he had enough energy to divide and rule, bringing down anyone who looked to be casting a shadow. General Lebed was the obvious first victim: he was allowed to negotiate peace in Chechnya and, this accomplished, unceremoniously discarded. (Only in May 1998 did he manage to get elected governor of the vast Krasnoyarsk Territory in Siberia, a base from which he can prepare himself for the next presidential race.)

The profiteers kept on accumulating, even if the Sinister Seven were no longer united. The banking barons duly reaped rewards for services rendered. Chubais, at once their agent and a player on his own, did best. Head of the presidential administration at the time of Yeltsin's illness and on good terms with the tsar's most politically-minded daughter, Tatyana Dyachenko, he was nicknamed "the regent," as for a time he was virtually running the country. The tycoon closest to him, Potanin, was then deputy prime minister in charge of the economy, a function Chubais took over when he returned to the government. Berezovsky was in the meantime appointed deputy head of the security council, the other seat of presidential power. But the tycoons were more interested in money than honors and it was over the public property still to be grabbed that they quarreled.

The dispute climaxed in July 1997 over the privatization of Svyazinvest, Russia's potentially lucrative national telecommunications company. The first stake of 25 percent was sold to Mustcom, a Cyprus consortium, with the financier George Soros supplying most of the money, along with Potanin's Oneksimbank. The losers raised hell. Chubais and his fellow "young reformers" replied that now, with the state badly needing funds, the plums had to go to the highest bidder, a candid admission by the chief architect of privatization that the deals hitherto had been rigged. Was it now all above suspicion? Not at all, judging by the handling of Svyazinvest, of the final sale of Norilsk Nickel and the dismissal of the minister in charge of the operation, Alfred Kokh. The crooked methods had not really changed, but there had been a shift in alignments: Chubais and Potanin versus the rest. Since Berezovsky and Gusinsky, like Potanin, had their own media empires, there followed a mud-slinging match, revealing to the vast public some of the minor scandals. (One nice bit was the advance of $90,000 each offered to Chubais and four members of his "team," by a subsidiary of Oneksimbank for a promised "History of Russia's Privatisation"; when a genuine history of this racket is written, such small bribes will obviously pale in comparison.)

While the moguls were making money in crooked deals, on the currency market, on the highly profitable GKOs, the Russian treasuries, their country was literally falling to pieces. There were, in fact, two economies side by side. A few big national companies dealing with communications or energy, a gas giant, a host of sizeable oil firms and other enterprises, predominantly in raw materials, all with outlets abroad. Around this core, a small army of speculators, importers, advertisers, hangers-on, and mafia-recruited body-guards sat in the modern offices, dined in the chic restaurants, drove in large limousines, stayed till the early hours in the nightclubs, bought fancy goods in the boutiques which gave to some sections of Moscow and to a lesser extent St. Petersburg an air of triumphant capitalism. But next to it was a country falling apart and an economy gone back to barter. Big factories somehow managed to carry on because clever intermediaries on their staff knew how and where to get rid of the various products received as payment for their own output. And the workers were paid in kind, when they were paid at all.

When between a half and three-quarters of a country's transactions take place outside normal accounting procedures, it is difficult to demand very accurate statistics. Taking the average of the best estimates, Russia's national product in the seventh year of Yeltsinian transformation is roughly half the level it was before "shock therapy" began. It is a terrible crisis, much deeper than the great capitalist depression of 1929-1932, a lasting one, with no prospect of recovery. Add to this the fact that, whereas the

Soviet Union had a narrower range between top and bottom incomes than capitalist Europe, Russia has already managed to beat Western records of inequality, and you will not be surprised by the price paid by the population: the revival of long-forgotten epidemics or the drop in life expectancy for Russian males by five years. Not surprised either by the contrast between the so-called New Russians, parading their wealth in Moscow or on the French Riviera, and the millions of old Russians barely saved from starvation by that precious companion, the private plot, on which one can grow potatoes and a few vegetables.

No wonder that the protests against the maddening delays in wage payment grew angrier. When the miners relaunched their campaign in the spring of 1998, they blockaded railway lines, interrupting traffic on the trans-Siberian. They were followed in their strike action and their demand for the president's resignation by nurses and other medical staff, by teachers, students and scientists, by workers in defense, including the nuclear industry. Russia, nevertheless, seemed solid for two reasons. Firstly, reduced now to the rank of a third world country, its exports of raw materials were sufficient to pay for growing imports, notably of foodstuffs. Secondly, as taxation, difficult to collect in an economy dominated by barter, proved insufficient to cover public expenditure, foreigners were ready to purchase the high-interest treasury bills and bonds. Indeed, in 1997 quite a lot of money flowed into Russia. The IMF congratulated the rulers for their successful struggle against inflation, as if it did not know that the government was really setting a bad example: to balance the books, it paid neither its debts nor its salaries on time. The fragile equilibrium was swept aside by the Asian crisis. The flight from "emerging markets" meant much higher rates to keep foreign money and, therefore, a much heavier burden for the budget. The sharp drop, by about a third, of oil prices caused a similar cut in Russia's export earnings, but also a declining interest of foreign investors for Russia's jewels, its fuel companies. The country was heading for the wall.

When, early in March, Boris Yeltsin decided to change the government, did he simply repeat his usual act of the good tsar, alas betrayed by a bad servant? Was he trying to get rid of Chenomyrdin because, after five years in office, he had become a rival? Or, sensing a crisis coming, did Yeltsin really believe that a new "young reformer" could save his skin? If he did, his idea turned out to be a flop. The thirty-five-year-old Sergey Kiriyenko, who like Potanin had graduated from the *Komsomol* into finance, did not have much of a chance.[22] Completely unknown, he had no backing in the country. It took time and a lot of bullying by Yeltsin to get him accepted by the Duma. When Kiriyenko and his team got down to the collection of taxes and the cutting of expenditure, the panic was such that they had to raise the rate for treasury bills to 150 percent; the extra budgetary cost much exceeded the rather verbal savings.[23] True, they sent Chubais—who else?— to Washington, from where he returned, in July, with an IMF-sponsored package amounting to $22.6 billion over two years (of which $14.8 billion, in principle, for 1998). But this was too little too late, and too obviously with strings, to turn the tide. The "young reformers," and not any "Soviet dinosaurs," had to resign themselves to the reality of the situation. It was absurd, in the name of financial orthodoxy, to keep on paying foreign lenders exorbitant amounts, when one was no longer able to pay the wages of one's nurses and teachers, miners and atomic scientists, soldiers and policemen. On August 17, to avoid an explosion, they proclaimed a provisional bankruptcy.

For a brief spell, there was unanimity. It was agreed that a historical period had come to a close, that seven years of Russia's forcible conversion to the monetarist cult of capitalism had ended in failure. But the rewriting of history began almost at once. Not to deny the bankruptcy, too obvious to conceal, but to shift responsibility. The Western inspirers of this policy got busy putting the blame on everybody except themselves and their Russian accomplices. Let us get the record straight before their whitewashing is taken as historical truth. The Russian rulers brought their country to economic disaster not because they refused to follow the wise advice of the international financial establishment; they did so because they listened to that advice. And the Russian people were led on this road to disaster not only by their apparatchiks and their moneybags, but in the first

---

22. Many former Communist Youth activists are to be found among the beneficiaries of the transition to capitalism; they were young enough to fit in and sufficiently connected to profit.

23. Don't shed tears over the poor Western bankers who lost their shirts in Russia. When you buy treasuries yielding 30 percent, let alone five times that level, you must be aware that you are not making the safest of investments; their mistake was to assume that the IMF would prop up nuclear and capitalist Russia no matter what happened.

place by our men in Moscow, by those whom we have simply christened "democratic reformers."

The first attempt was to put the blame on the old Soviet managers, like Chernomyrdin with his Gazprom connection. But Chernomyrdin was brought in at the beginning of 1993, because a "true believer" in shock therapy, Yegor Gaidar, had made such a mess—with galloping inflation and savings wiped out—that it was necessary to save the regime. Yeltsin tried to bring him back in August 1998 to repair the damage left by the "young reformer" Kiryenko. True, during his five years in office, Chernomyrdin made his own contribution to Russian calamity, but he was never allowed to act on his own. He was always under the close supervision of a keeper of financial orthodoxy. Indeed, throughout the seven calamitous years the Russian government always had within its ranks a man—Gaidar, Chubais, Fedorov—who could be described as "the eye of the Monetary Fund," watching that it should not depart from the line prescribed.

Another effort was made to shift responsibility to Russia's main profiteers, to Boris Berezovsky and his fellow financiers. It was rather amusing to discover that for some Western publications, after all, making profits was not by definition virtuous. More seriously, one could ask who had made these crooked deals possible, who had helped them to build their fortunes through privatization. The answer was simple: our man Chubais. And when it came to the presidential election in 1996 and they pooled their ill-gotten gains and their control of the media in order to turn Yeltsin's certain defeat into victory, who hailed their performance as a "triumph of democracy"? Our establishment might as well admit its role and that of its Russian associates, explaining on the same occasion the Orwellian sense of humor with which it calls them "democrats." Presumably because they are in no position to face the verdict of the people. Nobody seriously suggests that Yegor Gaidar, Anatoli Chubais, or Boris Fedorov should run in the next presidential campaign, as nobody believes that, even with an effective and expensive machine, they could get into two digits. Why? Because these Russian heroes of the Western world have a very different symbolism for their fellow citizens. They stand for collective calamity, personal greed, social injustice, and inequality that is both immoral and indecent.

Whose Millennium?

The whitewashing had its immediate purpose. It was a sign that, on reflection, the West is not ready to change its line. What is involved in the current Russian situation is not any return to Soviet economics. Even if Zyuganov were to form an all-Communist cabinet, he would not be moving in that direction. Nor is there any question of seeking socialist solutions. Primakov or Zyuganov are no more interested in the subject than Gingrich or Clinton. What is at stake is something quite different. Russia is performing acrobatics on the edge of an abyss. If nothing is done rapidly to unify the country through common economic interests, it may fall apart like the Soviet Union did. The immediate task is to pay back wages and back pensions, to provide a safety net for those threatened by catastrophe. The next step is to extricate the economy from barter by encouraging, wherever possible, the recovery of industrial production. For this, some subsidies and state intervention are required. The vulnerable industries will also need a degree of protection from foreign competition. This is not Marxism, but it goes against the religion of unfettered global expansion, preached hitherto and supervised by the Monetary Fund. Is the international financial establishment now ready for concessions?

You may have gathered from my tone that I have no great fondness for the political newcomers in Russia, no special sympathy for the society they intend to build, and no particular faith in their capacity to achieve what they set out to do. Why then favor them over their opponents? Because no people deserves to be tortured, and after seven years of disastrous experience, to proceed with the same treatment in Russia would simply be sadistic. The second reason is that what is being presented as an alternative is, in fact, a provocation. In today's ruined Russia, where tempers are on edge, to plead in the name of financial orthodoxy against the immediate payment of salaries to miners, nurses, or teachers is to ask for trouble, to invite an upheaval. It is like approaching a powder keg with a burning torch. And an explosion in Russia at this stage is much more likely to produce a jack-booted dictatorship than a society searching for socialism. Russia's young generation of workers, technicians, and intellectuals is learning a great deal and, one may hope that it is learning fast. It nevertheless still needs some time to digest its post-Stalinist past and to understand its capitalist present so as to start forging its own future.

It will be objected that I have been picking easy targets for attack. If the West vetoed the advent of a Communist regime in Russia, it had earlier accepted more civilized—read "truly converted"—Communists as rulers in other countries of Eastern Europe. Russia is also the country where shock therapy had its most disastrous results. So let us now turn to a country where a converted social democrat is president of the republic and which shock therapists present as their showcase. Let us look at Poland, where the collapse of the Soviet empire really began.

6.

The Sad Saga of Solidarity

Something was dead in each of us
And what was dead was hope.

Oscar Wilde, *Ballad of Reading Gaol*

A JOURNALIST or a businessman landing at the modernized Warsaw airport, grabbing a taxi for the Marriott or the Bristol and then shopping or strolling in the center of town, may be forgiven the impression that Poland is now part and parcel of the affluent West. The lights are bright, and the shops resemble those of Fifth Avenue or rue du Faubourg St Honoré; indeed, they are often the same. If the newsman is driven by his professional conscience to move beyond the posh districts and even to travel to the provinces, he will rightly report that there, too, the shops are filled with goods. The contrast with his recollection of the Communist era—with its long lines, empty shelves and the *babushkas* selling toilet paper in the streets—will lead him to draw the expected conclusion that shock therapy, like Guiness, is good for Poland.

What he will not explain is why the Poles are so ungrateful for this blessing. In July 1989, in the famous partially free election which spelled the doom of the Communist regimes throughout Eastern Europe, any minor candidate photographed together with Lech Walesa—symbolizing endorsement by Solidarity—was bound to be elected. Nobody imagined at the time that the Communists, thrown so spectacularly into the dustbin of history, could climb out of it in the foreseeable future. Poland's chief shock therapist, Leszek Balcerowicz, rendered this achievement possible. The former Communists, admittedly converted to social democracy, were the strongest party in the parliamentary election of 1993, though they still needed their Peasant Party allies to form a government.[1] Two years later, in the second ballot of the presidential election, when an absolute majority was required, the converted Communist, the smooth forty-two-year-old Aleksander Kwasniewski, defeated the outgoing president, Lech Walesa himself, who could not even save his skin with a red-scare campaign. After two years in government, the rechristened Communists could hardly be presented as a threat to capitalism.

Indeed, having in their essentials followed the economic policy of their predecessors, only in a milder form, the ex-Communist newcomers were, in turn, threatened with a backlash. Marian Krzaklewski, the leader of Solidarity, knew that his union could only recover by being more militant. Politically, he decided to unify the highly dispersed reactionary parties in a coalition— Solidarity Electoral Action (AWS)—around a platform that was populist in the worst sense of the term: it promised things—reversal of neoliberalism and hence only a conditional acceptance of Poland's entry into the European Union—without preparing the means to carry them out. The electoral success of this line revealed its hypocrisy. In the parliamentary poll of September 1997, the AWS won more seats than the Democratic Left Alliance (201 versus 164). It then formed a government with Balcerowicz's Freedom Party, known for its devotion to neoliberalism and European integration. The shaky alliance may not last as long as the time it will take to print this book, and we will return to the interesting contradictions it reveals. Here, it is enough to note that to regain popularity, Solidarity had to disown, and not to endorse, the policies introduced after 1989 by politicians issued from its ranks.

When an economic and social policy causes such deep and lasting discontent, one must look below the glittering surface, beyond the neon lights and the opulent shop windows. In Warsaw, one must cross the Vistula to visit the poorer districts on the other side of the river or take an hour's train journey to Lodz, the Polish Manchester, with a textile industry that is

---

1. The Social Democracy of the Polish Republic (SDRP) was the heir of the former CP. It formed the backbone of a coalition known as the SLD, the Alliance of the Democratic Left, which captured 20.5 percent of the vote and 161 of 460 seats in the Sejm. Its partners from the Polish Peasant Party (PSL) got 15 percent of the vote and 131 members. Their more than proportionate representation was due to the fact that many votes were "wasted," as several right-wing parties did not reach the threshold of 5 percent.

being "restructured." One can also travel to the one-factory or one-mine towns, torn by the closing or "downsizing" of their main sources of life and income; or to the rural areas of northeastern Poland, where the peasants driven from the land cannot find jobs in town. These gloomier impressions are confirmed by official statistics, and not only those referring to the big jump in unemployment from next to nothing to around 15 percent.[2] The immediate result of shock therapy was a sharp drop in output and living standards. It was only in 1996 that the gross national product topped its level of 1989, and real wages were still lagging slightly. What the Western press was hailing as tremendous achievement was merely a belated recovery.

The plight of the population in the intervening period may have been somewhat exaggerated in statistics by the emergence of tax evasion with the market economy: some income, obviously, went unreported. On the other hand, this is more than offset by the main feature of the new regime: polarization. Money has been changing relations in all walks of life, including health, housing, and education. While the poor, headed by a new mass phenomenon—the unemployed—were getting poorer, the new rich, led by the speculators, were getting incomparably richer.[3] Adding insult to injury, they showed off their wealth with aggressive ostentation stimulated by the new conviction that your money is your worth. To complete the Polish paradox, the pioneers of the new regime, the industrial workers, were victims of this transformation, not its beneficiaries.

In June 1996, to celebrate the twentieth anniversary of an important event in the history of Solidarity, at the Ursus Tractor Works outside Warsaw local Solidarity leader Zygmunt Wrzodak had the cheek to say about men like Jacek Kuron and Adam Michnik that "in their hatred of Polishness, they cynically exploited our misfortune, our blood and our naiveté." A few months earlier, during a protest march in Warsaw, demonstrators carrying the banner of the union dared to send—true, only verbally—the reds and the yids to the gas chambers. Granted, one faction cannot be identified with the union as a whole, yet the very fact that people

2. It was reduced to 11.1 percent in 1997, largely through "the severe tightening of the unemployment benefit regime." *Poland OECD Economic Survey 1998.*

3. Poland, where the range of incomes used to be narrower, has now overtaken the countries of Western Europe in polarity, and is approaching the American level. See *Polityka*, 16 May 1998.

like this are tolerated within Solidarity shows the road traveled by that organization since that glorious summer of 1980, when it was born in Gdansk amid the applause and admiration of an astonished world. To understand that degeneration, and also to grasp such Polish specialties as anti-Semitism without Jews or anticommunism without genuine communists, we must glance back at the country's recent history. After all, Poland is the only country of Eastern Europe in which the removal of the Communist regime was prepared by a real mass movement from below, spearheaded by the workers.

Nineteen fifty-six is a turning point in East European history. It opens with Nikita Khrushchev's not-so-secret indictment of Stalin and ends with the Soviet tanks in Budapest having crushed the Hungarian insurrection. Poland had its share of drama. In June, the "workers' state" had the first armed confrontation with its alleged masters, when police shot at striking workers in the Western city of Poznan. But the Polish Communist Party, unlike its neighbors, had an alternative leader in its ranks, a man whose rehabilitation was not posthumous. Wladyslaw Gomulka, while a faithful Stalinist, did genuinely believe in the postwar talk about "independent roads to socialism" and was discarded when the net was tightened with the onset of the Cold War. Though jailed, he was not executed, and was now in a position to take over. In October, Khrushchev, Molotov, and company descended on Warsaw to prevent his return to power. Seeing for once a Communist leader backed by the whole country, they changed their mind. The Polish "spring in October" was a moment of unity and euphoria, as peasants were allowed to disband collective farms, the Catholic Church was given more room for manoeuver and the repressive straitjacket was altogether relaxed. The Stalinist era was over, gone forever.

But the euphoria was built on a misunderstanding. Gomulka never had the intention of fundamentally challenging the regime and its Russian backers. His honeymoon with the so-called revisionists—the intellectuals still dreaming of an evolution within the system, with the help of the party, towards a vaguely socialist society—was over within a year, when the unorthodox weekly, *Po Prostu,* was closed down. Total rupture with the reformist intelligentsia took place in 1968, when Gomulka allowed his minister of the interior, General Moczar, to stage an anti-Semitic purge under an anti-Zionist disguise, and when incidents surrounding a famous Polish play with anti-Russian allusions gave the police an opportunity to club rebellious students.

It was easier to take on the intellectuals than the workers. When, in 1970, something had to be done to prevent consumption from outstripping output, the clever technocrats opted for a dramatic rise in food prices, scheduled for December, on the eve of Christmas. The response came from the country's northern maritime regions. In the harbors of Gdansk, Gdynia, and Szczecin, the shipyard workers led the offensive. They dropped their tools and proceeded to organize protest marches directed against town halls or Party headquarters. The repression was ruthless. Even in the official count, there were dozens of dead and more than a thousand wounded. Politically, if not militarily, the "workers' state" could not wage such a war against the working class. Gomulka was toppled and his successor, the pragmatic Silesian leader, Edward Gierek, who had started his professional life as a miner in France and Belgium, now traveled north to ask the shipwrights to give the regime a hand. The crisis came to an end only in February 1971 when, faced with the stubbornness of the women striking in the textile factories of Lodz, the government was forced to cancel its proposed increase in food prices.

Poland was thus in a strange stalemate. In one sense, the structure was unchanged, with the Party supreme and power flowing from above. But within this unaltered framework the Polish workers had conquered in blood a sort of veto: not a right to shape policy or to take part in the making of decisions, but a negative right to say *no* as a sign of resistance, a warning that such a policy will only be introduced over our dead bodies. To extricate himself from the resulting dilemma, Gierek chose the flight forward. With Soviet backing and Western credits, he embarked on a policy of expansion and, for a period in the early 1970s, Poland was upheld as exemplary. Then came the Western economic crisis, the difficulty of paying the debts through exports, and the realization that the investments had not been very wise. With the need to tighten the belt came the confirmation that *veto power* was not a figment of the imagination. On June 24, 1976, a Thursday, the government announced another tremendous increase in food prices, starting the following week. On Friday, striking workers from the Ursus tractor plant occupied the neighboring railway line, blocking the Moscow-

Paris express, while those from Radom, south of Warsaw, repeated the scenario of 1970, marching on Party headquarters and clashing with the police. This time, however, the movement did not last, because that very evening the prime minister proclaimed on television that the whole project was being postponed. He did so because alarming reports were heralding a strike wave sweeping the whole country.

The year 1976 was thus a shortened, condensed version of 1970, with one historic difference: it inaugurated the alliance between workers and intellectuals. In 1968, while students were clobbered and intellectuals purged, the workers did not rise. In 1970, as strikers protested in Gdansk, the students did not join in. This time it was different. The authorities, forced to yield, were seeking revenge. They were determined to jail and torment the workers involved in the riots. The victims, however, were not alone. A few intellectuals came to their rescue, doing what they could do best: spreading information and providing legal advice and social assistance. Out of this action was born the Committee for the Defense of the Workers, known on the basis of its Polish initials as the KOR. A famous writer, a celebrated actress, a few longtime socialists, and a group of younger people, of whom the activist Jacek Kuron and the essayist Adam Michnik were to become the best-known—they were not a legion.[4] But, despite arrests and continued harassment, they did their job well. After roughly a year, all the victims were released. The government, thinking that this was the end of the story, was mistaken. KOR carried on, helping in the setting up of a "flying university," sponsoring a series of dissident publications, notably a single page *Robotnik* (*The Worker*), propagating among its readers the idea that to defend their interests they would have to forge their own autonomous organization.

In its collision course, Poland had two special features. One was the massive presence, particularly in the countryside, of small property owners. The permission given by Gomulka to the peasants to leave collective farms meant their dismantlement. Over three-quarters of the arable land was thus in the hands of smallholders, and since farming still accounted for 30 percent of the labor force, a big chunk of the population wanted a change

---

4. Together with the brilliant young historian Karol Modzelewski, Kuron had already spent several years in jail for writing, in 1964, "An Open Letter to the Party."

of regime, convinced, wrongly, that capitalism would ensure the permanence of their claim to property. The other specificity was the prestige and
popularity of the Catholic Church. In prewar days, its power had rested on the
backing of the wealthy, of the big landowners, and on the backwardness of the
largely rural population. After the political and social upheaval, the new
Communist regime bestowed on the Catholic Church a new virginity, driving
it to the side of the downtrodden. Indeed, the popularity of the Church was a
measure of the bankruptcy of the ruling party. The more the CP stood for
injustice and exploitation, the more the Church appeared as the champion of
the oppressed. John Paul II's triumphant journey through his home country
in 1979, with the police forces out of the way, may have given some Poles
the idea that, after all, they could run things on their own. Yet the impending
confrontation was fundamentally between the industrial workers rediscovering their strength and the party claiming to be their representative.

The two protagonists faced each other in the summer of 1980 armed
with their previous experience. The rulers did not announce the increase in
prices dramatically, through the prime minister amid a brass of trumpets.
This time they did it quietly, simultaneously issuing secret instructions that,
wherever the workers resisted, they should be given compensation. The
workers, for their part, had learned to break their isolation, to establish
contacts between factories, notably through the KOR, so that each concession was a spur for another shop, for another plant, to ask for more. The
tide this time rose slowly and haphazardly. The first strikes started in
Warsaw on July 1, as soon as the prices went up. Then the wave moved
eastward to the Lublin region, where a sort of dress rehearsal was staged.
Yet the real drama, with an international audience, only began when the
Lenin Shipyards in Gdansk struck on August 14. There were specific
reasons for that stoppage, like the demand for the reinstatement of a popular
woman protester, the welder Anya Walentynowicz. As the crowd gathered
in front of the managerial quarters, another outcast climbed over the fence
and straight into history, a thirty-seven-year-old, mustachioed electrician—
Lech Walesa. Thus the stage was set from the start for the seventeen
momentous days which were finally to destroy a fundamental myth, namely
that the Communist Parties were, by definition or birthright, the spokesmen
for the working class.

The Sad Saga of Solidarity

This is not the place to revive those exciting days, but simply to draw some lessons from the events. The first is that in revolutionary situations ideas ripen at tremendous speed. The concept of an independent labor union was so heretical in Eastern Europe that the inspirers of the movement in Gdansk, connected with *Robotnik,* had not dared to put a demand for such a union in their original platform. Then the idea spread like lightning and became a profound, collective conviction, so that when the intellectuals, the so-called experts arriving from Warsaw to help, objected that the rulers would never accept such a labor union, they got the same answer from all the strikers in Gdansk: "That is not negotiable." Which brings us to the second lesson: at that stage, the workers were the masters making decisions and the experts—a handful of intellectuals from left Catholic or "revision-ist" backgrounds—were fulfilling their function of providing technical assistance and advice.

The other feature of this movement, despite the first signs of Walesa's predilection for personal rule, was its deep democracy, with delegates from various plants sitting together in an interfactory strike committee and negotiations with the government being carried in the open—a crowd outside the hall listening to loudspeakers. It was also very egalitarian, asking for wage increases, not proportionate but equal for all, the only exception being a supplement for those with the lowest pay. If you add to it that throughout this crisis the workers presented their interests as the superior interests of society as a whole, it sounds too Marxist to be true. Walesa wearing the Virgin Mary on his lapel and the class struggle conducted to the sound of Catholic hymns were reminders that matters were much more complicated. The regime they fought calling itself Communist, they could hardly be consciously Marxist. As was said at the time, if they acted and sounded socialist, it was like Monsieur Jourdain in Moliére's *Le Bourgeois Gentilhomme* speaking prose—they were unaware of it.[5]

The movement also had to be highly disciplined—keeping the workers inside the factories, banning alcohol—to avoid provocation, and it had to be very powerful to force the authorities to yield. The wave swept once again from Gdansk and Gdynia all the way to Szczecin, and the sit-in strikes

5. Daniel Singer, *The Road to Gdansk: Poland and the USSR* (New York: Monthly Review Press, 1982).

involved not just the shipyards but most of the factories in the maritime regions. Ten days of such pressure brought the government down, but its successor was just as reluctant on the essential point. The conflict continued amid rumors of imminent armed intervention, Russian or domestic. It took the extension of the strike throughout the country and concessions by the strikers—accepting the inclusion in the agreement of references to "the leading role of the party" and to "the established system of international alliances"—for the Gdansk charter to be finally signed on August 31. The impossible had become reality. Poland was the first Communist country to admit that its workers, for the defense of their interests, required their own autonomous organization.

There followed fifteen months of virtually dual power. The Party had history and geography—the division of Europe at Yalta and the Russian frontier—on its side. It had the control of the army, of the police, of all key appointments (the so-called nomenklatura) and no intention of giving up its prerogatives. But now it had to reckon with another source of authority. It had to bow to the inevitable: the recognition, formalized in November, of Solidarity, as a decentralized yet all-national labor union, growing like a mushroom after the political storm. Whether it had nine or ten million members at its peak does not really matter. For a time, Solidarity *was* working Poland, its claimed membership accounting for roughly three-quarters of the labor force outside agriculture. Nor was it quite accurate to describe the conflict as one between Party and union, since out of the alleged three million Party cardholders, about one-third also had the badge of Solidarity.

Both sides had to face an economic crisis aggravated by higher wages and falling output. For the Party the logical solution would have been to obtain from Solidarity through collaboration what it had failed to get from the workers through its bullying tactics, namely, the acceptance of a provisional tightening of the belt plus help in the reorganization of production. For this it would have been necessary to share power with the union, and the Party was unprepared for such a concession. Solidarity, too, preferred to act as a union defending its members, since any attempt to collaborate with the authorities would have revealed contradictions within its own ranks. The Party knew that, faced with a mass movement, if it went beyond a certain point, it ran the risk of another upheaval, while the union was aware that if it carried its action to its logical conclusion, the seizure of power, it was likely to precipitate the entry of Soviet tanks. And so it was a trial of strength with almost permanent brinkmanship; in March 1981, an open conflict was only avoided when Solidarity called off a general strike.

Yet the protagonists were also driven by circumstances to some form of collaboration. As the shortages became terribly acute, as the lines length-ened and the tempers reached breaking point, something had to be done to avoid an explosion. By the spring of 1981, several groups within Solidarity rediscovered the idea of self-management. For some this was a way of transforming society altogether, giving the working people the possibility of mastering their factories, their labor, their fate. For others, the workers' councils were, more modestly, a way of providing autonomy to the enter-prise within the existing system.[6] But they were also pointing toward a possible institutional compromise. Poland was to have two houses of parliament. The first, the existing Sejm, would, in keeping with the impera-tives of geography, be controlled by the Party. The second, a sort of economic chamber, would be the national representation of workers' coun-cils throughout the country. An agreement between the two would be required for the conduct of economic and social policy. The scheme could be conceived either as the institutionalization of dual power or as the preparation for the gradual, creeping transfer of that power. When, on November 4, Cardinal Jozef Glemp, acting as matchmaker, brought to-gether Walesa and General Wojciech Jaruzelski, promoted party leader the previous month, one could still hope they were seeking such a compromise. In vain: Solidarity, instead of a genuine share of power, was offered one seat in a body dominated by puppet Communist organizations. The other side had made up its mind. There was a purpose, then, in Jaruzelski holding the combined jobs of defense secretary, prime minister, and party boss. On December 13 at dawn, the general with the dark glasses was ready to move his troops into action.

Did he do it as a Polish patriot trying to avoid Soviet intervention? I am not very convinced by this now-fashionable version. Even after the

6. This was presumably the line of Balcerowicz, then still nominally a member of the CP, who was active in the so-called Siec (Network) advocating the development of self-manage-ment in the big enterprises.

publication of some Russian documents, we do not really know how the Kremlin would have reacted. If Solidarity had grabbed power, casting aside the party, the Soviets most probably would have sent in tanks. But what if Solidarity and the Party had reached an agreement and the Polish army was thus backed by the whole nation? All we can say is that the last thing the so-called Workers' Party wanted to do was to share power with workers' councils. What is also undoubted is Jaruzelski's professional skill. He did not bungle the coup, as Russia's putschist generals were to do in 1991. Neither was he bloodthirsty, like General Pinochet in Chile. While the miners killed by the troops in Silesia bear witness that anything would have been done to break the resistance, in retrospect it is fair to say that force was limited to what was needed for the success of the operation. The task was facilitated by the open, democratic structure of Solidarity. Almost its entire leadership, at national and local levels, could be arrested and deported in one huge swoop. With the "state of war" proclaimed, communications cut, the curfew introduced, and the harshest penalties reserved for the "militarized" key sectors of the economy, a beheaded and disorganized Solidarity could not offer active opposition for long.

In that sense, the military coup was successful. The regime could now raise prices without bothering about the workers' veto, without fearing a general strike. But the enemy, crushed, had not surrendered. Even after the end of martial law and amnesty for the prisoners, nobody of any importance rallied the regime. Passive resistance persisted. It was one thing to prevent the workers from organizing openly, quite another to mobilize them as participants in an economic reform. When in 1988 Solidarity managed to stage a strike in the maritime provinces, though it was only a pale echo of the vast movements of the past, Jaruzelski decided it was time to resign himself to sharing power. With the Soviet Union in the throes of perestroika, Poland's ruling class was ready to experiment with the market, to contemplate conversion to capitalism— anything to preserve its privileged position. For all this, it needed a partner.

The partner, in fact, was no longer quite the same. If the military coup had failed to crush and uproot Solidarity, it did change the balance of power within the organization. True, workers remained the backbone, and it was their non-cooperation which forced the authorities to seek an accommodation. The workers' role within Solidarity, however, had altered. During the seven years of underground activity, the center of gravity had shifted from the factories to the printing presses and the emphasis had shifted from strikes to propaganda. The control of intellectuals and central organs over supplies, notably financial resources, had grown. The Church, a place of shelter and protection, increased its weight still further, while foreign providers of money for the underground also gained some influence. We shall examine below the influence all this had on the political line of the movement, but it is worth noting here the revealing change in the conduct of the talks. In 1980, in the Lenin Shipyards, the strike leaders and their advisers carried on negotiations under the direct supervision of the striking workers. In 1989, in the seclusion of the Magdalenka resort near the capital, where the talks were prepared, and the Warsaw palace in which they were held, they spoke in the name of the labor movement.

Seldom is power transferred and the nature of a regime changed altogether by negotiators bargaining at a "round table," but in this case events were to go much further and move much faster than any of the participants imagined. In one sense, it was a meeting between enemies. General Czeslaw Kiszczak, the minister of the interior, presided over one delegation, whereas most of the members on the other side were his former "guests," inmates of his prisons or provisional detention camps. Here, however, they were seeking a compromise which each side hoped to turn to its advantage. The rulers (a definition more accurate than the Party, which was now dominated by the generals heading the army and the police who had imposed this negotiation on a reluctant central committee) were aware that they needed economic reform to survive and that they could not carry it out without the backing of Solidarity; they hoped to keep power by domesticating their new partner. The spokesmen for Solidarity were conscious that all the powers of coercion were in the hands of the rulers, who could also rely on Soviet support, though how much was uncertain given Gorbachev's perestroika. Solidarity hoped to turn, slowly and gradually, its share of power into the base for a takeover.

The talks were influenced by conditioned reflexes. Thus, the spokesmen of Solidarity, who soon would be preaching the monetary gospel of the Chicago school, still remembered that they were representatives of a labor union and obtained for Poland's working people a sliding scale of wages linked to price increases. Yet the whole relationship, with its tension and ambiguity, was best reflected in the institutional arrangement for the forthcoming election. In theory, the ruling coalition was bound to preserve its dominant position, as it was assured two-thirds of the seats in the more important lower house, the Sejm: only 161 of the 460 seats were open to free competition. At the same time, a deal was struck providing the president of the republic with important powers, notably over the army, the security services, and foreign affairs. The presumable presence of General Jaruzelski in the presidential palace was destined, notably, to reassure the Russians. As compensation, it was agreed to revive a second house, the Senate, with lesser prerogatives, but every one of whose one hundred members were to be elected in an entirely free vote.

God is supposed to first make mad those whom he decides to ruin, and the conduct of the Communists in this election was mad and suicidal. Were they blind or presumptuous? They could have weakened the shock, choosing proportional representation instead of majority rule in single-member constituencies. It was hard to understand what they hoped to obtain through these half-free and half-contrived elections. Even if the vote were free in only one constituency and Solidarity won it, all the other representatives would be deprived of even a pretence of legitimacy.[7] In practice, it proved a landslide. Solidarity won all of the 161 seats in the Sejm for which it was entitled to compete and 99 out of the 100 seats in the Senate. Quantity had a qualitative effect on this occasion. The Peasant and the Democratic parties, hitherto puppets of the Communists in the ruling coalition, faced with the dramatically shifting situation, suddenly discovered their own independent voice. Since the president was to be elected by the absolute majority of deputies and senators voting together, the outcome was no longer sure. To avoid a crisis and a possible collapse of the whole bargain, Solidarity had to provide some discreet assistance for General Jaruzelski to be elected. A price, however, was to be paid for this concession. In keeping with the headline of a controversial article by Michnik—"Their president—our prime minister"—and since Walesa did not want the job,

7. When Kuron mentioned to me the electoral deal contemplated, I argued that the Communists would never accept it, because it would spell their doom. While my analysis was accurate, my forecast was utterly wrong.

one of his chief assistants, Tadeusz Mazowiecki, was asked in August to form a Solidarity government and did so in September. A few months earlier, nobody could have imagined such a quickening of the historical pace.[8] Within the next three months, the political landscape of central and eastern Europe was to be entirely reshaped.

Poland was, once again, a pioneer. Solidarity, one could say, almost had the task of forming a government thrust upon it. It was unprepared and had to improvise. The most urgent duty was to cope with the deteriorating economic situation. The Mazowiecki government, with Balcerowicz surrounded by Western monetarists as economic overlord, embarked on what came to be known as shock therapy. With all controls abolished, prices skyrocketed. Checks were kept on wages so that they could not keep pace. Rationing by the purse replaced the long lines. While small savings were wiped out, the sky was the limit for the profits of speculators. All this was part of a conscious, relentless, primitive drive towards capitalism. The government turned a blind eye to smuggling from abroad or food and health regulations to attack the existing mechanism at its weakest, namely in retail trade. But big state enterprises were also handicapped by tax and salary advantages granted to the private sector. The drop in output and living standards proved much more dramatic and lasted much longer than the architects of that policy promised or even really expected. While economically disastrous, the move fulfilled its political purpose of smashing the existing system.

The big puzzle is how an organization whose very name spelled out the ideal of social solidarity came to preach a gospel based on selfishness. How could a movement, egalitarian in its origins, introduce a mechanism designed to prop up the privileged and damn the downtrodden? How could a labor union built by the industrial workers, particularly the proletarians from the big plants, preside over a program destined to hurt the fundamental interests of its very founders? Part of the answer is that the Solidarity of the rulers of 1990 was not the Solidarity of the rebels of 1980. This should not be taken to mean that the Polish workers were simply betrayed by the intellectuals. The so-called experts could not have done it on their own. If

8. I had lunch with Mazowiecki shortly before the poll and it clearly did not cross his mind that he might become prime minister as its result.

Tadeusz Mazowiecki or Bronislaw Geremek, to take Walesa's best-known advisers, were to go to the Lenin Shipyards or to any other plant to tell the workers to tighten their belts, they did not stand a chance. The workers *would* take it, for a limited period, from one of their own, like Walesa. Thus the whole leadership—workers and intellectuals—must take responsibility for the policy and the conversion.[9]

Who pushed them in that direction? While the Catholic Church had a reactionary influence on the governments of Solidarity in many other respects, it does not seem to have played a decisive part in determining its economic policy. Once the government was formed, the international organizations representing the interests of big business did play their role as extremely efficient pressure groups. But the ground had already been prepared. During its years in the underground, Solidarity received a great deal of assistance from the West, some of it coming from its European sympathizers, including the labor unions, with more coming from official sources, notably American. The CIA, it is now estimated, invested some $50 million in this operation—peanuts as an investment in the collapse of the Soviet empire, but a tremendous amount of money when translated into zlotys at the then-prevailing black market rate.[10]

All these factors mattered. They are not enough to explain the sweep of the conversion. In 1980, when they tied their fate to the workers' movement, Mazowiecki was a progressive Catholic (close to *Esprit,* a periodical of left-wing Catholics in France) and Geremek a "revisionist" Marxist historian. Ten years later, one was prime minister and the other the chief parliamentary backer of a government pouring bitter capitalist medicine down Polish throats, in keeping with a monetarist prescription. To understand such a shift, one must recall the change in Europe's general political climate during that decade. At its beginning, while the Polish workers dreamed of an egalitarian, self-managed society, part of the left in Europe

9. With the exception of Modzelewski, Ryszard Bugaj, and twenty-six other important activists who signed a protest against the Balcerowicz plan from the start. Together with others, they were to form Solidarity of Labor, later called Union of Labor, and thus remained true to the original aspirations of the movement.

10. About the links between the Vatican and the Reagan administration, particularly its security services, over Poland, see Carl Bernstein & Marco Politi, *His Holiness* (New York: Doubleday, 1996).

was still thinking in terms of a third way between neo-Stalinist antics and capitalist exploitation: the French Socialists got into office talking vaguely about "a break with capitalism." At the end of the decade, French Socialists were champions of financial orthodoxy and Thatcherist ideology was triumphant throughout Europe. In Poland itself, the "Communist" government of Mieczyslaw Rakowski was preparing the ground for the transition, lifting controls over food prices, while Solidarity during its underground years did little to translate its yearnings into a policy. Asked why they had departed so far from their original positions, the Polish leftists turned born-again capitalists borrowed a reply from the fashionable chorus: there was no alternative. Because of their record, the leaders of Solidarity managed to persuade the workers for a spell that this was the only way out. That is how Poland, the pioneer of a labor revival in Eastern Europe, was also a trend-setter in shock therapy.

Though it worked for a time, the price Solidarity had to pay for it was heavy. Seldom has such a capital of popularity and goodwill, accumulated over years of heroic action, been squandered so swiftly. The myth was weakened within a year, as was shown in the presidential race of December 1990. With the Berlin Wall down and the Soviet empire shattered, there was no longer any need for a Jaruzelski to serve as a "guarantee." But the political forces set forth by Solidarity did not face the electorate united. Angered by the independence of the prime minister he had sponsored, Walesa launched a "war at the top," a conflict within the leadership, which resulted in the presence of two candidates: himself and Mazowiecki. The "national hero" came first, though with only 40 percent of the poll. The prime minister was not even second. He was overtaken by a vulgar rabble-rouser, Stan Tyminski, a shady emigré come home having made money in business. True, Walesa defeated him easily in the run-off, yet Tyminski's original success was already a symptom of the sickness provoked by shock therapy. Both the dispersion of the forces once united under the banner of Solidarity and their decline were confirmed in the parliamentary elections of 1991.

Whatever his proclamations during the campaign, once elected, Walesa did nothing to reverse the economic policy. On the contrary, the first prime minister he picked was an even more zealous monetarist, Jan-Krzysztof Bielecki. The latter's successor, Jan Olszewski, a leader of

Poland's extreme right, was so busy seeking reds under the beds that he had no time for anything else; actually, the security files his government produced looked so suspicious that he was quickly voted out of office. Hanna Suchocka, Poland's first woman prime minister, who took over after an interval, presided over a coalition of conservative liberals and reactionary Catholics. She followed the same unpopular economic line (tempered once again by the presence in the government of Jacek Kuron as the defender of the downtrodden). By then Solidarity, taken here in its narrower role as a labor union, was exhausted and exasperated after two years of sacrifices. Without its active and then passive support, the policy inaugurated by Balcerowicz could not have been applied, but the cost was enormous. Solidarity, once the representative of the Polish working class, now had around two million members, less than the membership claimed by the OPZZ, the official trade unions reorganized by the previous regime under martial law. Solidarity could no longer take it. To recover, it had to show that it still had some connection with workers' interests. In the spring of 1993, the members of the lower house directly sponsored by Solidarity brought the government of Suchocka down. These obsessive anti-Communists did not know that they were bringing the converted Communists back into office.

The parliamentary elections of 1993 marked a stunning setback for both the remnants of Solidarity and for the Catholic Church. We had seen the Church at the height of its moral and political influence. In 1989, the hierarchy, wisely or not, decided to institutionalize that power. It asked for the restitution of property seized not just by the Communist regime but also by tsardom. It claimed a sort of moral control over the conduct of the population, reintroducing religious instruction, banning abortion, and obtaining the promise that TV programs would not clash with "Christian values." This tutelage from the classroom to the bedroom did not appeal to the Polish people. Women, in particular, were shocked by the clergy's relentless struggle against contraception as well as abortion. The stock of the Catholic Church slumped. The coalition of reactionary parties, which fought the 1993 election under a Christian banner, did not get the minimum of votes required to have representatives in parliament.[11] The influence of

11. That threshold was 5 percent for individual parties but 8 percent for coalitions.

the Catholic Church had not vanished, obviously, but its stranglehold was weakened.

Not all the parties tracing their origins to Solidarity suffered similar setbacks. The biggest among them, the Democratic Union, soon to be known as Freedom Union, including two prime ministers and most of the movement's dignitaries, came in third, with 10.5 percent of the vote. And it was followed closely by the Union of Labor, the only heir of Solidarity, which from the start rejected the economic policy of its governments. A party improvised at the last moment by Lech Walesa and a nationalist-populist movement just scraped through the 5 percent barrier, while the candidates put up by Solidarity as a trade union failed even that test. As a result of this dispersion and wastage, the new parliament was to be dominated by the two parties which came out on top and which both had their roots in the previous regime. In the election to the Sejm, first place was taken by the Alliance of the Democratic Left (initials SLD, based essentially on the converted Communists), followed by the Polish Peasant Party (PSL), previously a puppet of the Communists. Given a complicated calculation, with many votes not counted in the distribution of seats, this was enough for the two parties to get roughly two-thirds of all the deputies to the Sejm. Many commentators were struck by the coincidence. In 1989, to guarantee the Communists that proportion of seats, one had to do it by decree, excluding a number of constituencies from full competition. Now, the admittedly converted Communists were getting that share through universal suffrage, in free elections. This was the achievement of Leszek Balcerowicz and his sponsors, domestic and foreign.

But this was in no way a return to the old regime, shattered forever, nationally and internationally. The Peasant Party by now was nobody's puppet. It is the only Polish party with a social base, that of peasant smallholders, but one bound to be decimated if their country's agriculture were to follow the West European pattern. Their party could lean towards the Church and be reactionary on many social issues (notably abortion), but it had no enthusiasm for the uncontrolled reign of the market. Paradoxically, the Peasant deputies were less keen on the rapid conversion to capitalism than their ex-Communist partners, a much more complicated party.

Whose Millennium?

The Social Democracy of the Polish Republic (or SDRP) was founded early in 1990 on the ruins of the CP. The old leaders were replaced by younger men, even more pragmatic than their predecessors and remaining in the ranks were only those who assumed that the reorganized Party had a future in the new society. It was at the time a highly optimistic assumption. After forty-five years of monopolistic rule by the Communists, the scope for the spoils system was enormous. In one fell swoop, the Party lost its key posts in the national and local administration, and its privileged positions in television, radio, and the press. Because of the road chosen for the transition, there was no similar purge in the economy. Since it was agreed not to transfer the plants to the working people, but to create a capitalist class to run them, those with know-how, experience, or money (usually gained on the black market) were best placed in the new rat race, and many of them had a Party connection under the previous regime. Thus the SDRP had an electorate of three layers. The first and thickest was made up of victims of shock therapy: low-paid workers, civil servants, the unemployed, and pensioners, who were now worse off than before. The second consisted of people who, whatever their material fate, resented the proposition that nearly half a century in the country's life had been simply wasted; nobody likes to be told that whatever he did—in manufacturing, in science, or in education—was work for the devil. The third layer, most influential though not most numerous, was comprised of people who did well for themselves, yet were frightened that a purge of the "reds" might deprive them of their new privileged position. To reconcile these three threads, the SDRP had to appear as the party of gradual transition, conscious of the plight of the poor and allergic to any witch-hunts. It was as champion of "capitalism with a human face" that the Alliance of Democratic Left, which it inspired, successfully entered the parliamentary elections of September 1993.

Once in parliament, since the Freedom Union, though close in economic outlook, would not collaborate with ex-Communists, the latter had to make a deal with the Peasant Party, to whom they even granted the premiership for a time. The new governmental coalition had luck. The economy having reached rock bottom, its rule coincided with the recovery. It could thus reconcile its promise to improve things and its determination not to alter policy in any fundamental fashion. Production picked up, living standards

SDRP

122

rose, the transition was smooth, with no more basic change in foreign than in economic policy. The stage was thus set, in October 1995, for the final confrontation at the top between Lech Walesa, fatter-looking and spoiled by five years in presidential office, and Aleksander Kwasniewski, leader of the SDRP, the youthful and smooth champion of the converted Communists.

The polarization illustrated by this duel looked both inevitable and artificial. Inevitable once it became obvious that Jacek Kuron would not be a serious contender, but phony, because, in order to outbid his rivals, Walesa had to pretend that it was Solidarity versus the reds all over again, had to sound the tocsin as if Brezhnev's tanks were around the corner and ruthless commies were about to nationalize everything and jail all resisters.[12] It worked in the first ballot, with Walesa from Gdansk reappearing as the man most likely to repel the "red invasion." It did not work in the second. Though the media did favor Walesa, this was no dress rehearsal for the biased Yeltsin blitz soon to have the desired result in Russia. The West, for instance, had little to fear from a "Communist" pleading for Poland's admission into NATO and the European Union, or from a party which, during two years in office, had clearly confimed its conversion to capital-ism. Kwasniewski, sounding modern and moderate, defeated the aggres-sive Walesa. Six years after the collapse of the Communist regime, a man who, though born in 1954, had had time to reach a prominent position under the old regime, was chosen by the Polish people to be their president. The converted Communists now had control of both the government and the presidency.

This, however, was not the end of the story. Capitalism did not acquire a human face by being implemented with the assistance of recent converts. The discontent of the victims of the transformation did not vanish even in the period of recovery, only it now found a different outlet. With the Alliance of the Democratic Left in office and the critical left, the Union of Labor, unable to produce a credible alternative, the right took over as the main voice of discontent. Not the respectable right, bowing to Mammon

12. Kuron's party, the Freedom Union, picked him as a candidate by a very narrow margin and at the same time chose Leszek Balcerowicz as its leader. This symbolic choice really ruled out the simultaneous endorsement by the leftish Union of Labor, and the Kuron candidacy never took off.

but behaving with a degree of rational decency on matters of race, social conduct, or cultural freedom—no, the clerical and reactionary right, providing phony radical answers to genuine economic problems and genuinely dangerous proposals regarding the political organization of society. These ideas proved attractive to Solidarity, no longer hindered by its complicity with the government, in its bid to regain some strength as a labor union as well as some political influence.

It was difficult for Solidarity to claim that it had been against shock therapy from the start, since the Balcerowicz plan could not have been carried out against its opposition. The best it could do was to argue that this nasty program had been smuggled into the movement by alien elements, by people who were neither good Poles nor good Christians, people who were, to put it bluntly, Jews. The survival of anti-Semitism in the country where the Holocaust claimed the biggest number of victims is at once obscene and ridiculous. It shows, incidentally, the absurdity of theories about a threshold of tolerance for foreigners beyond which natives reject them. Jews in Poland are virtually non-existent. Of the original lively, colorful community of some 3.5 million people, accounting for a tenth of the whole population, even more in the towns, only fifteen thousand to thirty thousand are left. This does not prevent right-wing demagogues from hinting that a Jewish threat is hanging over Christian Poland or from suggesting that anyone they want to brand as a villain, be it Kuron or Mazowiecki, is probably of Jewish origin (or, in the best of cases, that other evil, a "freemason").

The snag is that such dirty ideological nonsense cannot really be used for practical purposes: there are not many jobs to be had by eliminating their Jewish holders. Red-hunting, on the other hand, could supply quite a crop, especially if it were extended to the management of the economy. Indeed, purging, cleansing, lustrating—to use a term fashionable in Eastern Europe—the former Communists is at the heart of the platform of the extreme right and it appeals to part of the electorate, since many Poles feel that, while the regime has changed, the faces of the people in the privileged layers of society have not: Jaruzelski gone, the nomenklatura has remained. Actually, the whole argument about the permanence of privilege reveals the duplicity and political dishonesty of the would-be purgers.

lustrating

If so many managers from the old regime have carried on, this is not due to the fact that Solidarity made a deal with the former rulers. It is due to the nature of that agreement. If it had been made on the basis of self-manage- ⚹ ment envisaged in 1981, if the working people had taken over the factories and were themselves to decide how and by whom they would be run, a number of managers would have disappeared. Those who stayed would have been endorsed by the employees. The negotiators, however, opted for a quick transition to capitalism which favored those with positions, contacts, and money, old-timers and latter-day speculators, the old nomenklatura and the new. The spokesmen of the extreme right do not abandon the capitalist goal. They simply invent an imaginary capitalist society, blessed by the Pope, in which all citizens (or should one say all truly ethnic Poles) are property owners, capitalists thanks to the national distribution of shares.

The cleverness of Marian Krzaklewski was to use the discontent of the Polish workers as the foundation of an anti-Communist crusade. With Walesa discredited as a loser, Krzaklewski had the full control of Solidarity and built around the union an electoral coalition—the already-mentioned AWS—regrouping all the shades of the Polish far right, ranging from the relatively rational social conservatives to the fanatical National Christians, for whom the secular European Union is a place of perdition where the ethnically pure Polish Catholics may lose their souls. The latter were reinforced in the coalition by candidates sponsored by the popular and ultra-reactionary station, Radio Maryja, which likens parliamentarians voting for abortion to "whores sleeping with the Nazis" and would probably suspect Jean-Marie Le Pen or Jesse Helms of liberal deviation. In immediate electoral terms, the operation proved successful. What once looked like a potential big party of the extreme right—Jan Olszewski's Movement of Polish Renewal (ROP)—was marginalized; in the parliamentary election of 1997 it barely crossed the 5 percent barrier and got only six deputies. Krzaklewski's AWS came out on top, with one-third of the votes cast and 201 deputies.

But 201 does not ensure the majority in a Sejm of 460 members. In seeking partners for the coalition, Krzaklewski gave the game away. Had his intention been really to reverse the economic policies followed since 1989, he would have picked as his partner the Peasant Party, electorally bruised but, because of its social base, hostile to European integration and the free play of market forces. Instead, as we saw, he chose the Freedom Union which, though at sixty deputies a junior partner, obtained two highly significant ministries. Bronislaw Geremek, a staunch European, was appointed foreign secretary, and the shock therapist Balcerowicz was made overlord of the economy.[13] This faithful follower of the Chicago school would not tolerate any monkeying with the market. Those who really believed in the AWS's promises to transfer to the people the wealth of the nation were now to lose their illusions. As all over Eastern Europe, this project of "distribution" would be at best a bribe and, at worse, a simple fraud.

This does not mean that Krzaklewski cannot keep his ethnic cleansers and purifiers of the economy together for a time. He could do so by offering jobs for the boys, and there are plenty in the administration. He can also keep his right-wingers happy, allowing them to hang crosses all over the place, to prohibit abortion and fight contraception, to try to impose a moral order on cultural life in general and the media in particular, in short, to turn Poland into a clerical backwater by comparison with which Ireland would look like a free thinker's paradise. But such an offensive is meeting resistance, including the president's veto, and with economic issues coming to the surface, Krzaklewski's motley coalition and the government itself are likely to fall apart.

The optimistic outcome would be that this short reign of the far right will clarify matters by destroying some myths still haunting Polish politics. Marian Krzaklewski may be putting the final full stop to the story of Solidarity, not only because workers, with the blessing of Balcerowicz, are being moved from the big state plants where Solidarity had its strongholds into small private enterprises where unionism is not tolerated, but essentially because, betrayed for a second time in succession, the Polish workers will not need a third time to grasp that Solidarity is not really defending their interests. Such a re-evaluation is necessary, if the Poles are to stop fighting the battles of yore and start preparing for the struggles of tomorrow. If it were not for conditioned reflexes, the neoliberals from the Freedom Union and those of the ex-Communist SDRP could together form a party

13. Geremek's Jewish origin gave Radio Maryja an opportunity to protest that the job should have gone to an "ethnic Pole."

representing the profiteers and beneficiaries of the transition to capitalism. The remaining majority of the SDRP could then join forces with the Union of Labor and the trade unionists to defend the interests of the workers, the public servants, the squeezed peasants, and all the downtrodden; in the process, they could start sketching the outlines of a different society. Only such a clear confrontation between right and left can gradually reduce the dangerous forces of unreason, of reactionary clericalism, to a marginal role. For when, in a country where Hitler put his gas chambers, the all but eliminated Jewish population is still being used as scapegoat, this is not a "Jewish question" (for which the Nazis, alas, had found a "final solution"): it is a sign of an irrational sickness within Polish society.

The gloomy version is that, if nothing is done to clarify the issues and fight the forces of unreason head on, they will keep on infecting the whole country. Many of my Polish friends, who showed great courage and abnegation in a long struggle for freedom, now sound very alarmed by the prospect of their country being swept by an irrational populist tide. They simply fail to perceive that they are partly to blame for this backlash because, however heroic their past, they did not have the courage to oppose shock therapy when it was being imposed as the only possible medicine and thus put off until tomorrow the struggle that should have been fought in 1989. Naturally, time may enable the Poles to find their bearings. Still, the political mess they have managed to make in their nine years of freedom contrasts with the hopes aroused in 1980 throughout the world by the Polish workers, led by the shipwrights of Gdansk, seeking their own, original way out of a seemingly desperate situation.

There is, I must admit, a personal reason for this emphasis on the Polish predicament. I was one of those who, in the heady days of 1980 or even earlier, saw in the Polish revival of the labor movement a possible example for Eastern Europe as a whole, a progressive and radical way out of the neo-Stalinist system. Let us not exaggerate my naiveté. I did not describe the workers of Gdansk as internationalist knights in socialist armor. I was aware of the weight of the Church, of nationalism, of the aversion to socialism provoked by its years of association with the regime. What I did not imagine is that this sustained mass movement of the Polish workers would lead to political suicide, to the establishment of a new system in which the power of the working class would be smashed, not strengthened, and this is why I thought it worth examining how this paradoxical ending was brought about.

It is necessary to draw another conclusion from this experience: spontaneity, the elemental force, is not quite enough. The movement of the Polish workers was powerful, it was not ephemeral, and yet it somehow fizzled out, failing to fulfill its promise. To achieve its historical task, a movement probably requires a fairly clear vision of its project and its purpose, but also some form of organization. It needs it not only to channel its force but to ensure that the wishes of the rank and file are not thwarted, that it is not led astray.

Finally, a lesson for the whole of Eastern Europe can probably be learned from the Polish events. Poland, after all, was the only country in the area where the transformation was not initiated by a perestroika from above, where the people did not enter the stage just for a short spell, where the dissidents were not a small, if heroic, band. Here the regime had to contend with lasting pressure from below, with dissident intellectuals linked to a vast labor movement. If Poland proved unable to produce an original, progressive alternative, maybe the time is not yet ripe for it in that part of the world. Thrown into the turmoil of a savage, primitive construction of capitalism, the workers do not yet seem able to clarify and impose their interests on society. The price we are paying for the Stalinist heritage is bigger than we thought. People are bewildered. They welcomed capitalism as salvation, only to discover that it was cornucopia for the happy few. Many then looked back with nostalgia. They still have to disentangle socialism from its neo-Stalinist connections and to distinguish the freedom they conquered from the new exploitation that went with it. They still need time for their education. For all these reasons, I have the impression that, to use the old-fashioned expression, the light will not come from the east in Europe in the foreseeable future. History may prove me happily wrong. Meanwhile, let us see what Western Europe has to offer as a potential battleground.

7.

French Winter of Discontent

If Winter comes, can Spring be far behind?

Shelley, "Ode to the West Wind"

ON NOVEMBER 15, 1995, Alain Juppé, the rather arrogant French prime minister, entered Palais Bourbon, seat of the lower house of parliament, the National Assembly, to present his plan for mastering social expenditure, particularly on national health. He did not know, nor did anybody, that he would precipitate one of those French upheavals which, while not necessarily shaking the world, do give it plenty of food for thought. Each time the storm seems to come out of the blue, and it is only retrospectively that one identifies clear warning signs. Barely a month earlier, France's public servants, the *fonctionnaires,* maddened by the government's decision to freeze their salaries, organized an impressive one-day strike and protest marches throughout the country which were surprisingly well attended. Roughly at the same time, student unrest started at the University of Rouen and rapidly spread all over France. It was also at the close of October that Jacques Chirac, the recently elected president, shocked the French with a spectacular volte-face performed on television: having promised in his campaign to right social injustices, he was now telling not the rich but ordinary people to tighten their belts.

The French people had plenty of reasons for discontent and impatience. For at least a dozen years—ever since 1983, when after two years in office the Socialists forgot their pledges and got converted to financial orthodoxy—they had been told by successive governments, left and right, that their sacrifices would soon be over, that there was light at the end of the tunnel, and that prosperity with full employment lay just around the corner.

For citizens, this program was reminiscent of the old joke: a sign outside the barber's promised, day after day, "tomorrow we shall shave for free." Chirac had sensed this mood of exasperation as well as fear, and this is how he became president in 1995. After fourteen years—two full terms—of François Mitterrand, probably no Socialist stood much of a chance. The danger for Chirac came from his fellow neo-Gaullist, whom he had sponsored as prime minister and who was now running well ahead of him in opinion polls.

To distinguish himself from the pompous, conservative, ostentatiously bourgeois (the French would say *Louis Philippard)* Edouard Balladur, Chirac had to run on a populist platform. From the beginning of 1995 he toured France, proclaiming that the "social fracture" was a mortal danger for the country and the struggle against unemployment the supreme task. He argued that higher wages did not clash with fuller employment (saying, literally, "the paycheck is not an enemy of employment") and added, rather demagogically, that finances would not be allowed to interfere with the equal medical treatment to which all French citizens were entitled. True, he was also saying that he was in favor of the Maastricht Treaty, the single European currency, and, therefore, of a tight budget. But he was doing it softly, without acknowledging the contradiction between the two policies, and in May he was elected president as the champion of the downtrodden. Once in office, the priorities were rapidly reversed. Still, when on October 26, speaking on television, he solemnly announced that balancing the books was now the categorical imperative, it proved too much. The French electorate is as cynical as any and has few illusions about its politicians. But you must at least take some time, respect certain rules, before you turn your coat. Here the contrast between promise and practice, as well as the haste, was so indecent that people were shocked. This may partly explain the country's mood, the sympathy for the strikers, during the winter crisis.

This, however, is hindsight. On that November afternoon, Juppé was full of confidence, "straight in his boots," to borrow his own words on a previous occasion—not only because of the natural brashness of the technocratic caste, but also because he felt on solid ground politically. The conservative coalition backing him had the control of all the political levers of command, the presidency, a comfortable majority in both houses, and most of the regional assemblies, and it had no serious electoral test to face for nearly three years. This seemed a good moment to carry out Chirac's orders about balancing the budget, and Juppé came to the chamber with his plan to cut the deficit in social services and reduce the cost of the welfare state. He asked for powers to act by decree in order to introduce a special contribution, a sort of additional tax, to repay the social security debt; transfer control over social expenditure, particularly on health, from bodies hitherto run jointly by employers and employees to parliament; raise the number of years after which workers could retire with a full pension; and so on.

But why the fuss? Was it not, asked the media, all very reasonable? After all, if you have a social services debt running to some 250 billion francs—about $50 billion at the then-prevailing rate—you must do something about it. Indeed, came the reply, but how was that debt accumulated, and who should bear the main cost now, the rich or those just above subsistence level? Wait a moment, the official argument went on: since the combined contributions of the employers and employees do not cover the cost of a system that should include everyone, and since the state has to pay the difference, then parliament (which in France really means the administration) should have control over the expenditure. Come off it, retorted the critics, even if you accept that control should be transferred from the users to the state—a very big *if*—then you should revise the financial procedures altogether, putting a larger part of the burden on *unearned* income. You should also, when raising money from wage and salary earners, do so by a progressive, not a proportionate, tax.

All these points, while valid, were really quibbles. Everybody knew from the very start that something bigger was at stake. The Juppé plan was merely the thin edge of the wedge. Once the government gained full mastery over the institution, it would gradually move in the American direction of a two-tier system, with minimal health services, minimal pensions, and an increased reliance on private insurance, pension funds, and all that profitable business French financial companies were dreaming of. In 1993, the number of years needed in France to get a full pension in the private sector had been lengthened from thirty-seven and a half to forty years (and the pension was based on the last twenty-five years, and no longer on the last ten); now the same was to apply to people working for public services and for the state. Juppé also tackled special pension schemes, like those run separately by the railways or by Paris transport for their employees. Indeed, he simultaneously announced a general reorganization of the public railways, prelude, it was taken for granted, to an overhaul and privatization of telecommunications, the post office, and so on.

This was, in other words, what the international financial establishment had been clamoring for. It was a frontal attack on the national health scheme, on the welfare state, on what the British call the "public utilities" and the French the "public service," that is to say, sectors that are not yet totally subservient to the forces and the logic of the market. And it was seen and praised as such by the media. It is hilarious today to read the newspapers of that period. Juppé, treated until then as a rather clumsy leader, was suddenly hailed as a hero.[1] Maybe he was not yet a great statesman, but what a man of courage, what a clever politician, capable of killing several birds with the same stone! The commentators soon had to eat their words as the prime minister almost became one of those birds he was to kill with his own stone.

On the very evening of Juppé's intervention in parliament, the third channel of French television quite cleverly devoted its current affairs program to the reform of the social services and brought into the studio for the occasion the top leaders of the three biggest French labor confederations. While their membership has dropped dramatically to less than 10 percent of the labor force, the French unions remain split politically. The biggest, barely so, is the General Confederation of Labor (CGT), still dominated by the Communist Party, though no longer its "transmission belt"; it was represented that night by its general secretary, Louis Viannet. The other CGT, known as Force Ouvrière (Workers' Power) is a splinter, a product of the Cold War, set up originally with the help of CIA money and for years the chief partner of the employers. It was seeking a role in the new circumstances, and it was particularly incensed by this interference with the organization of the health system, as it had a lot of members and officials in the administrative structure. Its leader Marc Blondel was present in the studio. So was Nicole Notat, head of the other major union, the French

1. "Juppé l'audace" ("Juppé the brave") was, for example, the headline of *Libération*, 16 November 1995.

Confederation of Democratic Labor (CFDT). That confederation dropped its Catholic connotation in the 1960s and, for a time, looked both modern and progressive. For years now, however, modernization has been concealing a reactionary retreat and the CFDT has been trying to replace Force Ouvrière as the favorite collaborator of the employers, public and private. Notat's conduct in the 1995 crisis was clear confirmation of this aspiration.

The three union leaders were asked their opinion on the Juppé plan. Viannet and Blondel—the first emphasizing the attack on welfare, the second the takeover by the state—expressed their hostility to the project and their determined opposition. Notat did not just beg to differ. She went out of her way to pick a fight. She contrasted the modernity of the Juppé plan with the anachronism of her colleagues. Since her position, we shall see, was to play a part in a split among French intellectuals, it is important to stress that she was not neutral, that she took sides from the beginning to the end of this conflict. Time and again, her words were to be quoted by official spokesmen and those of the *patronat*, the employers' federation; she was to urge the workers to go back, though she had never asked them to strike. For marvelous though it is that a woman is, at last, the leader of an important labor confederation, one must regretfully report that the lady was a scab. (Accepting real equality means recognizing that women, too, like Maggie Thatcher and Nicole Notat, can be black sheep and blacklegs.)

Though the steam was clearly there from the start, it took nine days for the discontent to grow into a protest movement. With the help of the unions, a day of strikes and marches was organized on November 24 and about three-quarters of a million people took part in the demonstrations, surprisingly well attended in the provinces.[2] In the capital, there was a small incident: booed by angry members of her own confederation, Notat had to be escorted by stewards to her car. Aggressiveness, particularly against a woman, may not be the best way to settle an argument, though if you want to speak for the government and march with the strikers, you are asking for trouble.[3]

2. Here and below I am taking a rough average between the enthusiasm of the organizers and the lowballing of the police.

3. The incident was blown up on purpose. For a sober description of what really happened, see the essay by Pierre Cours-Salies in Claude Leneveu and Michel Vakaloulis, eds., *Faire Mouvement* (Paris: Presses Universitaires de France, 1998).

Yet the key thing about the day of protest was that it was just a beginning. There and then, the railwaymen decided to extend their strike indefinitely and, confirming their determination through daily votes, they stayed out for over three weeks. Four days after the day of protest, on November 28, after another Paris demo, marked by a symbolic handshake between Viannet and Blondel (unthinkable not so long before), it was the turn of the public transport in the capital to be stopped by a strike. Both the Paris Métro—the subway—and the buses came to a halt. The strike then spread to the post office and telecommunications, and to such public utilities as gas and electricity. It affected trash removal and bus service in many provincial towns. Teachers, especially in primary schools, went on and off strike. Unrest among university students had started earlier, but the government, haunted by the memory of May 1968, was doing its best to bribe them back to the lecture halls.

Still, it was the stoppage of the railways, which are relatively more important in France than in the United States, and, above all, the general paralysis of Paris which impressed the outside world. When, deprived of public transport, the suburban commuters tried to get to the center by car they provoked the biggest confusion in the history of the capital, with traffic jams stretching over miles and miles. The attempt by the authorities to provide a substitute service of rented private coaches merely got bogged down in turn. People were hitchhiking, cycling, walking, and even, though this was rather for the benefit of the TV cameras, rollerskating to work in a general atmosphere that was astonishingly good-natured.

With trains idle and Paris paralyzed, the strike actually looked more spectacular than it was. Indeed, with the stoppages limited essentially to the public sector and the factories functioning, the country was not at a standstill, as it had been during the students' and workers' rising of 1968, the obvious point of comparison. Actually, the real novelty on this occasion was not so much the strike as the mass demonstrations, particularly the awakening of the provinces. People were marching almost all the time, at least twice a week, since there were six all-national demos in three weeks, not counting various local ones. It was a rising tide, each wave mightier than its predecessor, as if the incantation of officialdom and the warnings of its usually effective chatterers now had the opposite effect of sending more and more people into the streets. They were a few hundred thousand in November, climbing to around a million early in December and to nearly two million on December 12, the movement's climax. With transport unavailable, the marches were dispersed, the protesters demonstrating in their home towns, on their own turf. Thus Paris did not break any records this time, but many other towns did. At the heart of the movement, you had more than one hundred thousand people in the streets of Marseilles, nearly one hundred thousand in Toulouse, almost as many in Bordeaux, Rouen, and Grenoble, but also crowds of five thousand protesters in towns of fifty thousand inhabitants.[4] To have an idea of what this means, you have to think of, say, a million protesters marching in New York, two hundred thousand in Philadelphia, and nearly one hundred thousand in Atlanta. To return to France, in most towns the protesting crowds were larger on this occasion than in the famous month of May 1968, or than at any time since the war—indeed, bigger than ever before.

At the head of the demos usually marched the railwaymen and, as it was getting dark, the smoke from their flares gave a strange and rather menacing air to the processions. Otherwise, the protesters looked both determined and rather joyful. Their chanting did not have the surrealist imagination of the '68ers. They demanded—for the sake of rhythm and wit—the repeal *immédiat* of the *plan Juppé-Notat*. The main slogan about welfare was *la sécu*, short for social security but standing for all the social services on the national scale, *aux travailleurs* (to the working people), *nous nous sommes battus pour la gagner* (we fought to get it), *nous nous batterons pour la garder* (we shall fight to keep it). But the principal chant, the equivalent of the *ce n'est qu'un début* of 1968, was the rather simple, contagious *ouais, ouais, tous ensemble, tous ensemble* (oh yeah, oh yeah, all together, all together).

Who was supposed to come together? Those working in the public and the private sectors, women and men, the employed and the jobless—all these and more. Above all, the chant expressed the joy at being so many. After years and years during which they had been told to play according to

4. Juppé is the mayor of Bordeaux; in France you can be mayor of a town and at the same time hold national office. In general, the movement was stronger in southwestern than in northeastern France, presumably because public employment is more important in that less-industrialized part of the country.

the rules of the game, to obey the market because there is no way out, no other solution, they were delighted to find they were so many, with the same refusal, with the same basic message that shook the ideological foundations: *if that's the future you are offering us and our children, then to hell with your future!*

For an unyielding government, the terrible news was that this mood of defiance had the sympathy of the bulk of the population. As a rule, there is nothing more unpopular than a transport strike, when people have to get up terribly early and spend extra hours for their journey to work. This time, the travellers were not short-tempered. Monsieur Juppé discovered, to his horror, that in opinion polls the strike had the backing of the majority, hovering around 60 percent throughout the period. These findings were confirmed by other signs. The ruling neo-Gaullist party, acting by analogy with precedents from 1968, sent instructions to its local branches to set up "committees of users" to protest against the inconvenience caused by the strike. When these committees staged a pathetic demo in Paris of less than two thousand "angry users," the whole venture had to be given up. Simultaneously, a series of seven parliamentary by-elections, which just happened at the time, showed a net swing from right to left.[5]

At the height of the crisis, Chirac was being shown, on a witty satirical TV program called "Puppets," as a teacher giving a spelling lesson to the pupil Juppé who was mumbling "n-e-g-o . . . n-e-g-o . . . ," unable to complete the word negotiate. It was literally true since the prime minister took more than two weeks before mentioning negotiations, which made sense, as his original idea was not to bargain but to impose the wisdom of the international financial establishment on the unenlightened and reluctant French population. But as the strike, renewed each day by democratic decisions, showed no sign of weakening, and the strikers talking around the *braseros* exchanged subversive rather than submissive thoughts, as the tide of protest refused to recede and popular support failed to collapse, Juppé could no longer afford his arrogance and, on December 10 in a televised broadcast, he actually used the dreaded word, negotiation. By then, however, the problem was already one of retreat, and the government

5. In the second ballot, on December 10, the left actually gained two seats which belonged to right-wingers.

carried it out with greater tactical skill than it had shown in its all-out offensive.

Two days earlier, the government gave up the idea of a separate pension fund for public servants; they would continue to be paid out of the budget. Then, in his TV performance on December 10, Juppé dropped the project to extend the number of years required to get a full pension in the public sector and renounced his plans to revise downward special pension schemes. As for the reorganization of the railways, it was abandoned. Thus the government, more cleverly, while preserving its project for stricter state control of social-service expenditure, yielded completely to the transport workers, the backbone of the strike. These concessions, however, coincided with the climax of the movement. Two days later, on Tuesday, December 12, the protesters numbered about two million in the streets of some 270 French towns. And yet this was the beginning of the end. Not because the government and its servants were telling the strikers they had no reason to protest; they said that from the start. Nor because Nicole Notat proclaimed that the wage and salary earners "can only make a positive assessment of the results achieved," since, had they listened to her, they would have gained nothing at all. It was the beginning of the end because a social movement by definition cannot stand still; if it does not advance, it is bound to retreat. This time it could no longer gain ground, because it had failed to extend to the private sector and because it had no political agenda likely to mobilize people for further action. In the circumstances—with the specific, immediate demands of the transport workers, the spearhead of the movement, met—both the unions and the strikers in their assemblies thought it wiser to withdraw from the battlefield in orderly fashion, voting for a return to work. Naturally, the strike did not end overnight, and one more mass demonstration was organized throughout France.

Though Juppé had not yielded on the central issue of social spending, the last big all-national demo, staged on Saturday, December 16, was no funeral procession. The million or so marchers throughout France had mixed feelings. They were thrilled and proud to have rediscovered a voice, reasserted their power. They were uneasy about not using that power to greater purpose. The railwaymen, in particular, when you talked to them, felt rather guilty about releasing the pressure because they had got what they wanted. Still, with more trains and buses in motion, the strike was drawing to an end. An empty, waffling summit meeting between govern-ment, employers, and union leaders on December 21 was a face-saving device for them all. By Christmas, it was really over.

Not quite. A final conflict gave a taste of battles to come. The municipal transport authority in Marseilles thought it had invented an astute method to overcome the resistance of workers fighting to keep their acquired rights. It decided to leave the rights to old-timers and recruit newcomers on worse conditions of pay and security. Hoping to divide and rule, it actually drove the staff to united action. Together, the old and the new staged an egalitarian and successful strike. On January 9, 1996, they went victoriously back to work. This, admittedly, was a postscript. The main battle was finished. The government had not given up its intention to control and cut its expenditure on social services. Yet, having met an unexpected level of resistance, it will think twice before launching another big offensive.Thus, the confrontation was, for the moment, postponed.

Analysts in Paris could not help drawing comparisons between the revolt of 1995 and May 1968, when a student rebellion led to the biggest general strike in French history. The analogy came naturally to mind as this time, too, the unrest started, in October, on the campus, spreading quickly from Rouen to universities all over France. But this is where the similarity ends. French governments are now haunted by the fear that students can act as a fuse for a social conflagration, and so the minister of education was instantly allowed to negotiate. When the Juppé plan increased the risks of social explosion, he was given more money and more room for manoeuver. On December 3, the deal was struck: an emergency program provided the universities with additional funds, allowing among other things the hiring of two thousand more lecturers and as many administrators. The students did join in the demonstrations—even in great numbers in some towns, like Toulouse—but collectively they were only a minor actor in this perform-ance. The contrast is striking. In 1968, the students were at center stage: full of dreams and ideas, they called on the workers in the hope of turning a students' riot into a revolution. They actually talked as if there was no salvation in the world as it was, and they proclaimed that a critical university had to be used in order to overturn society. Their successors in 1995 were asking for better conditions to study so that they could fit into that society. (Their demands for more teachers and better halls would have been dismissed by the '68ers with the derisive slogan, *des gommes et des crayons!*—"give us rubber erasers and pencils!")

But this is only half the story. In 1968, there were only six hundred thousand students in France and the economy was still able to absorb most of them. There was an element of rhetoric, or premonition, when they proclaimed at the time that they were "the jobless of tomorrow." In 1995, the students were over two million and the prospect of unemployment was not a figure of speech. They fought for better conditions of work on the assumption that a piece of paper, a diploma, improves somewhat their chances of getting a job. But if they sounded much more reformist, the roots of their discontent are now much deeper, and this resentment will find its expression when they drop all illusions about being an elite and fully realize that their fate and their social function can only be really altered by radically changing society.[6] While the students in 1995 were a pale shadow of their predecessors, their potential is incomparably more explosive.

The second analogy, or rather difference, concerns industrial workers. In 1968, however ambiguous their relationship, and despite being blocked by the Communist Party, the students did manage to drive the workers to action. It was when the factories came to a standstill that the minds were really set to motion. This time, the awakening was brought about by the stoppage of transport. The factories kept on producing. Some industrial workers joined the demonstrations, but even token strikes in private industry were few and far between. On this occasion, the shutdown was performed essentially by people employed in the public sector.

Critics took advantage of this to present the whole action as the struggle of the privileged, enjoying the security of employment and defending their vested interests. The impudence of tycoons who earn millions or of academics, getting a nice bonus from the media for their mainstream views, describing the postal or railway workers as pampered or privileged is just indecent. Besides, their arrows were aimed at the wrong target. The strikers were not just defending their own rights. They were not saying, "Give us

6. In France, everybody graduating from high school, having got the *baccalauréat*, is entitled to a place in the university. To select its elite, the French system uses the highly competitive *grandes écoles*, such as l'Ecole Polytechnique or l'Ecole Normale Supérieure.

earlier pensions than the industrial workers get." They said, "If, thanks to our struggle, we keep our retirement rights, then those in the private sector can fight to win theirs back." It was an open movement. Associations defending the unemployed, immigrants, or homeless people were welcome in the demonstrations. Only opponents tried to brand it as narrowly self-interested.

Still, it is a fact that the industrial workers were not directly involved, though not because of any lack of sympathy. On the contrary, reporters and pollsters stressed that those in the private sector felt the public employees were fighting for them as well. Indeed, this "strike by proxy," as it was called, and the resentment over Chirac's volte-face are the two key reasons for the surprising acceptance of the usually very unpopular transportation strike. The question remains why, in spite of their sympathy, industrial workers did not enter the fray. The most likely answer is that in these days of mass unemployment and insecurity, the industrial workers are reluctant to take risks unless it is a crucial class confrontation, which it was not, or unless their vital interests are directly at stake, particularly if they are in a strategically strong position.[7]

What it really points to is that the situation today is very different from what it was in 1968. The questions raised at the time—about the nature and purpose of growth, about the beneficiaries who also set the pattern of production—are more relevant than ever, precisely because of the radically different social context of relative stagnation and mass unemployment and very different ideological framework, with profit and the enterprise sanctified by the new gospel of the market. Indeed the impact of the 1995 movement is largely due to the clash between its nature, its demands, and the seemingly established rules of the new religion.

This also explains why the political parties were completely taken aback, why they were onlookers and not real participants in this movement. (This criticism, quite naturally, does not apply to the ruling conservative

---

7. In November 1996, the truckers confirmed this thesis. They were mad about the terribly long hours, more than sixty a week, they were spending at work, while being paid for the much shorter driving time. They were in a strategic position, moving trucks like tanks to block roads, particularly petrol depots. Backed once again by the general public, they won the day, getting payment for waiting hours and the right to a full pension at age fifty-five. The employers not having kept their word, they struck again a year later, in November 1997.

coalition.) The Socialists, burdened in opposition with their recently acquired "culture of government," were at a loss. Throughout the crisis, the already mentioned satirical program, "Puppets," was showing Lionel Jospin, Mitterrand's successor as Socialist leader, repeating in worried tones: "Do I really have to say something?" The Socialists could attack the government for its clumsiness, for its undemocratic manner of consultation, but not for the substance of its policy, which was the extension of their own. As to the Communists, in an effort to break with the past they did their best not to appear as the party trying to seize the leadership and take over the movement.

Labor unions fared better than the parties. They had not initiated the current, but they went with it. True, the CFDT, the confederation of Nicole Notat, did what it could at the national level to reverse the trend. This did not prevent various unions within the confederation, notably those in transport and education, from being very active in the strike. The other two main confederations swam with the current from the start. They did so because they had learned their lesson. In several labor conflicts in the previous decade, in strikes on the railways, in hospitals, or in telecommunications, the unions had dragged their feet and the movement was led by the rank and file organizing themselves through self-ruling assemblies known as *coordinations*. After the postal strike of 1988, the CFDT expelled its most active members for excessive militancy. They founded their own union, SUD, standing for Solidarity, Unity, Democracy.[8] By now the SUD has more support among telecommunications workers than does the original confederation. All such trends meant the loss of prestige, influence and membership for the three big confederations. This time two of them, at least, backed the strikers from the beginning. They also allowed them to shape their own line, giving the whole movement a highly democratic character, with each railway station, each bus depot, staging every day a general assembly which, having examined and debated the situation, voted whether to carry on the strike. As usual, when the routine of everyday life is suddenly interrupted, it also drove the strikers to think about matters going beyond their immediate demands.

8. *Solidaire, Unitaire, Démocratique.* On the development of this union see Christophe Aguiton's essay in Aguiton and Daniel Bensaid, eds., *Le Retour de la question sociale* (Lausanne: Editions Page Deux, 1997).

Logically, this upheaval foreshadows a restructuring, a radical realignment of French unionism. I don't mean just the inevitable conflict between the advocates and opponents of the strike within the CFDT (whose leadership now shows a capacity for purging reminiscent of the Communist-dominated CGT in its Stalinist days). In a trade-union movement whose very existence is threatened by its failure to adapt to economic change, the persistence of splits going back to the Cold War makes little sense. If French wage and salary earners must be divided, they should belong to two broad confederations, one regrouping those resigned to bargaining within existing society (critics would say acting as the "transmission belt" of the employers), the other comprising those still believing in the possibility of altering that society. Such a duality would involve splits and separations in all present confederations. Everything that is rational, however, does not necessarily come about. Institutional conservatism, vested interests, inertia—all plead against such a realignment in the foreseeable future. The emergence in this conflict of new, young, bold labor leaders, the expansion of SUD, the remarkable success within the split teachers' union of the more radical branch, the FSU (Federation of Unified Unions)—all point to the possibility of such a rearrangement. The only thing that can be said safely is that the dramatic decline of organized labor will not be reversed without such a break.

The final surprise of this crisis was the reappearance of the intellectuals on the political stage. This may seem strange since between the Dreyfuss affair at the end of the last century and, say, 1968, French intellectuals were great signers of petitions and champions of moral or political commitment. The situation changed beyond recognition in the ensuing quarter of a century. By some curious aberration, it became the fashion to put the sociologist Raymond Aron above his school fellow from the Ecole Normale, Jean-Paul Sartre. *Engagement* became a dirty word and most intellectuals one heard speaking about matters beyond their field of specialization, particularly on television, tended to be more or less openly spokesmen for the establishment. Indeed, the *ruling ideology* seemed so dominant that the very term, dismissed as dangerously Marxist, had to be reinvented and rechristened as *pensée unique*. It is this reign of the consensus that was now to be broken and, paradoxically, the hostilities were opened by the "reformist" wing of the establishment.

The pretext was the alleged attack on Nicole Notat. A group of intellectuals and experts, loosely connected with a once-progressive Catholic monthly, *Esprit*, came chivalrously to her rescue. They were 167, including such names as philosopher Paul Ricoeur, historian Jacques Le Goff, and, last but not least, sociologist Alain Touraine, who had signed on when their statement was published in *Le Monde* on December 3-4, 1995. They praised the "courage and independence of spirit" of Notat's confederation. While questioning some aspects of the governmental policy, they hailed the essentials of the Juppé plan as "a fundamental reform going in the direction of social justice." In fairness, it must be added that at the time the petition was being written, towards the end of November, most of its signatories presumably had not grasped the scope and sweep of the events. Had they done so, they probably would not have signed, since it is difficult to preserve the leftist reputation many of them find precious while opposing the biggest social movement the country has known for over a quarter of a century. To travel to Chiapas and stand next to Commandante Marcos will not help that reputation very much if at home you stood in the limelight at the side of the strikebreaker-in-chief. Yet, having signed the document, they had no other solution but to defend their stand, accusing the movement of both "corporatism" and conservatism.

This put them actually on the other side, that of the officialdom and employers, and their backing for Notat provoked a passionate response. It is correct to speak of a response, even if the counter-publication was originally conceived on its own and not as a reply. A much larger number of intellectuals, some 560 by the time their text was published in *Le Monde* on December 10, including sociologist Pierre Bourdieu, philosopher Jacques Derrida, and historian Pierre Vidal-Naquet, issued a very different manifesto. They totally identified themselves with the strikers who "in fighting for their own social rights . . . are fighting for equal rights for all: women and men, old and young, jobless and wage-earners, workers with special statute, employees of the state or of the private sector." The commitment this time went beyond fundraising. On December 12, at the close of the biggest demo, many of the signatories, notably Bourdieu, met with strike activists in a hall belonging to the railway union, close to the Parisian Gare de Lyon—not to pretend that they already had alternative solutions, but promising to look for them in common.

Whose Millennium?

The seemingly undue emphasis here on the role of the intellectuals has its justification, because the ultimate impact of this French outburst of discontent is probably essentially ideological. Retrospectively, one may have the feeling of having been the victim of an illusion. Paris paralyzed, traffic jammed, millions in the streets, the world astonished—all this apparently left nothing tangible behind. The government was forced to retreat, to abandon temporarily some immediate targets. It did not give up its broader offensive against the welfare state. If something happened in those exciting days of December, it happened in people's minds.

No, it was not a figment of our imagination. To realize that, it is enough to recall the rage and panic of our established preachers, frightened because their spell was broken, their religion rejected, their ideology suddenly contested. True, there had been some earlier symptoms that the *pensée* was no longer as *unique* as the keepers of the cult tried to suggest. The struggle against the tightening of the immigration laws, the successful battles to take over and then force the authorities to requisition empty houses in the capital and in the provinces, the revival of women's liberation, with some thirty thousand marching through Paris on November 25, in the early days of mass demonstrations—all these were signs that the mechanisms of thought control were being slowed down. Yet it was only with the strikes and protest marches that, for a while, they ceased to function altogether.

The same talking heads went on repeating their usual message about the perils for profit, the fetters for free enterprise, about Maastricht, the money market, the Monetary Fund, about the imperatives of globalization. Only this time it was not working. Exasperated, they lost their composure, raised their voices, with no effect on the strikers or marchers and little on the population at large. This whole French episode has been loosely described as the first mass protest against Maastricht. This could wrongly suggest that it was mainly concerned with Europe and the outside world. For the definition to fit, one would have to conceive Maastricht as shorthand for all the changes brought about in the last two decades—the exaltation of private enterprise over public service, of individual greed over solidarity, of "creative" uncertainty over security of employment—changes imposed in the name of European integration and for the sake of that new god, globalization. It is the fatalistic acceptance of this religion which suffered a serious blow that December.

French Winter of Discontent

In their frantic efforts to restore the magic, the priests and preachers of the new global order accused the French movement of conservatism, of an anachronistic attempt to cling to the past. Starting from the correct premise that the strikers were struggling to defend their rights, the social benefits acquired or conquered in past battles, they drew the wrong conclusion that the protest movement was reactionary, backward, trying vainly to defy or rather to deny the future. If that were so, if the strikes and marches had been passé, obsolete, a last stand by people condemned by the inexorable march of events, the mighty would not have been so perturbed. The passion of the masters of our universe and the rage of their ideological servants had more solid reasons. After years of fatalistic resignation, the French protesters were not refusing *the* future but *their* future.

Seen in perspective, from a certain distance, France after its winter of discontent is at once unchanged and very different. Fundamentally, the society has not altered and even the main social front is as quiet as it was before; the number of strikes, for instance, has not increased. But at the same time many things that have happened in the last couple of years can only be understood in the light of an awakening. The first sign came early in 1997, a movement of moral indignation proceeding to that of social protest. The conservative government, probably with an early election in mind, and convinced, rightly or wrongly, that the bashing of foreigners was a paying proposition, introduced yet another law restricting the entry of immigrants. The bill was particularly obnoxious and one of its provisions came to be known as the informers' clause: you were to report to the authorities the date of departure of your foreign guests. As the xenophobic National Front of Jean-Marie Le Pen had just won yet another mayoralty in the south of France, this obvious wooing of his electorate was too much. When a group of young filmmakers published a text warning that if the bill became law, they would simply disobey it, innumerable people wanted to join them. In an unprecedented rush, some two hundred thousand signatures were collected within a few weeks and, on a sunny Saturday in February, more than one hundred thousand people marched across Paris, starting symbolically at the Eastern Station from which the Jews had been deported, and telling the authorities to seek solutions, not scapegoats. The government was forced to withdraw the silly clause and the Socialists, hitherto reluctant, had to promise that once in office they would abrogate the Pasqua-Debré laws.[9]

The parliamentary elections of May 1997 are the second example. If it had not been for the social upheaval, President Chirac probably would not have decided to stage that vote one year ahead of schedule, fearing the further deterioration of the mood; the "plural left" would not have won that contest and would not have formed a government dominated by the Socialists, and including one Green and three Communist ministers. Indeed, without that winter of discontent, Lionel Jospin, the new prime minister, would not be somewhat the odd man out within the converted and tamed West European left. The sixty-year-old Jospin is, in a sense, a walking contradiction. On one hand, he took an active part in the "normalization" of the Socialist Party under Mitterrand and as such does not differ fundamentally from Blair or Schroeder in his attitude toward the established order. But on the other hand he is the by-product of the social movement of 1995, without which he would not be in office. Naturally, the influence of this second factor will depend not on gratitude but on the strength of that movement, on the pressure from below. Jospin, however, cannot ignore it, because both the Socialists and even more so their Communist allies are aware that the more they move to the center, the more scope they leave to a left of social and moral discontent.

The third feature, in fact, is the increased activity of the various associations dealing with the have-nots, whom the French now call *les sans*, those without: people without shelter, foreigners without documents, workers without jobs. Organizations such as DAL (standing for "The Right to a Home") kept up their action of squatting in empty offices and apartments. Various associations defending immigrants and struggling against xenophobia had plenty of pressing to do as the left in office showed little enthusiasm to carry out its promises made in opposition. Among the unemployed, the protest movement gained the most ground. Here, too, associations actually involving many union activists had done some preliminary organizing on a national and even European scale. Yet the full

---

9. They only half kept that pledge, changing the laws but not having the courage, symbolically important, to abrogate them. The laws, incidentally, bore the names of the ministers of the interior who had introduced them: Charles Pasqua for the original bill, and Jean-Lois Debré for the latest version.

impact was only felt at the turn of 1997, when the jobless, demanding an increase in their benefits, invaded employment offices throughout the country and staged demonstrations in the streets of Paris and many other cities. Their message was plain: "We want to work, but if the society is unable to provide employment, it owes us a decent living allowance." Admittedly, the activists were only a fraction of the mass of unemployed. But for the first time since the hunger marches of the 1930s, the jobless re-entered the movement, not as objects of compassion, but as full-fledged protagonists.[10]

Finally, there is the undeniable, though not easily defined, change in the intellectual climate. It can be measured by the tone of the keepers of the ruling ideology. They used to speak with the quiet confidence of people dominating the scene. They now do so in the angry voice of those whose domain is threatened, and there are many signs justifying their apprehension: the frequent publication of texts questioning the reign of the market and of globalization; the continued success, say, of the non-conformist journal, *Le Monde Diplomatique*; the fact that books, admittedly small in size and cheap in price, in a new series sponsored by Pierre Bourdieu that attacks the role of the establishment, notably in the media, have been selling like hotcakes. Indeed, what is at once amusing and revealing is the number of violent charges against this professor of sociology, since his more active commitment, on the grounds that he is using the prestige of his membership of France's highest academic institution, the Collège de France, for his attacks against the established order. But we should not convey too rosy a picture, either. The most ambitious idea conceived in December 1995 has not been fulfilled. Intellectuals and activists, including important union leaders, have been meeting and discussing subjects of common interest, both in Paris and in some provincial towns, for a couple of years. Their efforts, however, were not crowned, as planned, with a great meeting to draw up the assizes of the social movement, nor did they produce the first outlines of a new vision. For this, much more work may be needed—and much more pressure from below.

---

10. On the movement of the unemployed, its background and prospects, see Marie-Agnès Combesque, *Ça Suffit. Histoire du mouvement des chômeurs* (Paris: Plon, 1998).

Each country has its own peculiarities. The resentment of Chirac's antics, the division of the labor unions, and the clashes between petitioners are all French specialties. But the general offensive against the welfare state was not confined to French frontiers. The attempt to improve the rate of profit by reducing the direct and the indirect cost of labor, the attacks on the social protection of the working people, had affected the whole of Western Europe for several years. And so did the resistance. At the end of 1994, Silvio Berlusconi, the TV tycoon turned prime minister who tried to reduce pensions, had to half-yield when Italians took to the streets in huge demonstrations. In Germany, in the autumn of 1996, the plans to cut sickness benefits had to be shelved when, staging demos and warning strikes, the labor unions showed both their strength and determination. In all these cases, including the French, it looks for the moment like a stalemate with an advantage for the government. The rulers give up individual proposals but not their strategy. The protesters win a battle and, then, lacking objectives, are unable to launch a counteroffensive.

On the ideological front, too, France is no exception and the battlefield is even larger, extending well beyond Europe. Indeed, the *pensée unique* may be a novelty for the French or the Italians, but not for the Germans, the British, or the Americans, for whom consensus politics is old hat. But in the last twenty years that consensus shifted dramatically to the right. Reaganomics, the collapse of the Berlin Wall, the "end of history" are all milestones on this road. It is Tina's twin, the idea that there *can be* no alternative, that the French protesters have now battered, ahead of their colleagues.

They did not, however, substitute an alternative of their own, and this may explain why Alain Touraine and his colleagues deny to the French strikes and protests the title of a "social movement," arguing that to deserve that name they would have to "combine a social conflict and a project for the management of society."[11] This dismissal seems strange, though a name, after all, is a question of definition. Maybe the authors wanted to stress that to be hegemonic, capable of long-term action, a movement must have a purpose and a vision or, to put it differently, that societies are not changed, any more than empires are acquired, "in a fit of absent-mindedness." Less

11. See Alain Touraine and others, *Le Grand Refus* (Paris: Fayard, 1996), 47.

charitably, one may conclude that having stood, to put it mildly, outside the movement, the authors quite naturally try to minimize its importance. Whatever their motives, they drew attention to an undeniable aspect of the French events. While the protesters rejected the blackmail that you cannot resist if you have no substitute for the established disorder, it is true that they did not offer an alternative project, the vision of a different society.

None of that diminishes the historic importance of their defensive action. After twenty years or so of total ideological domination, the very refusal, rejection, and resistance were vital. As long as the idea that there could be no alternative was accepted, explicitly or implicitly, the search for one was unthinkable. This is why the significance of this French break cannot be overestimated. It is a crucial beginning. But it is only a beginning. On the basis of this negative achievement, the genuine search for a radically different society must begin. Even if this "French flu" spreads rapidly, as it may well do, undermining the ruling ideology throughout western Europe, it will still be necessary to proceed with the constructive task of building a new project. The recurring refrain of the French winter of discontent, we saw, was the proclamation, "If this is the future offered us and our children, we just don't want it." Having rejected *their* future, the people of Europe must now begin the earnest search for *our* future.

Part Three
In Search of an Alternative

Introduction to Part Three

Mastering Our Fate

AN AIR OF AMBIGUITY inevitably surrounds this last part of the book, the purpose of which is to help in the resurrection of a left able to shape the future. The ambiguity is that while we have argued that, hopefully, the conception of socialism as a model handed down to an obedient population is forever gone, we have also maintained that people, though they may rebel, will not engage in sustained political action without a fairly clear vision of an alternative society. This last part of the book will try to find a way somewhere between these two only apparently contradictory pressures. Without providing ready-made answers, it will attempt to raise questions that the left must collectively debate.

The first chapter will be concerned with the function work assumes in our fast-changing society. In the advanced capitalist countries, we are offered the unacceptable choice between the European solution of growing mass unemployment and the American proliferation of the "working poor." What does the fashionable formula "the end of work" mean? Does it suggest that technological progress makes it possible to fulfill the old dream of eliminating the frontier between labor and leisure? This is hardly possible as long as work is labor, a special commodity but a commodity nevertheless, in a society in which the goods produced are assessed in terms of their exchange value and not their use value. The other fashionable idea, that of expanding the nonprofit sector in such a society without attacking the heart of the economy dominated by profit, seems also to belong to the world of fancy. Behind these questions lurks another: is the working class, profoundly altered in the years of restructuring, still a potential force for historical change?

Can one even envisage such a transformation in our increasingly inter-dependent world? This question forces us to examine the new cult of globalization. Is globalization God-given, imposed inexorably by techno-logical progress? Or, on the contrary, is the form that internationalization takes man-made, the response of capital to its structural crisis? Even if it is the latter, globalization exerts an influence on the politics of our world and raises a series of questions about what can or cannot be achieved within the frontiers of a medium-sized nation state.

Globalization focuses attention on the fantastic differences of wealth on our planet. It is no longer possible to pretend that inequality will look after itself, because instead of narrowing, it is widening. In the last thirty years the share of the richest 20 percent in the world's income has gone up from 70 to 85 percent; that of the poorest fifth has gone down from 2.3 to 1.4 percent. But the gap is growing also within national borders, notably in the advanced capitalist countries, particularly in Britain and in the United States. And the problem of equality is not limited to wealth. Women's liberation has put on the agenda an inequality affecting half the population which was being accepted as almost natural, because it was backed by the weight of centuries. Since racial oppression has lost none of its venom and discrimination against foreigners has invented new ways and conquered new recruits, egalitarianism, in the fullest meaning of this term, is now a vital and indispensable ingredient in any project for the real transformation of existing societies.

Equality leads us directly to democracy. The latter must be at the heart of any socialist revival and not only because of the Soviet experience. If that experience reminded us of the importance of so-called formal free-doms, we cannot be satisfied with their simple restoration. Our own system of rule from above, renewed every four or five years through a ceremony of popular abdication of sovereignty, in most cases a choice between Tweedledum and Tweedledee, each spending masses of money in a great television show, is clearly not enough. We need both egalitarianism and the reinvention of democracy at all levels, if we want people to acquire power in a radically different society.

Thus, the main lesson of the last part of this book is that tinkering with the prevailing institutions is not enough. We must fight within the prevail-ing system and yet provide solutions that ultimately take us beyond the confines of existing society. To ignore the latter is as unrealistic as to forget the former. The great achievement of the ruling establishment in the last thirty years or so has been to use every opportunity, notably the collapse of the Soviet Union, to persuade people that we are prisoners of a system from which there is simply no escape. Now, for the first time in years, the grasp of the establishment is shaken. But it will only be in serious danger on the day when people do realize once again that they are not doomed, that they can be masters of their fate.

8.

Beyond Labor And Leisure

The idea that to make a man work you've got to hold gold in front of his eyes is a growth, not an axiom. We've done that for so long that we've forgotten there's any other way.

F. Scott Fitzgerald,
This Side of Paradise

WE ARE ALLEGEDLY ENTERING a new era, facing an entirely new civilization, symbolized by The End of Work, to borrow the title of a successful book.[1] Since work is not only the source of livelihood for the bulk of the active population, but is also, within our system more than any previous one, a person's main link with other people, its disappearance would be epoch-making. The bare statistics do not confirm this dramatic prediction. Even in Western Europe, where unemployment figures have risen spectacularly, the actual number of jobs did not decline in the last quarter of a century, just failed to keep pace with the growth of the labor force. In the United States, seen as the prototype of the coming society, enough jobs were provided to keep unemployment roughly unchanged. What kind of jobs—precarious, hopeless, very badly paid—that is another matter. Indeed, what we may be watching is not so much the end of work as the end of an illusion.

Together with the myth of a capitalism without crises, of a magic mechanism of eternal growth, collapses the image of a capitalism with a human face, with its assumption that, at least in the advanced Western countries, almost everybody is entitled to a steady, more or less permanent, and decently paid job, with the prospect of improving living standards and,

1. Jeremy Rifkin, *The End of Work* (New York: G. P. Putnam's Sons, 1995).

last but not least, the prospect of social advancement for the children. In its American version, this story was summed up by the promise: tomorrow we shall all be middle class. All those fairy tales are no longer fashionable, and, significantly, they have vanished throughout the Western world at roughly the same time. When, in the 1970s, the established order felt seriously threatened, it fought back, picking labor as its main target. By the 1980s the offensive was in full swing, changing labor laws and withdrawing past concessions. Downsizing, outsourcing, re-engineering—to use trendy terms—and adapting the Japanese methods of exploitation, the establishment managed within fifteen years to redress the balance, shifting a substantial share of national income from wages to profits. The fundamental rule of our epoch, the domination of capital over labor, was thus fully reasserted.

Back to normal, then, and back to the past? Yes and no. While the rule of capital was never really endangered, the restoration is not complete, either. Although statistically wrong, the promoters of the saga of vanishing work are up to something. They sense the end of a reign. Our engine was always set in motion by two contradictory movements. On one side, in search of surplus, it had to reduce the time needed to produce a commodity, and, by introducing machinery, was eliminating human labor. On the other, in order to keep on extracting profits, it had to create new jobs. Its present difficulty in balancing the two, in compensating for destruction of the old with the creation of the new, is symptomatic, especially in that it is due to the increasing role in production of technology, science, and knowledge. Nearly a century and a half ago, Marx argued that "the theft of . . . alien labor time" was "a miserable foundation" for the calculation of our wealth, which we should measure by free time, not labor time. "Truly wealthy a nation," he quoted a contemporary with approval, "when the working day is 6 rather than 12 hours."[2] What may have seemed visionary then is realistic today. At least in the advanced Western countries, we are potentially equipped to start dismantling the frontier between labor and leisure. Yet the gap is tremendous between the potential and its realization. To advance, we would have to re-examine the purpose of growth, we would have to switch from expansion driven by the search for profit to the

2. Karl Marx, *Grundrisse* (New York: Vintage, 1973), 705-6.

establishment of production targets by the people, democratically, on the basis of their social needs and not their bank accounts. In other words, we would have to change the very nature of our society.

But first we must drastically reduce the field of our investigation, the area in which the question actually arises. True, as capitalism spreads across the globe, it destroys existing structures, uproots people, so that everybody is affected. Yet this does not mean that all areas are now directly concerned with the move "beyond work," be it in the factory or in the office. This is certainly not the case of the poorest, of the 1.3 billion people to be found primarily in south Asia, Africa south of the Sahara, and Latin America, whose income is estimated at less than one dollar a day.[3] Numerically, they account for roughly a third of the so-called developing world, and their preoccupation, clearly, is subsistence and survival. In the remaining two-thirds, with their traditional rural surroundings shaken, people are driven to sprawling towns, seeking a living in the informal economy. Manufacturing, far from dwindling, has been absorbing more labor. Between 1970 and 1990, the share of developing countries in world manufacturing employment went up from 43 percent to 53 percent.[4] The rise was particularly striking in the fast-growing Asian states: South Korea, Indonesia, Malaysia, Thailand, the tigers and dragons presented to us as models of capitalist virtue and then, after the financial crash of 1997, suddenly dismissed as addicts to all sorts of anti-market vices. *Sic transit. . . .*

China, a latecomer to the Asian club of rapid capitalist expansion but in sheer size its most significant member by far, provides here a logical link with Europe. The number of jobless Chinese is enormous, and this now barely concealed unemployment is the result of China's conversion, its transition from exploitation by mainly political means to exploitation by more classical capitalist ones. A similar phenomenon is taking place in the former republics of the Soviet Union and in the East European countries which used to belong to the Soviet bloc. Here, too, while not quite as long as in China, the lines of the jobless are extensive—and growing tremendously. Open mass unemployment is clearly the price that must be paid for

3. *UNDP Human Development Report 1997* (Oxford: Oxford University Press 1997), 3.

4. Richard Freeman, "A Global Labour Market" (World Bank, July 1994), quoted in *World Employment 1996-97* (Geneva: ILO, 1997), 4.

admission to the capitalist club. This scourge is the effect of the global extension of our model, as is the starvation in Africa and debilitating poverty in Asia. But this is not really what theoreticians mean by the disappearance of work, resulting from technological and managerial development. They refer, artificially, to countries accounting for about one-fifth of the world's population but about four-fifths of its resources and its output, in other words the advanced capitalist states: Japan, Australia, New Zealand, Western Europe, and North America.

And even in these countries, it only applies if one does not confuse the "disappearance of work" with the reduction of employment. Because the number of jobs has actually increased during this period, particularly in the United States. Between 1973 and 1996, what the economists call the participation rate, in this case the labor force divided by the population of working age (fifteen to sixty-four) rose in the United States by nearly ten points from under 68.4 percent to over 77.9 percent, the small drop in the men's share more than offset by the impressive climb in women's participation from just over half to 71 percent.[5] With further slackening of the growth of labor productivity, already low by European standards, and employment rising, though not regularly, by 1998, at the end of an exceptionally long period of expansion, the rate of unemployment was brought down to 4.6 percent, back to its level of the early 1970s. It could be argued that, workers' resistance rapidly broken, the American establishment could relax its economic policy, the monetary weapon no longer required to keep wages down.[6]

In Europe, in any case, where labor resistance proved stronger, the battle over employment is still unresolved. The European Community did not experience a trend comparable to the American, with a rising proportion of people going to work. Between 1973 and 1996, the labor force participation

5. Figures taken from *World Employment*, 19. Separate data for women and men refer to 1973 and 1993. Figures for Europe below taken from same source. American figures differ from those in *The Economic Report of the President*, but ILO data (based on OECD figures) is used on purpose for the sake of comparisons with Europe.

6. In the debate over the use of interest rates to slow down expansion, it was openly argued that "heightened job insecurity" may allow a lower rate of unemployment without serious wage pressure. For this class language, showing that a primary purpose of monetary policy is to keep wages down, see for instance the semi-annual testimony before the Senate Banking Committee by U.S. Federal Reserve Board chairman, Alan Greenspan, 28 February 1997.

rate remained roughly steady in most countries of Western Europe, the increase in the share of women—not as rapid as in the United States—balancing a decline in men's participation, faster than the American. The European lag behind the United States is due to a sharp reduction of the proportion of people working among those younger than twenty-five and older than fifty-five. France is the extreme example, but the length of the working life seems to be drastically shortened throughout continental Europe.[7] Yet, in spite of this and the slower growth in labor productivity, the jobless, an almost forgotten term, returned to Europe with a vengeance. Unemployment, which was merely "marginal" at around 3 percent during the postwar period of prosperity, jumped to nearly 12 percent in the depression of the 1990s and finds it difficult to get down to single digits in the ensuing recovery. This resurrection of an old calamity may be interpreted as a sign of the solidity of capitalism: who could have guessed a quarter of a century ago that such a revival of unemployment would take place without a major political upheaval? However, it can also be taken as a sign of the sickness of a system no longer able to make up for its "creative destruction." Yet whatever the gravity of the crisis, the jobs are not literally vanishing. Even in Western Europe, employment has actually been rising in the last twenty years by an annual average of 0.2 percent, which is much less than the American rate (1.8 percent), but only fractionally lower than its own growth before 1973.[8] The prospect is not so much the disappearance of work as its radical transformation. The theoreticians of the end of work are contrasting a rather idealized version of work in the "golden age"—permanent, secure, backed by social guarantees—with the employment of today: precarious, uncertain, stripped of its social benefits.

To examine this properly, one must look both at the long-term transformation of the structure of the labor force and at the quickening of this

7. For French case and comparisons, see INSEE *Données Sociales 1996*, 165-73.

8. The European lag is not new. Its average annual growth between 1960 and 1973 was 0.3 percent compared with 2 percent in United States. See ILO, *World Employment 1996-97*, 20, table 2.3. The opposite is true for labor productivity. Here, in the business sector, the average annual growth for the European Union was 5.1 percent between 1960 and 1973; 2.6 percent between 1973 and 1979, and 1.9 percent between 1979 and 1997. The comparable figures for the United States are 2.6 percent, 0.3 percent, and 0.9 percent. *OECD Economic Outlook* 63, June 1998: 284. The difference is mainly due to productivity outside manufacturing.

process in the last quarter of the century. The postwar changes deepened the secular trend. The sharp increase in agricultural productivity enabled the continental countries of Western Europe to follow the Anglo-Saxon example, and by now the share of the population actually working on the land (excluding those employed in related spheres of agribusiness) is marginal not only in the United States (2.4 percent) and Britain (1.8 percent) but also in the countries that only yesterday were semi-peasant: 4.4 percent in France, 6.7 percent in Italy and still dwindling.[9] For a time, migrants from the countryside continued to move into urban factories. But, in the 1960s in the United States and in the 1970s in Europe, the proportion of people working in industry began to decline. Only that loose catch-all, the service sector, has been growing since, and by now it absorbs about 65 percent of total employment in Western Europe and more than 73 percent in the United States.[10] In Europe, the industrial phase of this development involved an important inflow of immigrant labor, though that was radically reduced by the economic crisis. Throughout the Western world, the second phase, loosely defined as the transition from blue to white collars, coincided with the massive expansion of women in the workforce, a process that is still not completed.

With productivity in manufacturing rising rapidly and working hours barely changed—a contrast that is a striking feature of postwar development—it may seem fairly rational that labor resources were shifted to, say, health, culture, and education. Yet when one looks at the employment in the services, these were not the only growing sectors. Advertising, financial services, various jobs linked with law and order, that is to say professions connected with the perpetuation of the prevailing organization of society, were also expanding fast. It may be objected, rightly, that commercialized culture, an education preparing young people to fit rather than to question, or health services partly designed to preserve the labor force are also there to prop up the system. But the doctor, the teacher, or even the TV producer are not fulfilling that function as obviously as the investment adviser, the property lawyer, the janitor, and the jailer.

9. See *Quarterly Labour Force Statistics,* no. 2, 1998, OECD.
10. *OECD in Figures,* 1998.

And the system badly needed to be propped up. Together with the sixties went the "golden age," though not its illusions. The pace of growth began to slacken, the rate of profitability declined. The French general strike of 1968, the Italian Hot Autumn the year after, more generally the "blue-collar blues," as it was called in the United States, revealed mass discontent with the existing form of exploitation and a potential for resistance. For the system to survive, it was imperative to reassert its basic principle: the domination of capital over labor. After a quarter of a century of highly profitable and safe collaboration, however, the establishment was reluctant to destroy the complex mechanism. It made a last effort to improve profitability and extricate itself from the predicament through expansion, and it failed. The big jump in oil prices further complicating calculations, it managed to combine no growth in production with a sharp rise in prices, giving rise to an economic neologism: stagflation. The seventies were, thus, a decade of transition, after which capital embarked on a full offensive.

The attack was preceeded and accompanied by ideological bombardment. It spread throughout the Western world, though, quite naturally, it was not simultaneous. The Reagan administration, by crushing the air controllers' union, PATCO, in 1981-1982, gave a signal to business the world over that it was time to take back concessions in negotiations with labor unions. The biggest confrontation took place in 1984-1985 in Britain, where Maggie Thatcher's government, after intensive preparations, took on the miners and finally managed to defeat them as the leadership of the trade unions chose not to back the strikers with the full strength of the organized labor movement. Altogether, it was easier to pare back social benefits in the United States, where they were gained or lost in separate bargains, firm by firm, than in Western Europe, where the dismantling of the welfare state had to involve national deals and parliamentary legislation. In Italy, the *scala mobile*, the sliding scale indexing wages on prices, was not finally abolished until 1992-1993.

For capital, victory could only be consolidated by changing its relations with labor, notably on the shop floor, and this was achieved by adapting Japanese methods of management. This shift is worth studying, because it is supposed to put an end to a period, to the era of so-called Fordism, taken here in two meanings: F. W. Taylor's "scientific management," with its time and motion studies and its strict separation of physical from mental work, culminating in the auto assembly line, and Ford's "five dollar day," standing for the attempt to broaden the consumer market through higher wages. Fordism is thus a shorthand for a method of management evolved at the beginning of this century but which had its period of glory during the thirty years after the Second World War, when the rapid growth of production, particularly of durable goods, coincided with the development of their mass consumption. This expansion exhausted (after many had assumed it to be perpetual), the mechanism had to be altered. One car symbolically replacing another, Fordism was said to be replaced by Toyotism. This does not mean that in the earlier period all factories were modeled on Henry Ford's famous River Rouge plant, simply that at one stage from the point of view of the employers, his was the most efficient and therefore the dominant way for the utilization of labor. The "lean production" illustrated by Toyota is capital's response to a new challenge, at a more advanced level of technological development. I will not even pretend here to describe how the Japanese economy is run and how its managerial mechanism was shaped after the war against the background of a highly hierarchical society. What we need for our purpose, and what I shall try to summarize using the vast literature on the subject, is the gist of the method, its main features, particularly as they were absorbed by the western world in its transition to a new mode of exploitation.[11]

The first point to remember is that the Japanese managerial transformation was carried out once labor resistance had been smashed. Japan had fairly militant trade unions immediately after the Second World War, but

11. For a thorough but apologetic description, see J. Womack, D. Jones, and D. Roos, *The Machine That Changed the World* (Rawson-MacMillan, 1990); for a more critical approach see Bennet Harrison, *Lean and Mean* (Basic Books, 1994); Ruth Milkman, *Farewell to the Factory* (Berkeley: University of California Press, 1997); Laurie Graham, *On the Line at Subaru Isuzu* (Ithaca, N.Y.: ILR, 1995); and Mike Parker and Jane Slaughter, *Working Smart, A Labor Notes Book* (Detroit: Labor Notes, 1994). For problems facing unions in the context of globalization, see Kim Moody, *Workers in a Lean World* (London: Verso, 1997). For Japanese background see William Tabb, *The Postwar Japanese System* (New York: Oxford University Press, 1995). For Swedish experiments see Christian Berggren, *Alternative to Lean Production* (Ithaca: ILR Cornell University Press, 1992). See also Paul Burkett and Martin Hart-Landsberg, "The Use and Abuse of Japan as a Progressive Model" in *Socialist Register 1996*. For the whole problem of deskilling, see Harry Braverman's fundamental *Labor and Monopoly Capital* (New York: Monthly Review Press, 1974).

they were defeated in the late 1940s and early 1950s in a red scare offensive launched as part of the Cold War. The new managerial mechanism, introduced afterward and imposed from above, can only function where there is no organized labor or where the unions are sufficiently domesticated to accept their total subservience to the firm. This postwar battle also throws some light on what is considered the bright side of the Japanese pattern, namely job security (though "life employment" really ends at fifty-five) and wage increases according to seniority (admittedly tempered by personal evaluation—*Satei*—and bonuses accounting for about a third of the annual income). These gains were preserved to give the obedient unions some credibility, but they were limited to the very big corporations. Thus, the relative privileges hailed as typical of the Japanese process of production apply in fact to barely one-fifth of that country's labor force, because conditions differ greatly between the core firm and its periphery.

Indeed, one of the characteristics of the Japanese model is its loose, many-layered form of vertical integration. Toyota, at one stage, had "168 first-tier contractors, 4700 second-tier subcontractors and 31,600 suppliers in yet a third tier." [12] Social conditions and benefits go down with each level, and at the lowest, where women and temporary work are concentrated, wages are a mere quarter of those in the main plant. [13] The whole setup has been compared to a web, with the core firm as its spider. The suppliers are subordinate without being subsidiaries. They are legally autonomous but highly dependent. The main firm provides financial aid and technical know-how, particularly to first-tier contractors, who in turn control their own suppliers.

Herein lies one secret of lean production. The core firm is stripped of everything that may be delegated—cleaning, catering, security, accounting—and contracts out anything it can. This is even more striking in electronics than in the car industry. Thus the NEC, Panasonic, Mitsubishi, and Sony contracted out almost three-quarters of their color television production. [14] The close

12. Harrison, *Mean and Lean,* 156. For more up-to-date figures (230 first-tier suppliers, approximately 5,000 second-tier and 20,000 third and fourth-tier), see W. Ruigrok and R. van Tulder, *The Logic of International Restructuring* (London: Routledge, 1995), 53.

13. Parker and Slaughter, *Working Smart,* 230.

14. Harrison, 158.

and complex relationship dictates another specificity of Japanese production, the *kanban*, literally the name of the tags on each part, here used collectively to describe the method of just-in-time delivery, which radically reduces the cost of inventories, passing part of the burden on to the suppliers. The core plant, however, must be flexible in a more general sense, since ideally the purpose of the operation is to produce only when the orders have been registered. A car factory must be quick at recording, shifting supplies, setting up new lines. It is within this flexible factory that the utilization of the labor force must be examined.

It has been argued that Toyotism is the opposite of Fordism, having reversed the separation of brain from brawn that Frederick Taylor had developed into a fine art. The best way to assess the truth of this proposition is to look at Japanese methods applied on American soil in the transplants—the joint ventures or factories organized on the Japanese model. In most cases, the hiring process is more careful, more selective, than in the traditional American counterparts and much more time—weeks instead of days—is spent training the newcomers, instilling in them the "spirit" of the enterprise and teaching them new ways of working, notably in small teams. In teams they are to *kaizen*, that is to say, to meet regularly to discuss how to improve efficiency and reduce defects. While the assembly line persists, it is also through teams that the workers are involved, each one able to perform the task of his partners, to replace them, so that the team leader is there as just the rescuer of last resort. Among the other relative advantages described by people employed in these new plants, one should mention the clean and bright surroundings, the polite language, the apparent respect for blue-collar workers. (The Japanese have not yet managed to export to the Western world the mood prevailing in some of their enterprises, where employees "volunteer" to do overtime at normal rates or to give up days of holiday to which they are entitled.)

The attractiveness of the Japanese organization diminishes as you look at it through the eyes of the performers and not its hagiographers. *Kaizen* is not an Asian version of workers' control. The employees have no say on such matters as overtime, line speeds, or shift rotation.[15] All key decisions are made from above, and within this framework workers have the right, nay,

15. Graham, *On the Line,* 125; but the same point is made in all the books.

the duty, to permanently improve their performance, that is to say to deprive themselves of the pockets of autonomy and freedom they managed to "steal" from the employers in the traditional plant. The team, in this context, means merely peer pressure. Nor should one confuse job rotation with a passport to liberty and skill. The tasks are still broken down to time-measured fractions, in perfectly Taylorist fashion. The worker's tasks are multiplied, not his knowledge. Indeed, when the Toyotist factories are recruiting in the United States, they look for people who are young, energetic enough to cope, and ready to collaborate; they are not seeking skilled workers.

The ambition of F. W. Taylor, epitomized at one stage by the Fordist assembly line, was to transfer all knowledge to management, reducing the worker deprived of his skill to an appendix of the machine. Even if the Toyotist factory had restored some mental functions to workers, it would not have been the reversal of Fordism but its final fulfillment, producing that strange creature: the thinking cog in the machine. But it restored nothing of the kind. If anything, it reduced the working people to an even more subordinate role. In those plants where its thought control is successful, it may have managed the Orwellian feat of disguising coercion as consent, with some people really deceived. But its real achievement, starting with Japan, is to have spread throughout the Western world what has been aptly described as "management by stress," by comparison with which Charlie Chaplin's predicament in the movie *Modern Times* seems like child's play.[16]

Naturally, a higher form of exploitation is not unconnected with the superior technological means at capital's disposal. Without robotics, without computerized communications and computerized controls, there is no just-in-time management and no Toyotist firm as it functions today. But the Japanese model was born without the bulk of the technical features it now uses. Indeed, the technological progress, the programs, the software, were largely developed to fill its needs and the system then moved beyond the frontiers of Japan because there was a demand for it, because Western employers required a new strategy and new methods to preserve their domination over their workforces. The new mechanism can no longer be

---

16. The term "management by stress" is at the heart of the analysis in Parker and Slaughter, *Working Smart.*

imagined without the available technology, but the technology, though the indispensable instrument, was not the begetter.

Can mass production, like that of cars, ever be reconciled with a genuine form of self-management, the mastery of the working people over the conditions and the meaning of their work? This question was raised in a fashion, during the 1970s and the 1980s, in connection with Sweden. That country was, at the time, an exception to the rule. Unemployment was almost negligible, four-fifths of the labor force was unionized, and with a narrow range of wages it was difficult to recruit young people ready to accept work on assembly lines, which they found strenuous and demoralizingly dreary. The two Swedish car manufacturers, Saab and Volvo, were driven to do something to make that employment less unattractive. Volvo, in particular, made several efforts. In 1974, it set up a plant at Kalmar, where highly fragmented work was replaced by much longer cycles. Eleven years later, in the new plant at Uddevalla, the assembly line was abolished altogether, with teams of ten or twelve workers assembling a car from beginning to end. The same principle was applied in the truck factories.

The Swedish experiment is at once instructive and inconclusive. It is interesting to see that job dissatisfaction diminishes as workers get more knowledge of what they are doing, more control, more initiative, and also that the highest levels of Swedish (though not international) productivity were rapidly reached despite this shift to a different method. On the other hand, it is inconclusive, because the main preoccupation of the employers was to maximize profits, and as soon as Sweden ceased to be exceptional, the growing pool of jobless altering the mood on the labor market, the employers gave up experimenting. Still, some lessons can be drawn. The operation proved most successful and lasting in the truck plants, where the unions, backed by the rank and file, had managed to impose a favorable balance of forces. Mass unemployment turns out to be a perfect cure for the humanitarian zeal of employers who, even in their most reformist period, had no intention of transferring real power to the workers. As André Gorz rightly points out after studying the Swedish case, at no stage was the product itself and its social usage allowed to be examined by the producers and the "citizens-users." To put it even more baldly, you can't build self-managing socialism in a single factory. By the mid-1990s,

Sweden was, in turn, converted to lean production and the just-in-time regime.[17]

The Japanese strategy was adopted so quickly because Western business was in need of new methods. The big U.S. corporations in the car industry or consumer electronics began to study seriously their Japanese rivals when these, thanks to higher productivity, started to encroach on their home territory. The American giants then discovered that they could gain substantial advantages through imitation, as the Japanese model provided solutions to their twin problem of profitability and labor relations. It taught them that there was no virtue in size and no need for formal vertical integration. You could enjoy industrial command and financial control without costly direct responsibility. As workers tended to be unionized in the big plants, lean production, with reduced staff at the core, meant reduced resistance, lower wages, and fewer social benefits. Conditions could be downgraded at each remove until, at the very bottom, sweatshops were revived. Why seek cheap labor in a distant land when you can get the third world at home?

The process, in fact, was one of adaptation rather than pure imitation. Since the Japanese methods were imported into the United States at a time when financial capital was gaining ascendancy over the industrial one, the whole transformation was subordinated to the imperatives of almost immediate profitability. If downsizing was the first phase of this process, re-engineering was its higher stage. Savings on inventories, thanks to just-in-time, and on labor, thanks to the dismissal of workers or their transfer to less protected jobs: drastic cost-cutting was extended to all forms of economic activity, including the service industry, in a frantic search for bigger dividends or, rather, an always rising value on the stock exchange. This mixture of Japanese shop-floor exploitation and American financial management, nicknamed corporate governance, is both spreading and beginning to meet resistance. Europeans in particular, after years of hope and illusion, find it difficult to accept the idea that you can have a job without earning your subsistence or that health and other social services should be sacrificed to boost the profits of private enterprise.

17. On the Swedish experiment, see Berggren, *Alternative*. See also Lars Hendriksson, "The Swedish Model," in Parker and Slaughter, *Working Smart*. The reference is to André Gorz, *Misères du présent Richesse du possible* (Paris: Galilée, 1997).

Naturally, everywhere the method has to be adapted to local circumstances. It has been argued, for instance, that a European reply to the new challenge can be found in the famous "networks" of northeastern Italy, the industrial districts where the agglomeration of small specialized firms—working together in, say, ceramics or textiles or custom-made engineering equipment—enables them to find their place in the international division of labor. But it may be more accurate to call this another version of the same model, since here too the smaller family-owned suppliers survive thanks to self-exploitation (as well as, whenever possible, the avoidance of taxes). The whole setup has been aptly described as one of "concentration without centralization."[18] The networks may prove transitional, as leaders such as Benetton for textiles or Luxottica for spectacles tend to gain control. How long Italian webs will resist international spiders is debatable.[19] However, our preoccupation here is with the phenomenon itself, not its variations, with the fact that within less than two decades labor relations have been overwhelmed, that sophisticated theories about a secure "salaried society" have collapsed as wage labor under capitalism has revealed its fundamental precariousness, and that all this has happened as a result of a managerial, rather than a technological, revolution.[20]

Revolution may be too strong a word, since it suggests, wrongly, that the system has changed its essence rather than some of its manifestations. Because it is called lean and mean, or because it can determine production in precise response to received orders, our model should not be perceived as one of conservationist development, guided by rational and ecologically responsible social decisions. There is no need to substitute the legend of controlled, limited expansion for the shattered myth of eternal growth. Capitalism may have changed its spots, but it has not changed its nature. Spurred by the search for profit, capital is still driven inexorably forward by its obligation to expand, by the inner necessity of enlarged reproduction. "Armaments, universal debt, and planned obsolescence," in keeping with

18. Harrison, 9. For his critical assessment of Italian networks, see chapter 4.

19. The resistance may be stronger in regions like Emilia Romagna, where the ex-Communist local authorities provide technical assistance to small enterprises than, say, in the Veneto.

20. For a serious study of the rise of this "société salariale," see Robert Castel, *Les Métamorphoses de la question sociale* (Paris: Fayard 1995).

Aldous Huxley's epigram, remain the pillars of the Western world, resting on what István Mészáros has called the "decreasing rate of utilization." Since what matters is exchange value and not use value—that is, whether the product can be sold, not whether it is needed—the more waste, in a sense, the better. It is more profitable to have private cars than public transport, to sell consumer goods that have a short life span rather than a long one. The perfection, however, is reached with the production of arms, which may not be used at all, but which are easy to sell.[21] This law applies more than ever. Considering that the Cold War has ended, the reduction in arms expenditure is marginal, and the military-industrial complex remains at the heart of our production. Elsewhere, the rate of utilization goes on decreasing. The life cycle of a computer, a micro-processor, a chip are getting shorter and shorter. We have managed to reduce the time needed to produce new models and the cost of the operation. Expenditure on advertising, on salesmanship, on any trick to get people to purchase is rising. Capitalism can be accused of not giving a damn about the genuine needs of the people, but not of restraining production in order to keep it under control.

This brings us to the mystery we must still tackle before moving to possible remedies, namely the contrast between the striking growth in the number of the jobless and working poor and the slowdown in the rise of productivity. The dramatic story of instability in the last two decades coming after a long period of steady rise in employment would suggest that productivity had been increasing regularly during the "golden age" and then jumped frantically under the impact of technological change, playing havoc with jobs. The figures actually tell the opposite story. The productivity of labor climbed spectacularly, particularly in Europe, up to 1973 and rose much more slowly afterwards. Admittedly, these figures must be taken with more than a grain of salt. The calculation of labor productivity in general is a perilous exercise, and in the case of the service sector quite often a phony one.[22] But here logic seems to be working strangely in

21. István Mészáros, *Beyond Capital* (New York: Monthly Review Press, 1995), particularly Part III, chapters 14, 15, 16.

22. For an analysis of the difficulties, see Harry Magdoff, "The Myth of Productivity," *The Nation*, 27 March 1982, and the ensuing debate, 10-17 July 1982. See also Magdoff and Paul Sweezy, *The Deepening Crisis of Capitalism* (New York: Monthly Review Press, 1981), chapter 11.

reverse: it is as the pace of its productivity slackens that labor gives the impression of becoming increasingly superfluous.

Some reasons for this slowdown in labor productivity can be ventured. The obvious one is the continued shift of labor from industry into the services, where progress of productivity is, as a rule, less rapid. Even this, however, has to be qualified. With electronics entering the office, secretaries, communication workers, and bank tellers have seen their jobs disappearing as fast as in the factories, and junior managerial staff is now following suit. Nevertheless, the rule is still valid. Jobs are cut in production and created in the services, though no longer in sufficient numbers to absorb the slack. Car workers being replaced by car salesmen is a classic example. More generally, there is the tendency mentioned earlier to develop sectors contributing more to the preservation of existing society than to its productive development: jobs in all sorts of financial services and law offices, in advertising firms, or security agencies. There is also, in keeping with the law of decreasing utilization, the wasteful use of allegedly productive investment, the abuse of electronic equipment, with the computer as a glorified typewriter only a minor example. Finally, there is the traditional reason why jobs that are barely productive are kept or created in sweatshops or pizza halls: their cheapness. More research and reflection is certainly needed to explain the apparent contradiction, but one point is clear: worsening conditions for working people, the plight of labor in recent years, is not due to a sudden rise in productivity resulting from technological innovation.[23]

For there is at least one conclusion with which everyone agrees. In the last couple of decades the employers have gained ground and the workers have suffered serious defeats. This does not mean, as some people do suggest, that up to the 1970s, capital and labor ruled together; if the reign of the former had not been supreme we would have witnessed the dawn of another epoch. It is simply that capital, no longer able to rule in the old

---

23. Robert Brenner in "The Economics of Global Turbulence," *New Left Review,* no. 229 (May-June 1998), helps to solve the puzzle. He shows how in U.S. manufacturing downsizing and re-engineering finally has an effect and labor productivity picks up, notably in the mid-nineties. But, outside manufacturing, productivity grew by the lowest rates in U.S. history (an annual rate of 0.3 percent between 1979 and 1990 and 0.2 percent between 1990 and 1996). The slowdown in overall labor productivity thus reflects "the rise of a labor-extensive low wage economy outside manufacturing."

manner, chose to squeeze its subordinate partner—and did so with striking success. The weakened position of the workers can be illustrated in many ways. One is the decline of organized labor. Most workers are still unionized in Scandinavian countries. The share of union members in the labor force, while greatly reduced, is still substantial in Germany (29 percent), in Britain (34 percent) and in Italy (39 percent). It is now barely in double digits in France or the United States and it keeps on dwindling.[24] Worker militancy, as measured by readiness to strike, has dropped even further.

There are other, deeper signs of deterioration of the condition of the working people. In Europe, the obvious symptom is the reappearance and permanence of mass unemployment. In the United States, where real wages are now lower than at the time of the Vietnam War and the gap between the haves and the have-nots is widening, the striking feature is the "working poor." Yet the differences, although significant, should not be exaggerated. If you take into account the jobless not figuring in the statistics—those who just dropped out of the labor force or those in jail, representing 1 percent of the male workforce in the United States—the proportion will be much closer to the European average. On the other hand, the "working poor" ceases to be an American, or an Anglo-Saxon, prerogative. For instance, a report shows that between 1983 and 1997 the share of French workers earning low pay went up by nearly half to 15 percent of the workforce, and this was entirely due to the increase of those with very low pay (less than half the median wage or less than $620 a month), whose proportion climbed from 5 percent to 10 percent of the total.[25]

The two sides of the ocean are somewhat united by the gradual disappearance of what used to be considered normal employment and the rapid extension of provisional, temporary, part-time jobs—of so-called contingent labor. True, statistics do not always confirm the most dramatic versions of this transformation. Thus, in the United States temporary work apparently rose only from 16.6 percent in 1973 to 18.8 percent in 1993 and is

24. *OECD Employment Outlook,* July 1997: 71. Data are for 1994, except for Germany (1993) and Italy (1992).

25. *Les bas salaires en France: Quels changements depuis 15 ans?* (preliminary report published by French Ministry of Employment and Solidarity, November 1997)

still "voluntary" for about three-quarters.[26] Naturally, the "choice" of women, predominant among part-timers, might have been different if public day care was available and normal working hours were shorter. But beyond all the disagreements about the scope of the change, there is the undoubted impression of greater instability, uncertainty, insecurity. The working class in the Western world looks, at this stage, dispersed, divided, and demoralized.

How lasting is this defeat, and what can be done to transform retreat into a counteroffensive? In seeking solutions to the present predicament, let us start with a trend which, though initiated in the United States, has gained ground on the left in Europe, with a school of thought which, while accepting the inevitability of unfolding developments, seeks an escape, some will say a shelter, in the expanding and loosely circumscribed territory known as the third sector, neither market nor state. The vagueness is understandable since, depending on the definition, the frontiers will vary greatly. If you include all the work carried in health, education, culture, and other social services subsidized by the state and the local authorities or paid by the church and the foundations, if you lump together charitable, voluntary, and community work, and add that performed by the non-governmental organizations, you will get a sector accounting for a few percent of the national product and a slightly larger share of the workforce.[27] If you confine it to cooperatives refusing the rules of the market and various local exchange trading systems, the territory shrinks to marginal proportions.[28] This uncertainty, we shall see, is connected with the other, highly ambiguous name used to describe this area: the nonprofit sector.

26. For American figures, see L. Mishel, J. Bernstein, and J. Schmitt, *The State of Working America 1996-97* (Armonk, N.Y.: M. E. Sharpe, 1997), chapter 4. For official definition of contingent work see *Monthly Labor Review* 119, no. 10 (October 1996), particularly the article by A. E. Polivka. See also B. Bluestone and S. Rose, "Overworked and Underemployed," *The American Prospect,* March-April 1997.

27. According to *Giving USA,* quoted by *The Economist*, 30 May 1998, in the United States in 1997 the nonprofit economy accounted for 8 percent of GDP and 10 percent of the workforce.

28. In Britain, France, and Germany, local exchange trading systems—under various names—provide an alternative limited system of exchange based on services rendered with working time as a unit of account. For its alleged potential for a future egalitarian society, see Gorz, *Misères,* 165-74.

Whose Millennium?

It is best to begin with Jeremy Rifkin, who, judging by his text, cannot be suspected of trying to overthrow the existing order. *The End of Work* is stunning for its discrepancy between the dire diagnosis and the mild remedy. The prospect we are facing is one of a workerless world, a planet without jobs, in which states are dwarfed by huge transnational corporations. With the third sector providing the only way out, what concrete proposals, beyond appeals to the "transformation of consciousness" and "commitment to community" does the author propose? Essentially, various forms of tax concessions and deductions to encourage both sponsors and participants. Amid means of payment, we may leave aside the proposal to introduce the value added tax in the United States, because that has existed for years in Europe, where unemployment looms larger than ever. Bolder, though less concrete, are the suggestions to shift some resources from armaments and to tax the transnationals more heavily. Finally, some ideas, such as a guaranteed annual income or "a social wage in return for real work in the social economy," are put forward without being fully elaborated. Yet the real puzzle is why should business, big or small, accept additional taxes and subsidize a sector much wider than what is needed to have a "reserve army of labor," thus boosting the general level of wages? Rifkin argues that big business has little room for manoeuver, since the choice is between building prisons or financing "alternative forms of work in the third sector." He is entitled to appeal in this way to the self-interest of the establishment, since nothing in his text really threatens the structure of power and property.

The same cannot be said of some of his European companions. Take, for instance, the latest book by André Gorz, the well-known and original social critic.[29] Its rhetoric is inspired by the *Grundrisse*, the book in which Marx insists more than in any other on the contrast between the crucial role played in modern production by technology and science and the absurdity of measuring that wealth in terms of labor time, a contradiction that will only disappear when the associated producers take over, putting an end to the reign of capital. Echoing this in parts of the book, Gorz does assert that in the society he contemplates, "wage earning must disappear and with it capitalism." Elsewhere, however, he gives the impression that capitalism will just tiptoe off the stage, that it will vanish—nay, that it is already vanishing, with the

---

29. Gorz, *Misères*.

173

disappearance of big plants and mass production.[30] Marco Revelli, one of the most coherent and lucid advocates of the third sector, does not even go as far; he does not tackle the issue of an alternative society. Less optimistic, he paints the third sector as a sort of a breathing space, the terrain for a historical respite, and describes the ground conquered for the social economy as a "liberated" area.[31]

This expression, probably deliberately, takes us back more than a quarter of a century. Though the situation has changed completely, there is something in the writing of the advocates of the third sector that is reminiscent of the mood of that period when, the hope of a rapid and radical change having gone with the 1960s, the activists, the militants had to get ready for a march much longer than they had originally expected. The period of the existentialist belief that instead of passively accepting the imposed condition you could change it into a means for action finds echos today in the argument that the young can turn their precariousness into a source of self-affirmation. That was the period when some people already believed that the world would be changed by Marcuse's "outcasts and outsiders." It was the time of red bases and liberated territories, a time of communes. There was, indeed, something moving about young people opting out of their commercialized environment and something valid in their contention that a revolution requires altering people's consciousness and not only changing structures and institutions. Less realistic was their implicit belief that the communes would multiply and, like the "countryside surrounding the towns," would ultimately submerge the capitalist citadel. Alas, the walls of that Jericho will not be brought down by moral trumpets.

The number of outcasts and outsiders having grown in the meantime by the million, it will be objected, the situation is totally different. Undoubtedly. To clear up any possible misunderstanding, let me stress that the political involvement of the swelling ranks of the victims of the crisis is, in my opinion, vital. In Europe, it is particularly important to mobilize the unemployed, and this is why the entry on the French political stage of the

30. Marx makes it clear that the contradiction will disappear and the emphasis will be put on "disposable time" only when "the mass of the workers . . . appropriate their own surplus labor" *(Grundrisse,* 708), but for Gorz it seems to happen on its own momentum, without any change in property relations. See, for example, his praise for the social project of the Centre des Jeunes Dirigeants, *Misères,* 128-31.

31. Marco Revelli, *La Sinistra Sociale* (Torino: Bollati Boringheri, 1997).

jobless, at the beginning of 1998, was so significant. Since the current mode of development produces the contingent and the precarious en masse, their participation in any movement from below is crucial. Let us go further. Any money that can be got from a foundation for progressive research or interesting social experiments is welcome. Any funds that may be obtained from local or national authorities to boost social services, especially if these can be run in more democratic fashion, are to be grabbed. If by social and political action combined, one can conquer a sizable minimum wage, a not indecent unemployment benefit, or a shorter working week without loss of income, if by persistent pressure one can force the system to grant concessions that, to a certain extent, clash with its logic—splendid! Yet what I am trying to convey is that the system has its logic, its hard core, and will not be compelled to yield by peripheral action.

The problem with the advocates of the third sector is that they have a rather variable conception of the state and the big corporations. Accepting as a rule the most extensive interpretation of the influence of globalization, they talk in this context of the famous thirty-seven thousand big transnationals which account directly for one-fifth, and indirectly for another fifth, of the total employment in the industrialized countries. But when we come down to individual nations, the power of these corporations seems somewhat forgotten. On the contrary, the state, which had nearly vanished in the global setting, re-emerges, admittedly in a rather abstract, classless reincarnation. You may expect from it, for instance, a decent "social wage," irrespective of whether you work or not, an innovation that would seriously upset the labor market as it now functions.

It is here that all the talk about "post-market" or "nonprofit" appears in its full ambiguity. *Nonprofit* is supposed to mean neither fish nor fowl, neither state nor market, but something in between. The trouble is that state and market are not sheer abstractions. For all their conflicts, they are part of the same social formation, the capitalist society, in which the scope for nonprofit institutions is, by definition, marginal. Profit will only disappear when society ceases to be driven by the accumulation of capital and the pattern of production is no longer determined by exchange value, by the weight of the purse, but is democratically decided on the basis of genuine needs. Meanwhile, isolated, squeezed in the pores of capitalist society, even the most idealistic cooperatives are likely, in the long run, to be corrupted by their environment. This is not a call to surrender or to inaction. Quite the contrary. The movement must be aware that the radical transformation of society will not happen overnight and that it will not be accomplished without the active participation of the main victims of the current crisis. But it will not be the work of outcasts and outsiders alone. A central confrontation cannot be avoided. And this implies different allies and a different strategy.

The ambition cannot be to resurrect the past—not only because the objective is impossible to reach, but also because it is undesirable. The "golden age" only glitters in the nostalgic vision provoked by current discontent. Who would dream of reviving the Fordist conveyor belt when automation makes it possible to eliminate a great deal of painful and monotonous labor? The aim should be to look *beyond* present society.

The structure of the labor force has been profoundly reshaped in the advanced Western world, by both a secular trend and its sudden acceleration. While this quickening of the pace in the last fifteen years or so has dramatized the change and focused our attention, the long-term trend is more fundamental. Scientific progress, technological innovation, and improvements in management have made it possible to radically reduce the human resources required, first, to produce the food needed for our subsistence and, then, to manufacture the bare necessities of life. It will be rightly objected that much more than that is necessary for the full development of the human being. The snag is that the development of the individual is the last worry of capital preoccupied with its own expanded reproduction and this is why capitalism has long ceased to perform its so-called "civilizing function"—boosting in a revolutionary way the productive forces so as to enable humankind to rise above a mere struggle for survival. For a very long time now, it has presided over a growth that is artificially distorted.

Let us limit ourselves to the second half of the twentieth century. The first striking feature is the contrast between the impressive rise in human productivity and the relative stability of the hours each worker has to perform. Before the Second World War the labor movement conquered, at least in France and in principle, a forty-hour working week. After the war, and well after the reconstruction which could have justified a temporary lengthening, the effective working week hovered around forty-three and

forty-four hours. It was only after the economic crisis, coupled wit
of unemployment, that the working week dipped below the forty-l
in Western Europe, while in the United States the hours worked actually
rose slightly despite that crisis. Taking the second half of the century as a
whole, even allowing for the longer holidays won by the European workers,
the reduction in the hours performed annually by a worker varies from
almost nothing to, say, 30 percent. During the same period, production,
depending on the country, climbed by 400 or 500 percent. The contrast is
instructive. Free time, though indispensable to allow people to develop
their personality, is not an important item for our society, which is more
preoccupied with the commercialization of the limited leisure time available.

The second key feature of the latter half of the century was the elaboration of a complicated structure based on the principle of the decreasing rate
of utilization. One of its pillars is planned obsolescence, reinforced by the
ever-expanding investment in advertising. The other is the military-industrial complex, which not only provides scope for the minimal rate of
utilization—weapons produced not to be used or to be destroyed on the
first occasion—but also is by far the main recipient of government subsidies for production, research, and development, subsidies which can be
adapted to the state of business, and may, therefore, be used as an
instrument of economic management. With all such aids at its disposal, our
society is somehow able to proceed with its distorted and now artificial
growth.

So far and so near. It is clear that, sticking to the advanced capitalist
countries, we are, in a sense, very close to the era imagined by Marx, when
"the measure of wealth" is no longer "labor time, but rather disposable
time," or "free time, i.e., time for the full development of the individual."[32]
Not that the available equipment can be simply switched to a mode of
production with a completely different purpose. To say that the "machines
will not cease to be agencies of social production when they become, e.g.,
property of the associated workers" is not enough.[33] The machines, the
programs, the methods of organization designed for exploitation will not

32. Marx, *Grundrisse,* 708, 711.
33. Ibid., 833.

177

be automatically transformed into tools of liberation. Some will be adaptable, others will have to be dropped altogether. What is certain, however, is that the state of our knowledge, developed and applied otherwise, makes it practical to imagine a radically different society. The ideal, let it be stressed once again, is to abolish the frontier between labor and leisure by eliminating work that is tough, dreary, and unpleasant. In the meantime, it is possible to reduce substantially that still-indispensable socially necessary labor, to spread it evenly, so as to give much more "disposable time" for all. The trouble is that this different life is at once within our grasp and inaccessible. The present system can continue its distorted expansion until it meets its ecological limits or is brought down by the people, who finally find the reign of capital unbearable.

It may seem strange to think about the funeral of a social order which, judging by most reports, has actually managed to bury its would-be gravediggers. Capitalism, according to Marx and his followers, was mass producing its future executioners, the proletarians. The analysts today, even if they do not say goodbye to the proletariat, describe it as a shrinking, not ascendant, force. If you look almost metaphysically at a working class personified by miners, engineers, and shipwrights—male, blue-collared, and highly concentrated in the very big plants—the description is not inaccurate. Not that their social weight has disappeared. Having witnessed two of Europe's major upheavals—France in May 1968 and Poland in 1980—I can testify that it is when the big factories come to a halt that people's minds start working. Nevertheless, sticking to a frozen, narrow definition and to the Western world, the proletariat is declining. But if, unimpressed by the color of the collar, one treats the working class as a living body, having to adapt itself to the distorted expansion of the economy, then the trend is in the opposite direction. With the peasant smallholders marginalized, wage and salary earners now account for about 80 percent of the working population in most Western countries, and it is within this loose and all-encompassing mass that one must dig to discover the size and shape of the new working class.[34]

34. Wage and salary earners now account for 89.6 percent of the labor force in the United States, 80.8 percent in the United Kingdom, 79.9 percent in Germany, 75.9 percent in France, and 62.3 percent in Italy. Figures for 1997 (except France, 1996) based on data in *Quarterly Labour Force Statistics,* no. 2 (OECD, 1998).

In describing the working population, it is now customary to begin with the big earners. The fashion is, borrowing the vocabulary of Robert Reich, to call the top 3 or 4 percent "symbolic analysts" and the next 16 percent or so "knowledge workers."[35] This has the advantage not only of concealing the role these people play in the process of production and the organization of society, but also of creating the flattering impression that we are ruled, if not by philosopher-kings, by princes of science and knights of enlightenment. The reality is much less inspiring. In our increasingly unequal society, wealth is highly concentrated. It suffices to recall that the share of American wealth owned by the richest 1 percent of the population climbed from 20 percent in 1975 to 36 percent in 1990 or, on the world scale, that the wealth of the richest 225 people is almost equal to the combined income of the poorer half of the earth's population.[36] These super-rich share the biggest incomes not with scientists but with businessmen, with managers who are part-owners, since CEOs now owe their obscene salaries to stock options.[37] Bill Gates has a proud place amid "symbolic analysts" as a moneymaker, not as Einstein's successor.

The erudition of the so-called knowledge workers of the second rank is also highly specific. Whether they occupy key positions in the financial or accounting services, in the law firms, or in industrial management and research, or whether they are crucial in the manipulation of people and ideas as TV performers or advertisers, their skills are essentially those required for the capitalist regime to function and their positions are linked with its survival. Come to think of it, even among those financially at the top, only actors, singers, or other artists, if they have not sold their soul to Mammon, could continue, more happily, to perform their role without basically changing its purpose in a radically different society.

Though these privileged groups figure in statistics as salary-earners (primarily for tax purposes), it is not among them that you will find your working class. To locate it we must look at the changes in the structure of

35. Robert Reich, *The Work of Nations* (New York: Knopf, 1991).

36. *Human Development Reports* 1996 and 1998 (Oxford: Oxford University Press).

37. In America, the managers of the one thousand biggest firms are now estimated to own around 10 percent of their shares. See *The Economist,* 28 February 1998.

employment over the last half century. The two biggest cuts we already know: the sharp reduction of employment in agriculture and the later and lesser contraction in industry (which still accounts for 37.5 percent of the work force in Germany, though for only 23.8 percent in the United States).[38] The shift from industry to the service sector should not be identified with the disappearance of the working class. The women at the cash registers in the supermarkets are paid worse than the men on the assembly lines in the car industry, and their conditions of work are similarly alienating. Generally speaking, the women whose numbers in the work force have increased greatly as a result of rather natural growth (nurses and other staff in the health services, teachers and various personnel in education), and more artificial expansion (in trade or at the bottom of the bloated administrative services of management) can, on the whole, be integrated in a flexibly defined working class.

What other changes? Acute observers have noticed that extreme polarization has brought about the revival of trendy restaurants, elegant boutiques, and beauty parlors which, with expensive cars standing outside renovated houses, have altered the look of old posh districts and the newly gentrified ones, particularly in metropolitan capitals.[39] Numerically more significant than this proliferation of personal services for the rich is the expansion of professional services for their enterprises, though here one must be careful about a statistical illusion. The big corporations, striving for a lean look, got rid of all sorts of departments dealing with accounts, transport, security, catering, or cleaning. As these functions were outsourced, they also changed their statistical nature: the same people doing the same job were no longer counted in industry, for they were in the services. Finally, there is the much-discussed development in independent, autonomous work, a progress highly exaggerated. Taking the period as a whole, this sector has actually declined with the squeezing of peasant smallholders and small shopkeepers. People working on their own outside agriculture are only really important, accounting for between a fifth and a quarter of the labor force, in the countries of southern Europe, like Greece, Italy or Spain. Elsewhere, the proportion hovers around 10 percent. It has risen

38. Data for 1996 from OECD in *Figures,* 1998.

39. See Saskia Sassen, *The Global City* (Princeton, N.J.: Princeton University Press, 1991).

substantially in the last twenty years in Britain (from 7.3 to 11.9 percent), Ireland, and Belgium.[40] Most of these new independents are not luxurious nomads offering their services to the highest bidders across the planet. They are quite often people who, to avoid unemployment, are doing on their own a job they would formerly have performed in a firm with greater security and better benefits.

In general, the changes in the work force are profound but not fundamental. Though even in the rich countries there is now plenty of misery not only among the unemployed, the "reserve," but also in the growing precarious sections of the army of labor, it would be wrong to define the workers, as it was once possible, as people who "have nothing to lose but their chains." Today many of them fear to lose homes and cars, even camcorders and cell telephones. What unites them potentially, as always, is their role in production. Deprived of the mastery over their means of production, they have no control whatsoever over the purpose, the meaning, or even the organization of their work. But latter-day craftsmen, have they not, with the computer, recovered their tools? The woman working at home on her terminal is no less a prisoner than was the seamstress sweating over her sewing machine. This issue of subordination will come to the surface as social tension builds up. Take computer programmers, key figures in the fast-expanding information industry. Skilled performers, they are still relatively well paid. But only a tiny fraction among them are the "symbolic analysts" inventing the programs which help the establishment increase its control over labor, extend its financial network, and strengthen its mastery over the media. The huge majority is doing hack work on strict orders from above. As the social conflict intensifies and the myth of a triumphant middle class collapses, these technicians, researchers, and a host of others will have to decide whether they side with the masters, in the declining hope of clinging to their privileges, or whether, in search of autonomy and self-fulfillment, they side with the workers whose interest is to bring the whole system down.

In the decisive historical question of whether the working class is still the main agency of radical transformation, the problem is not one of size. Numerically, it is far from dwindling. The problem—not new, but more acute than in the past—is how to unify this class, how to give it a common

---

40. See ILO's *World Employment,* 26, British figures 1973-1993; by 1996, the proportion rose to 13.2 percent (OECD in *Figures,* 1998).

purpose, despite its apparent divisions and real diversity. Paradoxically, developments which should ease the building of a different society are rendering the transition more difficult. The breaking up of big plants into smaller units should facilitate the self-management by the producers, while the enormous progress in communication and transmission of data, duly adapted, should help facilitate democratic co-operation on a larger scale. There is no denying, however, that the concentration of the big proletarian battalions was an asset for their mobilization.

The new labor movement has a complex and tremendous task if it wants to bring together its various sections. It must persuade those employed in the relative safety of the public sector that if resistance is crushed in the private sector, their job security will not last for long; Europe's telecommunications workers have a foretaste of things to come. But it will also have to convince those working in the big plants of the large corporations, with their unions and their social benefits, that there are no more safe havens, that once the employees of the suppliers, the smaller firms, are sufficiently squeezed, it will be their turn; in other words, that they have common interests both with the "contingent" and the jobless. It will not be much easier, in the present climate, to explain to those at the other end, in the modern equivalents of the sweatshops or enterprises surviving at the margin, that their enemy is not the big factory worker but their boss, or, in the case of enterprises run by single families and friends, the system which drives them into self-exploitation. In the new circumstances and the resulting disarray, workers must relearn some elementary rules of solidarity. Judging by what happens, they must also be taught again that it is in the interests of the bosses to divide them by nationality, ethnic origin, and the color of their skin.

Or by gender. The problems connected with the employment of women illustrate the full complexity of union activity. In the OECD countries, women now account for over 40 percent of the work force and, based on present trends, they should approach parity around the fortieth year of the new millennium.[41] Whatever progress may have been made, they are still suffering serious discrimination in terms of pay, promotion, and even access to various professions. Because of their role in society, because they keep on fulfilling two functions, they are very prominent among those apparently "favoring" part-time work. In 1993, they accounted for about

41. See *Données Sociales* 1996, 113.

two-thirds of that work in the United States and for around four-fifths in many European, notably Scandinavian, countries; these are countries where part-time work is rather important, representing about a quarter of total employment in Norway and Sweden, and over a third in the Netherlands.[42] These countries are also being upheld as an example of what could be done for women, which is more debatable. Admittedly, if some form of flexibility has to be accepted, it is preferable that it should not be imposed by the employers but negotiated by the unions so as to select the hours and preserve some benefits. Yet this tendency to reserve for women a special position, driven to its logical conclusion, could revive the belief that women's real place is in the kitchen, the church, or the nursery—Germany's notorious *Kinder, Küche, Kirche*—while the resulting loss of revenue might consolidate the only slightly shaken chauvinism of the males.

This example shows not only the complexity but also the political nature of union activity. If a renewed labor movement wants to advance once again, it cannot afford the old division reducing the trade unions to bread-and-butter issues or to corporate action, leaving the political sphere to the parties. If it wants to unite, it will have to be political. The only thing that can bring the various types and levels of workers together is their common desire to gain mastery over their fate, their concerted quest for control over their work, not just its organization but also its social function. As science feeds technological progress, accumulated dead labor in the shape of capital dwarfs by now its living counterpart. The only way out is to smash that capital and its power so as to recover the machinery and the knowledge as instruments at the disposal of the associated producers. This is the distant objective, and the task to get there is immense. On the road, the movement will have to elaborate its project, bound to include an important egalitarian contribution and new forms of democracy. But first we must answer another nagging doubt: can working people play a historical role in a world where national frontiers are apparently being swept aside by the gale of globalization?

42. OECD *Employment Outlook*, July 1997: 177.

9.

Internationalism Versus Globalization

The tendency to create a world market is directly given in the concept of capital itself.

Marx, *Grundrisse*

The hour of flight, alas, will be the hour of trespass.

Rimbaud, *Une saison en enfer*

THE RELIGION OF THE MARKET losing support, because it provided hardships instead of the promised cornucopia, the cult of globalization came to the rescue. To people protesting against unemployment and insecurity, against the growing gap between rich and poor, and against erosion of social services, the new priests could reply with a message of deep sympathy and fatalistic resignation. As a French minister of finance put it at the end of a G-7 meeting in Lyon in 1996: "Don't dream! We are living in a globalized economy." Using true and impressive figures about the size and speed of movements of money, they conjure up a rather futuristic vision of our universe, with electronic currency, information highways, and footloose, cosmopolitan companies ready to move, lock, stock, and barrel, at the smallest sign of a wage differential. With such a picture as the background, the preachers of the new cult can use a sterner language when addressing the unbelievers who, undeterred by warnings, dare to fight for higher wages or defend their social benefits. "If you win," they say, "you will be flooded by cheaper goods from overseas or see your factories transplanted abroad by owners in search of lower labor costs and, should you try to resist on a national scale, you will be brought to ruin and forced to surrender by the flight of capital, foreign and domestic."

Faced with such obvious propaganda—the latest version of Tina—the temptation is great to score counter-points and show to what extent the whole argument rests on oversimplifications, half-truths, and statistical stratagems. It is true that in the last quarter of a century, with restrictions removed, new means of communication were used and new instruments invented, so that we have witnessed a fantastic expansion of financial capital throughout the planet. But this explosion is partly due to the preceding period of unusual controls and restrictions. If comparisons of the opening of frontiers or the dependence on foreign investment are stretched not thirty but more than one hundred years back, to the sterling-dominated gold standard, the differences will not be quite so impressive. Similarly, if the world's population is dominated by a few hundred huge transnational corporations, their output outside domestic frontiers still accounts for roughly 15 percent of total industrial production. And, though these giants are clearly guided by profit rather than patriotism, they have strong national roots. With few exceptions, their directors and top management are recruited in the home country and the bulk of their research is also carried out there.[1]

Finally, productive investment should not be confused with hot money. Factories are not faxed abroad. Wages are not the only factor determining plant location. Three-quarters of direct foreign investment has found its way to the highly industrialized countries. Even in 1995, despite China— the new attraction—the relatively rich, high-wage countries absorbed about 60 percent of the total flow of new investment. The United States and Western Europe are by far the biggest recipients.[2]

1. The exception for top management is in big corporations from small countries like Holland (Shell, Uniliver, Philips), Switzerland (Nestle), or Sweden (Electrolux, ABB). On this, see Winfried Ruigrok & Rob van Tulder, *The Logic of International Restructuring* (London: Routledge, 1995), 152-62.

2. *UN World Investment Report 1996* (Geneva: UNCTAD, 1996). When statistics for 1998 are published, they will naturally reinforce the argument, since the share of Asia in federal foreign investment has dropped dramatically as a result of the 1997 financial crash and the ensuing slump in production.

Whose Millennium?

It is important to repeat such basic facts in order to destroy myths peddled with a purpose. Important, but not quite sufficient. In order to dispel the mood of defeatism, the feeling of impotence bred by the cleverly imposed vision of an inexorably deregulated, globalized world, as well as to prepare moves necessary to counter the undeniable and important changes that *have* taken place in recent years, it is crucial to put the whole phenomenon in historical perspective. For all its technological innovations, globalization is the renewed attempt to impose and extend the rule of capital on a world scale. Capital, by its very nature, tends to jump over borders. It had an earlier period of rapid expansion in the nineteenth century, when Britain, the "workshop of the world," ruled the waves. Though its rule had been shaken before, the international reign of sterling really ended in 1914, with the outbreak of the First World War. Then came the Bolshevik Revolution, which prevented capitalists from running things in quite the same way, the Great Depression, the rise of fascism and, finally, the Second World War. The new international monetary system, introduced at Bretton Woods by the Western powers in 1944, was supposed to eliminate the two major evils of the recent past: nationalism, by providing a new international framework, and speculation, by allowing state controls over international capital movements. The collapse of this structure in the early 1970s made room for globalization.

Hence, the second point: namely, that globalization is a response to the crisis. Faced with the declining rate of profit on one hand, and the crumbling· of a monetary mechanism resting on the absolute, unquestioned hegemony of the United States on the other, capital took to the offensive on both fronts. Restructuring and globalization are twin weapons wielded by a capitalism struggling to recover its raison d'être, its very essence—profitability.

But this, in turn, drives home the third vital point: contrary to the establishment's pundits, globalization is not a natural phenomenon, an inevitable destiny thrust upon us by economic progress and technological advance. The shape the internationalization of the economy has been taking is politically determined. At the root of the fast financial expansion lies not the computer but the decision taken by governments to lift all restrictions on the international movements of capital. Once the decisions were imple-mented in the 1980s, the technology came into its own. The speed of communication and calculation helped the movement of money to reach astronomical proportions. Indeed, it offered scope for a frenzy of financial speculation. Less than a tenth of the huge foreign transactions—the value of which is now estimated at about $1.5 trillion a day—has any direct connection with foreign trade or investment.[3]

Have our wizards unleashed a financial Frankenstein? The nature of capital has always been to expand, to cross foreign frontiers and penetrate still unconquered territory at home. Today, with the Soviet Union crushed and China wooing the capitalist invader, the goal seems nearly reached. Does the close of the journey announce the twilight of the reign, the capitalist system requiring, as Rosa Luxemburg famously suggested, new lands to conquer in order to survive?[4] Or, to put it differently, should the growing difficulty the regime seems to have in generating enough new jobs, the cancerous growth of financial capital, or the folly of speculation be interpreted as symptoms of an impending doom—and the international repercussions of the Asian slump as the first warnings signs of that collapse? Too many premature obituaries of the system have been published to rush into print with yet another. Besides, capital will not leave the stage until it is pushed off it, and for the time being it is very much doing the pushing.

Free trade, somebody quipped, is the protectionism of the hegemonic power. It took Britain, the economically dominant state of the nineteenth century, some time to get fully converted to free trade. The abolition of the Corn Laws—the subordination of agricultural interests to those of the exporting manufacturers—marked, in 1846, this conversion on the home front, while the Cobden-Chevalier treaty with France, signed in 1860, marked its extension to the foreign one. In the 1870s, the gold standard, favored by Britain since the end of the Napoleonic Wars, spread throughout the capitalist world.[5] Britain had then the highest income per head. It accounted for 24 percent of all foreign trade and a much higher proportion of foreign investment. Its moment of power and glory, however, was

---

3. See John Eatwell, ed., *Global Unemployment* (Armonk, N.Y.: M. E. Sharpe, 1996), 10.

4. Rosa Luxemburg, *The Accumulation of Capital* (New York: Monthly Review Press, 1968), particularly chapter 26.

5. The gold standard is a system under which the currency is defined as equivalent to a fixed amount of gold. The currency must be convertible into gold at its face value; gold must be freely imported and exported, and there must be sufficient reserves of gold to meet demand.

already foreshadowing its relative decline. In the 1880s the United States overtook Britain as the main manufacturer, and Germany was not far behind. Indeed, the last quarter of that century witnessed an economic depression, a scramble for colonial markets, and the beginning of monopolistic competition between capitalist powers.

But a monetary system, too, can be guided for some time by conditioned reflexes. For many years, London remained the center of international finance. Nearly 60 percent of the world's trade was being carried in sterling bills. Changes in the London bank rate reverberated in all the main financial capitals and provoked tremors throughout the globe. No wonder that John Maynard Keynes could describe the Bank of England of that period as "the conductor of the international orchestra." By then, however, it was a discordant band performing music for an impending funeral. In 1914, a horrible war engulfed British hegemony, gold standard and all.

One of the results of that bloody slaughter was the victory of the Bolshevik Revolution. The metaphorical ghost haunting nineteenth-century Europe now had a real face. The moneybags and their political subordinates could no longer run their business by concentrating on measures to preserve the rate of exchange. Wages and working conditions were bound to matter. Once the vanquished emerged from galloping inflation, the victors tried to restore the old monetary order in a slightly modified version, as a gold exchange standard with a reserve of strong currencies, such as the pound. But this substitute, prepared by the Genoa conference of 1922, did not last. Britain was no longer strong enough to rule, and America was not yet ready to take over. International monetary disorder and speculation helped to precipitate the worst slump the capitalist economy had known, the Great Depression that reached its depth in 1929-1932. Production collapsed and unemployment climbed to unprecedented heights, approaching a quarter of the labor force in Britain and the United States, nearly half in Germany. (Without keeping in mind, first, galloping inflation, which wiped out savings after the First World War, and then this army of the jobless, it is impossible to understand the age of darkness that was to invade Europe with the rise of Nazism.)

The gold exchange standard was swept aside by this storm. Foreign trade contracted dramatically as frontiers closed. Each country was trying to fend for itself with protective measures or competitive devaluations. Economic rivalry foreshadowed military confrontation. True, there was some recovery from the bottom of the slump, but Europe, and with it the world at large, was heading for its second catastrophe in quick succession: two bloody tragedies within thirty years, less than the lifetime of a generation. "Never again," the feeling of revulsion against such massacres, was so strong that even the politicians and their financial advisers who, in the spring of 1944, met at Bretton Woods in New Hampshire had to take it into account. Their task was not only to restore capitalist order throughout the largest possible portion of the globe. It was also to prevent another calamity, like the big slump, which could prove fatal for the reign of capital.

On paper, the draftsmen set up a multilateral, international institution to deal with the financial problems of the world. At its heart was the International Monetary Fund (IMF), which was to authorize the very exceptional adjustments in the fixed rates of exchange, but also to act as a supplier of liquidity. (Gradually it became a lender of last resort.) It was to fulfill this function thanks to a fund filled by members' contributions according to a complex mechanism of quotas, determined by the given country's economic strength, which also signalled the amount of money that country could borrow. To supply capital for long-term investments, another body—the International Bank for Reconstruction and Development, known as the World Bank, was set up. To show accurately the crucial role of the United States, it is not enough to point out that the American quota in the IMF, by far the biggest, prevented any decision from being taken without Washington's consent or even to stress that the new monetary arrangement was in fact a gold-dollar exchange standard, since all currencies were linked to the dollar valued at $35 per ounce of gold. To do it full justice, one must describe the arrangement itself as an instrument of American domination.

Though there were forty-four delegations at Bretton Woods, only two really had a say in the drafting of the original document: the British, inspired by Keynes, and the American, led by Harry Dexter White. The plans of each of these delegations were significantly amended during the conference proceedings. The final document, however, was patterned after the original draft introduced by the U.S. Treasury Department, although considerably modified under pressure from Congressional and financial circles. The reasons for the precedence given to the American delegation and U.S.

business interests are plain to see. At the end of the war, in economic terms, there was only one victor. The United States accounted for about half the world's manufacturing production, one-third of its exports, and 61 percent of the gold reserves.[6] Bretton Woods was, in a way, a belated transfer of power. The nineteenth century had been economically dominated by Britain. The second half of the twentieth was to be American. The system worked, not because the IMF provided the liquidity or the World Bank the capital, but because it fitted for a period the interests of the dominant power.

The ambition of the United States at the time was to preside over the largest possible capitalist horizon and, therefore, if it could be done, to drive Stalin back behind the Soviet frontiers. In Europe, to achieve this task, it was necessary to prop up Western regimes threatened by popular discontent and to reclaim countries that the advance of the Red Army had put in the Soviet orbit. The Marshall Plan, launched in 1947, served both purposes. It thus antagonized Russia and helped to fix the frontiers of the Cold War. The triumph of the Chinese revolution in 1949—though Stalin had nothing to do with it—exacerbated Washington's passion and strengthened its determination. In order to achieve its objective, America was ready to assist the economic recovery of its former—and future—rivals in Europe, to send troops to fight in Korea, and to help double Japanese production in the process. The monetary mechanism worked because wealthy America was willing to pay.

Indeed, the combination of economic assistance, military spending, and direct investment was soon to exceed the American trade surplus. From 1953 onwards, with only a few exceptional years, the United States was to experience a substantial and growing payments deficit. For a time this did not matter as the central banks of other countries were perfectly happy to pile up dollars in their coffers. The mood, however, changed in the 1960s. Germany, France, and Italy had by then more than recovered. In 1956, together with the Benelux countries, they had set up the Common Market. Having, admittedly prodded by Washington, re-established the convertibility of their currencies, they were ready for competition. So was Japan. But the terms of that competition were not really equal. Though America no longer distributed aid to Europe, its imperial expansion and takeovers

6. Paul Kennedy, *The Rise and Fall of the Great Powers* (London: Fontana, 1989), 461.

of foreign firms exceeded its resources. By the mid-1960s, the dollars in the hands of foreign governments were worth more than the gold reserves of the United States, and the imbalance increased as America embarked on war in Vietnam. Yet Washington showed no intention of mending its ways. America, it was beginning to be whispered in Europe, with the dollar as the reserve currency, is the only country which can print its way out of balance-of-payments difficulties. Still, General De Gaulle, the odd man out within the Atlantic alliance, was the only one who dared to insist upon it and reveal in the process that, if the emperor was not quite naked, he was nearly broke. In 1965, instead of piling up the greenbacks, France asked for its dollars to be converted into gold. (Germany was doing the same without fuss.)

Let us stop for the moment, because the incident shows something important about the ambiguous relationship of rivalry and complicity between capitalist powers. Here was the brave general, the only one who dared to question and challenge the American leadership of the alliance. But even he couldn't go the whole distance. When it was pointed out to him that the entire system would collapse along with the dollar, he retreated, and France actually took part in measures, such as the setting up of a "gold pool," designed to uphold the gold parity of the American currency. By then, however, Washington had realized that it no longer had the means to preserve its supremacy in the old fashion and would, therefore, have to find other ways to perpetuate its domination. It needed to devalue the dollar to resist German and Japanese competition. In August 1971, President Nixon declared that the little window was closed: the United States would no longer exchange dollars for gold. Two years later, fixed rates of exchange were abolished. The Bretton Woods era was over. It had lasted roughly as long as the so-called golden age, just shy of thirty years. The capitalist world was now floating into the realm of deregulated speculation, into chaos.

Naturally, there was never a neat divide, and historians will not be able to erect 1973 as an unmistakable frontier post between two eras. The old system contained much more than the seeds of its own destruction, and its demise was followed by a period of transition. The old, regulated monetary mechanism was worn from within by hot money, by an expanding sector of speculation. I am not referring here to the offshore tax havens, which incidentally could not have prospered without the "benign neglect" of the mighty. I am referring to the hotbed of speculation at the heart of the system, to the eurocurrency market in London. *Eurodollars* was the name given to dollars deposited abroad and not submitted to American jurisdiction. Paradoxically, the first such deposits were made by the Soviet Union through its Narodny Bank. This is the anecdote. The serious story is that a big eurodollar market *(eurocurrency* market as other moneys followed suit) was allowed to thrive in London, that by 1970 eurodollar deposits reached the value of the U.S. gold reserves, and that such a development was utterly impossible without the more-than-tacit approval of American and British authorities.[7] Those who argue that, later on, the governments had no choice but to deregulate under the pressure of the markets usually forget to describe how these very governments had prepared the ground for their allegedly inevitable surrender. In allowing the branches of American banks to use eurodollars and its transnational corporations to deposit them there, Washington was probably already beginning to think of an alternative way of preserving its domination.

The eurocurrency market changed size altogether with the inflow of *petrodollars,* the huge profits made by Middle Eastern sheiks and sultans thanks to the sharp increase of oil prices in the 1970s, gains which they promptly placed in Western banks. Incidentally, much of that money was then recycled in developing countries. So far so good. Except that a shift in the economic policy of the rich countries at the beginning of the 1980s, involving a tightening of the screws and a sharp increase in interest rates, meant that the borrowers had to cut imports and boost exports in order to make the unattainable repayments. The resulting debt crisis caused in many countries, notably in Latin America, the "lost decade," an economic euphemism for social disaster and untold personal misery.

The inflation following the oil shocks is a reminder that the 1970s were a period of transition. Faced with a slowdown in growth, a declining rate of productivity, and a falling rate of profit, aggravated by the rise in the

---

7. As Susan Strange put it succinctly: the eurodollar market "could have come into being only with the permission of the U.S. and British governments; the one allowed offshore dealings to go on free of U.S. bank rules and the other allowed dealings to go on free of British rules and regulations." Yoshikazu Sakamoto, ed., *Global Transformation* (UN University Press, 1994), 236. For figure of 1970 eurodollar deposits, see S. Corbridge, R. Martin, and N. Thrift, eds., *Money, Power and Space* (London: Blackwell, 1994), 58.

price of petroleum, the system was going to abandon its provisional compromises and social contracts for the sake of the old laws of the capitalist jungle. But after a quarter of a century of comfortable class collaboration, there were voices in the establishment warning against the risk of open class conflict. The clash within the British Tory party between the liberal "wets" and the future Thatcherites was an illustration of this dilemma. In fact, the 1970s saw the last attempt to get out of the structural crisis through some form of expenditure. The result was a slowdown in production and an accelerated increase in prices: stagflation. This was the signal for change. Stagnation would remain, but combined this time with deflation and an attack on all the gains of the postwar period. The 1980s were the years of the all-out offensive.

As usual, that offensive was first prepared and then reinforced by an ideological campaign. Economics, dubbed by Carlyle the "dismal science," was, quite naturally, a crucial element in such a drive. Symbolically, the recently created Nobel Prize for economics was bestowed in 1974 on Friedrich von Hayek, the arch-reactionary free trade crusader, and in 1976 on Milton Friedman, guru of the monetarists.[8] Not just Marxists, but Keynesians, too, were now out of fashion. The trendy economists were preaching a "natural rate of unemployment," below which an economy ventures at its peril. While the erudite were thus arguing about the Phillips curve, mass propaganda was reviving the old clichés about the inherent vice of the public and the intrinsic value of private, "free" enterprise or about the perfect wisdom of the markets guided by a benevolent "invisible hand."[9]

Propaganda was closely linked with practice. In order to shift the balance substantially from wages to profit or, to broaden the argument, in order to re-establish firmly the rule of capital over labor, all sorts of measures were

8. Eric Hobsbawm in his *Age of Extremes* (New York: Pantheon, 1994) draws attention to the attribution of the Nobel prizes.

9. Michal Kalecki anticipated the conduct of his fellow economists, back in 1943, in a text arguing that full employment would meet the hostility of business leaders: "The workers would 'get out of hand' and the 'captains of industry' would be anxious to 'teach them a lesson.' . . . A powerful block is likely to be formed between big business and the rentier interests and they would probably find more than one economist to declare that the situation was manifestly unsound." *Selected Essays on the Dynamics of the Capitalist Economy* (Cambridge: Cambridge University Press 1971), 144.

taken on the domestic front. Battles were picked, strategically, with the air traffic controllers in the United States or the miners in Britain to serve as "an example." Labor legislation was altered to weaken unions. Sliding scales protecting wages against inflation were abolished. To widen the scope for profits, every kind of public property was sold in the European privatization drive, starting with industry and banks, then moving to railways and telecommunications. Encouraged by their success, the sponsors of this action extended their campaign to dismantle public expenditure as such—naturally, not on arms or on subsidies for private industry, but on all the welfare services, health, and education. Globalization must be seen in this context. The opening of frontiers, the lifting of controls over capital movements, the unification of markets, the purchase of a country's state bonds by foreign institutions, the fantastic expansion of hot money—all are designed to impose the rule of capital, the tyranny of the market, on any government which, under the pressure of its electorate, would dare to question the new gospel that what is good for profit and the firm is automatically good for the people.

This movement of financial deregulation did not proceed at the same pace everywhere. The United States lifted all restrictions on movements of capital in 1974. There was no surprise that Britain should follow, since the interests of the City of London, historically, seemed to outweigh those of British industry; Margaret Thatcher duly dismantled controls once she became prime minister in 1979. In fact, some suggested that the formerly dominant country and the one trying to cling to its hegemony were interested in shifting the emphasis to finance to compensate their relative loss to Germany and Japan in the industrial race and in the struggle for shares in the world commercial market. In any case, by the early 1980s the trend was contagious. Germany removed controls in 1981, and Japan, becoming the world's biggest lender, moved, though with restrictions, in the same direction. Ironically, in France the decision to reform radically the money markets so as to get them ready for international capitalist competition was taken, in 1984, by a Socialist government. By 1988 a directive announced the end of controls for the European Union as a whole. This general lifting of restrictions was accompanied by a mind-boggling multiplication of deals. The figures in the following quotations may give an idea of its scope: "In the midst of the currency crisis in March 1973, $3 billion were converted into European currencies in one day. In the late 1970s, daily turnover around the world was estimated at $100 billion; a decade later, that figure had reached $650 billion."[10] By 1995, daily turnover was estimated by the Bank of International Settlements at $1.24 trillion and the sky—or catastrophe—seemed to be the limit.

There is no denying that this staggering development has been facilitated by revolutionary changes in the means and cost of communication and calculation. In 1960, a transatlantic cable was able to carry 138 conversations at the same time. By 1995, a fiber-optic cable could carry 1.5 million conversations simultaneously. A laptop computer of today can achieve several times as much as did a $10 million mainframe computer of twenty years ago, and it has been estimated that the cost of computing has now been reduced to .01 percent of what it was in the early 1970s.[11] Such cheapening of instant transmission did not only alter the relationship between the main plant and its suppliers or between the national headquarters and foreign subsidiaries. It made it easy to establish twenty-four-hour trading throughout the globe and close links between various markets across vast expanses. And the reduced speed and cost of calculation provided an incentive for the elaboration of new financial instruments.

The extraordinary human inventiveness when it comes to money-making is not to be denied, either. Deregulation offered plenty of opportunities. With fixed exchange rates abandoned, currencies floated. The spectacular rise and decline in the 1960s of the main trading currency, the dollar, drove people involved in foreign business to look for cover. The international vagaries of money, in turn, spurred the manipulation of interest rates, another unknown that traders now had to take into account. The lifting of rules and regulations had opened the way to many innovations in domestic finance, and the process was extended to the international field. A customer worried about the risks involved in his transaction was offered various ways to hedge his bet: buying on the futures market the promise to supply a certain amount of a given currency (or commodity or security); getting an

10. J. B. Goodman and L. W. Pauly, "The Obsolescence of Capital Controls," in J. A. Frieden and D. A. Lake, eds., *International Political Economy* (New York: St. Martin's Press, 1995), 303. See also "Survey of the World Economy," *The Economist,* 19 September 1992.

11. "Survey of the World Economy," *The Economist,* 28 September 1996.

option to buy or sell, a warrant guaranteeing the delivery by a certain date; against a fee, obtaining a swap with somebody wanting to buy the currency you want to sell and vice versa; or manipulating the much more complex derivatives invented to satisfy all kinds of general or specific demands. Derivatives, as the name indicates, derive their value from real movements in the rate for a currency, share, or commodity, and from the assessment of their likely trend. It is by now best described as an immense system of reinsurance, in which you can both cover your bet and gamble. Since in the reports most favorable to this innovation, it is admitted that less than a fifth of all the international transactions have any connection with actual deals in foreign trade or investment, the obvious conclusion is that in this reinsurance racket, hedging has yielded pride of place to speculation.

One international consequence of the multiplication of derivatives is that speculators gambling against a currency, say hedge funds attacking the pound in 1992, are in a stronger position. Not only can they borrow from the banks much more than they risk, but now "the power of that money is magnified, because only a small fraction of the notional cost, or face value, of a derivative contract is needed up front. In other words, hedge funds can take huge bets . . . without putting up much of their own money."[12] The hedge funds, registered offshore or in the United States, where regulations were lifted earlier, are now the fashionable heroes, or villains, of the story. Yet as the analysis of the successful operation against the lira and the pound shows, they were only an element of a much larger offensive.[13]

Recent years saw both an extremely rapid expansion of financial markets and changes in the relative importance of players. In the United States, the obvious model, the pace was dictated by mutual funds, of which the hedge funds are the most active branch. Between 1980 and 1995 the assets of the mutual funds climbed almost ninefold from $293 billion to about $2.6 trillion. They did not quite catch up with the giant pension funds—whose assets rose during the same period from $668 billion to about $4 trillion—but they did narrow the gap, for the simple reason that, prevented by legal

12. Ruth Kelly, "Derivatives: A Growing Threat," in J. Michie and J. Grieve Smith, eds., *Managing the Global Economy* (Oxford: Oxford University Press, 1995), 220.

13. International Monetary Fund, *International Capital Markets, Part I: Exchange Rate Management and International Capital Flows* (August 1993).

constraints from doing certain things, the pension funds bypassed the obstacle by shifting money to mutual funds. Their huge combined appetite was satisfied during that period by the vast supply of bonds by an American administration piling up debts and by the purchase of securities of varying quality, including junk bonds. Their nominally brilliant performance was greatly helped by the unbelievable success saga of the stock exchange. Satisfied at home, they ventured abroad. The hedge funds showed the way as champion speculators. The pension funds followed, helped by deregulation, by derivatives as insurance, and by the removal of controls, notably in Europe, ensuring the mobility of their investments. They now could buy foreign stock or government bonds and shift their investments whenever they chose. But they were not alone. Big investment banks, such as Goldman, Sachs or Morgan-Stanley, major commercial banks, and hedge funds have all played leading parts in the riot of speculation that convulsed financial markets. The growing financial departments of the international companies must also be taken into account. Those were the big battalions which brought down the pound sterling on Black Monday, September 16, 1992.

Pension funds are an Anglo-American specialty, presumably because without them old Americans would starve and retired Brits, *pace* Beveridge, would have a very hard time. While other countries, for instance Japan, have put a lot of money into life insurance, pension funds are mostly either British or American, and this is why their mass entry into foreign markets has been presented as an "Anglo-Saxon" invasion.[14] Mutual funds, however, are essentially American and it would be more accurate to describe this international penetration of institutional investors as American. It would be grotesque, however, to suggest that America is bringing capitalist methods to Europe and the world. While capitalism is universal, it acquires specific features in different countries. In Germany, unlike in the United States, banks were allowed to invest directly in industry and their crucial role in production led Rudolf Hilferding to invent the concept of *finanzcapital* at the beginning of this century. In France, on the other

14. In 1992, according to the IMF, their assets amounted to $3.3 trillion in the United States and $671 billion in the UK, compared with $192 billion in Japan and $63 billion in Germany. Quoted by Richard Farnetti in François Chesnais, *Le Mondialisation financière* (Paris: Syros, 1996).

hand, the relative weakness of the big industrial groups drove the central-
ized, Colbertist state to play a more direct role in the organization of
production. It would be equally wrong to maintain that American capitalism
is not propped up by the state. Indeed, considering the part played by
Pentagon procurement, and to a lesser extent by NASA, in the development
of IBM and other computer and electronic firms, in the fortunes of Boeing
and McDonnell Douglas, not to mention the histories of General Motors
and Eastman Kodak, such a claim is simply ridiculous. The propping,
however, can take different forms.[15]

One must also dismiss another suggestion, made for obvious propaganda purposes, namely that the entry of institutional investors on the world
market marks the international triumph of a "share-owning democracy,"
the victory of the little man. It marks exactly the opposite. The privileged get
the big slices in this system, while the small savers are bribed and silenced
with crumbs. But the latter have no say in shaping policy. The power of
decision is being restricted to smaller and smaller circles. And this is true
not only because of pension or mutual funds. The banks, squeezed by
competition, asked and obtained the right to venture into new fields. You
now read regularly not just about the merger of the very big orthodox banks
in the same country, like Chase and Chemical in the United States or the
Union Bank of Switzerland and the Swiss Bank Corporation, but also about
a record-breaking deal between a commercial bank like Citicorp and
Travellers, the financial conglomerate; about ING, a Dutch bank, taking
over Barings, the old London merchant bank, or the Deutsche Bank buying
Bankers Trust Corporation; about concentration in insurance in Europe
as well as across the ocean, and so on. It is no longer the big eating the
small. It is the giant swallowing the giant in order to acquire the right size
for tough international competition. Small is beautiful—that's for the
birds. In reality the world is dominated not by the small savers but by the
mighty corporations still centered essentially in the three financial capitals:
London, the old-timer; New York, the dominant; and Tokyo, the now-ailing
newcomer.[16]

15. On this, see Ruigrok and van Tulder, 216 ff.

16. On the concentration, the role of these cities, and the contrast in them between rich and
poor, see Saskia Sassen, *The Global City* (Princeton, N.J.: Princeton University Press, 1991)

The attempt to impose the U.S. financial model on the world at large must be interpreted in another way and in a different context. After a historically short spell of less than thirty years of unprecedented growth and of exceptional concessions, capitalism is restructuring itself. It is getting back to normal, to its old ways, though naturally in a new framework and, therefore, a new fashion. The Japanese methods of organizing production proved helpful in this effort to reassert its authority, and the American model of management, as it has evolved in the last fifteen years or so, with reinforced financial control and the emphasis on immediate profits, is similarly seen as the most appropriate for the consolidation of the system in the new historical period. With the strengthened power of institutional investors, with a much smaller proportion of shares required to control a company than in Europe, with the ease for the discontented investor to shift to a more profitable sector, the emphasis in this model has been on the quick gain and the quarterly report. Its first important achievement, quite naturally, has been "downsizing," in practical terms—an attack on labor, on the number of workers, their wages, and their benefits. And this is only the beginning. Other aspects, notably research and development, could suffer from this short-term approach. Raised from the level of the firm to that of the nation, this attitude dictates sharp cuts in taxes on profits or on higher incomes and a reduction in public expenditure, except on defense, provider of juicy contracts, and the police as well as prisons, indispensable to deal with social discontent.

It is this model which, under the pompous name of "corporate governance," is now being exported. Its peddlers and advertisers are the usual suspects: international organizations like the OECD, which in its annual country report scolds Germany for still departing from the prescribed pattern; the businessmen who meet once a year in Davos to attend the free trade mass; *The Economist,* which is the house organ of the cult; and the other convinced or paid followers in the media throughout the world.[17] Despite such backing and the acquiescence of officialdom, in Europe, as in France in 1995, the drive has met strong popular resistance. Its sponsors,

---

17. Some of the main beneficiaries are beginning to wonder whether the movement of the pendulum has not gone too far. George Soros, the celebrated head of the Quantum Fund and known as the slayer of the English pound is a striking example. See his article "The Capitalist Threat," *The Atlantic,* vol.79 (February 1997): 45-58. But his second thoughts do not go as far as to approve a tax on capital movements. On the Tobin proposal, see note 25 below.

however, remain convinced that they will carry the day, thanks to "globalization." With the movements of capital completely uncontrolled, a high proportion of public debt in foreign hands (figures fluctuate, but the average for the OECD is between a quarter and a third), with the possibility for discontented investors to sell shares or bonds and shift to a more convenient destination, no government, it is argued, will be able to resist. They now have to obey not only the domestic but also the international rules of the capitalist game. Thus, from Buenos Aires to Tokyo, from Helsinki down to Cape Town, the United States should appear as both champion and model.

It would be rash, nevertheless, to describe the end of this millennium and the beginning of the new one as the era of American hegemony. To be sure, the leading role of the United States cannot be doubted. With the other superpower barely out of the way, Washington reminded its partners through the Gulf War that they and the world at large still needed a sheriff. There are also economic proofs. A quarter of a century after the collapse of the Bretton Woods agreement, the dollar is still the pillar of the international monetary structure, despite the fact that the United States has been, since 1986, a net debtor and is by now the world's biggest borrower. When, in the 1980s, it ran a big deficit, domestic and foreign, the British, the Germans, and the Japanese, above all, came to the rescue, massively buying American treasury bills. And this does not prevent the dollar from remaining the reserve currency and the main instrument of international exchange. When Washington decided in the early 1970s to preserve its domination by other means, it did manage a fairly successful operation.

And yet American supremacy is not exactly what it used to be. The Japanese, who cannot quite speak for the whole of Asia, particularly given China's growing role, and the West Europeans, who despite the euro cannot quite speak with a single voice, are clearly not ready to attack the dollar, because breaking the main pillar would bring their common temple down.[18] But they are no longer willing to fully accept Washington's dictation either. The IMF, the World Bank, and their rules—all that is fine for the poorer brethren. When the mighty representatives of the dollar, the yen, the mark— and tomorrow the euro—meet at the G-7 sessions, they either avoid issues

18. In September 1997, Japan proposed to organize a regional rescue operation for the Asian crisis. The IMF under American direction turned it down and Tokyo did not insist. This was a sign that Japan is no more ready than Germany for a real confrontation with Washington.

or fight it out, like their respective transnational corporations fight it out in the world market. Washington is not at the head of some world government. It is first among unequals in a complex, still unformed, triangular arrangement.

Unformed and unstable: the sudden collapse of the New York Stock Exchange, overwhelmed by selling orders on October 19, 1987, Black Monday, precipitated a panic in markets on all the continents. In 1992-1993, successive blows by a host of speculators shattered and nearly destroyed the European monetary system. In December 1994, Mexico, presented as a success story and as an example to follow, saw the peso and quotations in the financial markets drop dramatically, as money, Mexican as well as foreign, took flight, thanks to the framework of vaunted "freedom," bringing the government to the verge of bankruptcy and the country's economy to ruin. By the summer of 1997, it was the turn of those postmodern heroes, the "Asian tigers," to suffer a speculative attack against their currency and stock markets, but these were tremors of a different notch on the Richter scale.

Consider the growing importance of east Asia in the world economy just during the dozen years or so after 1985. This is the period of the fast expansion of direct foreign investments in developing countries—reaching $100 billion in 1995—and most of the increase is accounted by east Asia. The transnational corporations, attracted by relatively cheap labor and favorable conditions, are investing heavily. The Japanese are particularly active, because this is the decade of the strong yen vis-a-vis the dollar, and all the countries potentially within Japan's sphere of influence are either pegged or otherwise tied to the American currency. If you add up the four "old tigers" (Hong Kong, Singapore, South Korea, Taiwan), the four new ones (Indonesia, Malaysia, the Philippines, and Thailand) and, last but not least, China, you get nine countries. The share in world exports of those expanding nine climbed from 13.1 percent in 1985 to 23 percent in 1995. This was more than the slightly increased share of the United States (15.4 percent) or the declining share of Japan (11.7 percent) and even of the European Union (19.4 percent).[19]

19. The superiority is exaggerated, because intra-trade is included in the Asian case and excluded in the European. The exaggeration is not as great as this would suggest, since intra-trade accounts for one-quarter of the total in the case of the nine in Asia and for two-thirds in the case of the European Union. *OECD Economic Outlook* 63 (June 1998), 205-20.

If China or Indonesia still export mainly consumer equipment such as textiles, toys, or footwear, most of the others ship computers, electrical goods, or communications goods. The nine countries have thus contributed to overcapacity and overproduction in those sectors and helped to precipitate their own fall. As the dollar started climbing in relation to the yen in 1995 and the east Asian currencies followed suit, speculators began to wonder how long these countries would be able to bear the pressure, and hot money took off.[20] When the Thai baht was brought down on July 1, 1997, panic spread like lightning. Currencies and stocks tumbled in quick succession in Malaysia, the Philippines, Indonesia, and South Korea. The Hong Kong dollar came under attack. So did the Chinese yuan on the black market. While all this aggravated the Japanese crisis, the flight from "emerging markets" knocked down the tottering ruble and threatened currencies from Brazil to Venezuela.

From the earlier episodes, commentators drew the optimistic conclusion that the international monetary edifice was no longer as fragile as it used to be. The original fall of prices on the New York Stock Exchange in 1987 was more abrupt than in 1929, but this time the financial authorities, both in Washington and in New York, intervened quickly to provide liquidity, and then foreign banks came to the rescue to soften the subsequent decline in value of the dollar. In Europe, while the lira and the pound were swept out by the first wave and the French franc was nearly engulfed by the second, the European monetary system survived and is now crowned by a common currency. In the Mexican case, though President Clinton had problems carrying along Congress and his international partners, he managed to find the $50 billion required to salvage the Mexican government and the—heavily American—investors. (The Mexican people, it goes without saying, paid a heavy price in high inflation, mass unemployment, and a sharp drop in their living standards, but this is in keeping with the nature of the game.)

This time, however, it was not working. The IMF, despite the shortage of its own money, managed to sponsor rescue operations involving some $140 billion for Thailand, Indonesia, South Korea, and Russia (exceeding

20. Between April 1995 and April 1997, the Malaysian ringgit rose by 55 percent, the Thai baht by 49 percent, and the Indonesian rupiah by 46 percent in relation to the yen. See *Conjoncture*, published by Paribas, July 1998, 24.

$180 billion if the package for Brazil is included). Acting quite openly as a Western, or an American, agent, it seized the occasion to force South Korea or Thailand to open up more widely to foreign investment. Yet, though the potion was at least as bitter as ever, with the jobless growing by the millions and those below the poverty level by tens of millions, the remedy seemed to have the opposite effect. The recession turned into a depression that kept on deepening. And it did not spread for purely psychological reasons. If Russia or Latin America were affected, it was not only because investors moved out of emerging markets. The drop in demand from the Asian nine plus Japan was enough to bring the prices of raw materials down, particularly those of oil, and Russia as well as Latin America are still heavily dependent on raw materials for their export earnings. The trouble deepened because the world economy is increasingly integrated. The unfinished depression that started with the fall of the baht may well become known as the first big overproduction crisis of the fully globalized economy.

Will there be many more? Will our rulers, who clearly learned a lesson, always be successful with their salvage operations? There is a reason to view the system as fragile, unstable, and even threatened by catastrophe. It is the growing gap between fact and fancy, between economic reality and its fictitious financial representation. We already saw this contrast in relation to production. Listening to tales about the information revolution, epochal change, and the end of work, one could imagine we were living in a period of exceptionally fast expansion, with working people eliminated by the sheer pace of technological progress. Quite the opposite is true. We are in an era of relative stagnation. The rate of growth of output and labor productivity is barely more than half of what it used to be during the "golden age." The same illusion operates as we shift to international relations. Listening to all the talk about inexorable globalization, one is bound to conclude that the expansion of international trade has reached unprecedented speed. Wrong again: it has slackened. The annual rate of growth of foreign trade went down from an average of 7.2 percent between 1950 and 1973 to 3.9 percent between 1973 and 1990.[21] True, foreign investment has gathered speed, but even this is deceptive. About half of that growth

21. M. Kitson and J. Michie on trade and growth in Michie and Smith, 7.

was accounted not by new investments but by mergers and acquisitions in other advanced capitalist countries, as the big transnational corporations jockeyed for position in their intensified struggle for supremacy.

The new rule of financial capital is not pure fiction. It has a clear connection with economic reality. It has served as the framework and the cloak for a change in the distribution of the surplus, for an important transfer of wealth. In the last quarter of a century or so, most countries witnessed a significant reduction in the share of wages in their national income. This has been coupled with increasing differentiation, a growing gap between high and low incomes. The trend has been most striking in the two countries closest to the new model, the United States and Britain. Yet even there the real changes—the defeats of labor and the victories of capital—do not justify their financial representation. The relatively slow recent progress of profitability is not enough to account for the rise of the Dow Jones. In the international domain, foreign trade and investments grow in arithmetical terms, and financial accounts in geometrical, nay, *astronomical* ones.[22]

It is this frenzy of speculation, this flight into financial fiction, that makes one think that Rosa Luxemburg was prophetic when she argued that the reign of capital can only survive as long as it has new territory to conquer. With Russia and China now swallowed, though far from digested, there is not much more to go. The irrational expansion of fictitious capital might be the first sign of ultimate convulsions, an attempt to extend its life by artificial means. For us, to paraphrase Rimbaud, the flight, the escape from this system, can only be its trespass, with the "alas" completely superfluous in this context.

Instead of seeking consolation in prophecies of doom for the established order, we should look for means to resist its present ascendency and, therefore, turn to the question of the nature of internationalism raised at the beginning of this chapter.

---

22. For a carefully argued and documented explanation of why profitability, particularly in the United States, did not rise substantially till the 1990s, despite the reduced share of wages, see Robert Brenner, "The Economics of Global Turbulence," *New Left Review,* no. 229 (May-June 1998).

Globalization is not singular: it corresponds to the essence of the capitalist system and its expanding nature. It marks a return to normal after a short and exceptional period. *Mutatis mutandis:* taking into account the differing structure of production and stage of development, the international inter-penetration today is not very different from what it was on the eve of the First World War. If we take as a criterion of openness the share of foreign trade in the national product, we overtook the level of the nineteenth century in the 1970s and have moved beyond since. But if we take as a test the share of direct foreign investment in world output, then in 1991 we were still apparently lagging behind the high point of 1914.[23] The claim that our current position is unique and incomparable rests on an optical illusion due to an ignorance of history.

But once it is admitted that globalization was and is a natural tendency of capital, the differences between the present and the period before the First World War are also undeniable. Then, for the imperial power the colony was essentially an outlet for its goods and a source of raw materials. Now, many third world countries have their own manufactures and cheap labor is one of their attractions for transnational firms. While the main purpose of having a colony was to gain an exclusive position behind sheltered walls, today the big corporations are fighting on the international scale for a larger share of the world trade. The battles and mergers between giants are not limited to international finance. The takeover of Chrysler by Germany's Daimler-Benz, producer of Mercedes cars, was the biggest industrial merger so far, though judging by the overcapacity, not the last to come in the auto industry. The breakup of state monopolies in telecommunications has led to a frenzy of national deals and international joint ventures between such mammoths as AT&T and British Telecom. But international concentration is also proceeding apace in petroleum, pharmaceuticals, electronics, the aircraft industry, and radio and television. Mergers and acquisitions on a world scale reached in 1997 the record level of $1.6 trillion, a peak that was likely to be exceeded, since they climbed to over $1 trillion in the first half of 1998 alone.[24]

23. See R. Kozul-Wright's essay in Michie, 157 and table, 158.

24. *International Herald Tribune,* 4 June 1998. According to Security Data Company, quoted in *The Economist,* 4 July 1998, American mergers and acquisitions reached the record of $926 billion in 1997 and topped that with $949 billion in the first half of 1998. The process, slowed down by the fall in share prices, resumed after the recovery of the Stock Exchange.

A small number of increasingly huge firms dominate production and trade in most sectors. But they do not quite carve up the world. These transnational corporations can no more make peace and divide the world economy than capitalist states, even assisted by such institutions as the IMF, can set up a world government.[25] Even the capitalist monopolies are doomed to some kind of competition.

So while "globalization" has in no way altered the fundamental nature of capitalist society, it has changed the way in which it functions. The impact is greater than before the First World War, because capital has in the meantime invaded new territories, penetrated more deeply the world economy, and, directly or indirectly, affected the life of many more people. This process has taken place essentially in the last half century. Encouraged by the reduction of tariffs and the removal of other barriers, foreign trade has been growing steadily since 1950 at a rate about 50 percent higher than the growth of production in the same period. We have seen that this expansion of foreign trade was actually much faster during the "golden age" phase, whereas the bonfire of regulations on capital movements and the ensuing boom of international finance took place after 1973. Yet, whatever the periodization and the motivations, did not this lifting of controls and the resulting upheaval alter the situation completely, reduce radically the autonomy of individual governments, and eliminate the nation-state as the initial terrain for the radical transformation of society?

As we try to answer this crucial question, it is important to repeat that the financial upheaval is not an inexorable result of technological progress. It is not imposed by fate but made on earth, as one of the responses of the capitalist system to its structural crisis. This is important, because what humans can do, they should, as a rule, be able to reverse, though it must be admitted that any present-day attempt to reintroduce controls over the movements of capital would meet with tremendous resistance. (How serious it would be can be gathered from the outcry provoked by a much

25. In 1994, out of the one hundred top transnational corporations (rated by their share of foreign assets), forty-four were European, thirty-two U.S., nineteen Japanese, three Canadian, and two Australian. Together, they had $1.4 trillion of assets abroad and accounted for one-third of global stock of direct foreign investment. In 1993, these top one hundred TNCs employed roughly twelve million people or about 16 percent of the estimated seventy-three million employed by all the TNCs worldwide. See *World Investment Report* 1996, XVI and 29-32.

more modest proposal, made by James Tobin, another Nobel Prize winner in economics, to introduce a small tax on international transactions in order to reduce the scope for speculation by "throwing some sand into the wheels.")[26] Remember the origins of today's impotence of the nation-state: liberalization was not imposed from above on reluctant governments. They neither resisted nor were neutral when it came to neoliberalism. Governments around the world were *active participants* in this transition, including many ostensibly left-wing governments which, accepting the existing society, had to accept its changing rules of the game. What this episode shows is not the vanishing, or the withering away, of the nation-state but its adaptation to a new historical phase. Incidentally, the very idea of stateless capitalism is a contradiction in terms. Take away the institutions for the protection of private property (the police, the prison, the judiciary), the more sophisticated instruments for the production of consent, and the myriad financial devices propping up the system, and the capitalist social order would collapse like a sand castle at the beach.

During the postwar years of relative prosperity, indeed, the state *widened* its scope. It increased its function as supplier of a skilled labor force through the spread of mass education and its function as the provider of a "second wage" through health insurance, pensions, family allowances and other benefits. To help firms, it ventured into basic production and acted as a juridical matchmaker in social relations, keeping a watchful eye on the "social contract." The so-called welfare state emerged under the combined impact of these concessions and pressure from below. But, as soon as the mechanism of expansion got bogged down and the whole process of accumulation was threatened, the movement was reversed. Instead of smoothing social relations, governments now faithfully produced anti-labor legislation to strengthen one side in the class conflict. They attacked welfare expenditure, growing notably as a result of rising unemployment. They privatized not only to artificially balance their books but also to help profits. In short, the state is not supine. It has instead intensified its repressive and, above all, its ideological functions: it was not so easy to transform the gospel of growth into that of alleged "freedom"

26. James Tobin, "A Proposal for International Monetary Reform," originally published in the *Eastern Economic Journal* in 1978, reprinted in *Essays on Economic Theory and Policy* (Cambridge, MA: MIT Press, 1982).

and the sanctity of the firm. The state also increased its assistance to "private enterprise," particularly to the transnational corporations, over-reaching their nations but still needing their help. One of the difficulties in building the European monetary union is the fact that, for all the corporate mergers, there are still relatively few European-wide corporations, and Brussels has not replaced other capitals as the protector of transnationals.

There is still one aspect of globalization that we must get out of the way before coming to the key question about the present potential to use the nation-state for the transformation of society, namely the effect on manu-facturing employment in the advanced capitalist countries of the switch of production to the third world, which has led to increased exports. Although the last thirty years saw a widening gap between rich and poor both within nations and between nations, a certain number of formerly third world countries in southeast Asia, the so-called NICs (or newly industrialized countries), by combining initial domestic controls with foreign investment and technology, have managed to boost production and trade at a very fast rate and to export increasingly more sophisticated products. Altogether, it is estimated that in the G-7, that is in the most developed countries of Europe and America plus Japan, in 1968 only 1 percent of manufacturing consumption was satisfied by imports from the third world; by 1993, that proportion had climbed to 4 percent and third world countries accounted for 10 percent of all manufacturing imports.[27] This was bound to affect employment, either directly or through resulting changed methods of production, particularly in shoes or textiles but also in consumer electron-ics. The impact proved greater in Britain or the United States than in Germany or Japan. Because the NICs were also serious importers of techno-logical goods, the influence on the reduction of manufacturing employment in Western countries should not be exaggerated. More important is the effect this highly publicized threat has had on labor relations, on the aggressiveness of the bosses and the tacit acceptance by the unions that, if they do not moderate their demands, the employers, and especially the transnational corporations, will just migrate to more hospitable shores. If a radical left-wing government were to take over in an advanced country,

27. Eatwell, *Global Unemployment*, 7.

the bluff would be called, since the big corporations are really dependent on their home governments. Which brings us to the key question: can a radical government do something within the nation-state, or are those confines now too narrow for a struggle aimed at the real transformation of society?

In its extreme form—there is no possible struggle now but international—the argument is obviously farcical. Even national battles depend on the militancy gained in local conflicts. It is naive to assume that, say, German or French unions, passive and defensive on their own soil, will suddenly show a fighting spirit as soon as the confrontation is extended to the European Union. Indeed, this excessive version, insisting that only comprehensive European action is relevant, is really a call to passivity, since one can hardly hope that all the labor movements of Western Europe will reach simultaneously the same level of discontent, political maturity, and consciousness. The serious argument is that in the deregulated world, in which everything has been done for capital to move freely and impose its laws, labor or the progressive movement will be rapidly driven beyond the frontiers of the nation-state; in other words, that internationalism has been thrust upon us.

To examine this issue of changed circumstances, let us look at a concrete case. In 1981, the united French left won office, with François Mitterrand as president. Its program, including the nationalization of industrial conglomerates and merchant banks, while not sufficiently far-reaching to really transform French society, was radical enough to provoke the antagonism of the international capitalist establishment. The left-wing government, however, neither considered refusing to respect the capitalist rules of the game nor mobilized its supporters to back it in such a confrontation. Thus, the inevitable happened. When it met the hostile forces of the international market as well as its domestic allies, it simply surrendered. After 1983, Mitterand did exactly the opposite of what he had promised. He "normalized" France. He did his best to adapt it to capitalist competition and consensus politics, damaging in the process the heritage of the French left, its belief that fate can be altered through collective political action.[28]

---

28. The reader interested in my critical analysis of Mitterrand's reign can consult Daniel Singer, *Is Socialism Doomed? The Meaning of Mitterand* (New York: Oxford University Press, 1988).

He did not, however, destroy it altogether. When attempts to impose the American model intensified, the French people rebelled against the logic of neoliberalism. Their winter of discontent, described earlier, changed the political climate, led to a snap election, and in June 1997 brought the united left back into office, this time with the Socialist Lionel Jospin as prime minister. It was a normalized left, not even pretending like its predecessor that it was seeking "a break with capitalism." But under the influence of that social movement, during the electoral campaign it did promise things—a reduction of the working week to thirty-five hours without loss of income, the rejection of austerity and of the deflationary implications of the Maastricht Treaty—which clashed with the new orthodoxy. The odds, and already the first indications, are that, sticking to the imperatives of the established order, it will betray its pledges once again. The slender hope is that, under pressure from below, it will be driven to keep them and will thus buck the international trend.

The fundamental problem thus remains unchanged. It is whether a radical government determined to carry out its project is willing to break the capitalist rules of the game and is ready to mobilize for this purpose. The framework in which this conflict would take place, however, has been modified in sixteen years. Mitterrand, who would have faced serious resistance from the bosses had he dared, had more room for manoeuver, more time to prepare. Jospin would be bound to internationalize his struggle more rapidly. We may now venture a tentative answer to our dilemma: because it has not withered away, the nation-state is still the ground on which the movement begins, power is seized, and the radical transformation of society is initiated, but sooner or later, to survive, the movement must shift to a wider battlefield. How rapidly? The question can only be answered pragmatically, taking into account the country's size, its degree of integration, and the extent of its autonomy. If a government determined to reshape society were to triumph in the United States, it could defy the rest of the capitalist world for decades (probably it would not need to, because its desertion would have precipitated comparable events elsewhere). In a medium-sized European state, the respite would be counted, at best, in years. Nobody now thinks seriously of the radical transformation of Lancashire, Lombardy, or Louisiana on their own.[29] The countries belonging to the European Union have not yet been reduced to the rank of provinces. But because of economic and legal integration, they are no longer fully fledged sovereign states, either, and the introduction of a common currency, the euro, has speeded up this process. Potential radical governments must take it into account when they elaborate their projects. These must be contagious, since the new regimes will have to spread in order to survive. Their proposals—to reduce working hours, to increase social benefits, to fight together against the dismantlement of the welfare state—must appeal to the electorate of member countries, if need be above the heads of their governments.

While urgency varies, the need for an international vision is general. After all, solidarity across frontiers is one of the most attractive features of the socialist heritage. When fighting against NAFTA in North America or the Maastricht Treaty in Europe, it is degrading, demoralizing, and therefore, in the long run, counterproductive, to do so in tones that could be confused with the jingoist language of a Pat Buchanan, a Le Pen, or the Tory Euroskeptics. The progressive opposition must make it plain that it is fighting not for an abstract nation but to prevent the reinforcement of the rule of big business and, therefore, that it would be willing to sacrifice sovereignty for joint action with the labor unions and other social movements in member countries to defend the interests of working people. These are elementary internationalist principles which, in our day, need to be restated.

"Socialism in a single country," that Stalinist contribution, is a contradiction in terms. Whatever version of socialism emerges from the current turmoil, it will have to be internationalist to be genuine. You cannot have a movement struggling against exploitation, injustice, inequality that is not universal. You cannot have islands of purity surrounded by a dirty ocean. Capitalism is driven by its engine to invade the whole planet, and socialism, in its own way, is also universal. If globalization is the way in which profit conquers the world, internationalism must be the reply of the working people. A new world is waiting to be born. The contradictions of the big corporations, which are defended by their states and are at the same time

29. I stand corrected. Such are the strains of the European transition, that rich regions are thinking of going it alone. The Legha is pleading for the independence of Padana, meaning the practical secession of northern Italy.

in conflict with the interests of their population, the way in which nation-states are torn at the seams by the development of productive forces—all these are symptoms of impending change. The computer could be an instrument of cooperation instead of exploitation. Information highways or digital television do not have to be vehicles of commercial culture any more than the Internet has to be subordinated to trade. I do not mean that the same tools modify their nature in the hands of a socially different user. The relations between science, technology, and the social system they serve are more complicated than that. I am simply suggesting that our level of scientific and technical development permits a much higher stage of international organization.

And people are instinctively yearning for it. We saw that, shocked by the atrocities they are shown, whether in Algeria, Bosnia, Rwanda, or Kosovo, people are demanding not just immediate intervention to stop the massacre but some form of international government, with its tribunals and its means of coercion. The problem is that, at this point, such an institution is bound to be biased. Can you imagine such an organization condemning and punishing the United States, say, for its intervention in Guatemala or Nicaragua? Can you envisage even clients of the United States, like Saudi Arabia or Israel, getting harsh treatment? Or encroachments against human rights being measured by a yardstick unconnected with American commercial interests? Yet, if you institutionalize such a body, under the sponsorship of the United Nations or otherwise, and put armed forces at its disposal, you will merely strengthen the forces for the preservation of the status quo. And nevertheless the humanitarian yearning is natural.

This need for a genuine international authority is even more striking when one considers our ecological predicament. The efforts to ensure the survival of the planet must, by their very essence, be planetary. Problems such as pollution of land, air, and water, ozone depletion, and global warming must be tackled locally but can only be *solved* on a world scale. Every few years a UN Conference on Environment and Development is held, like the jamboree staged in Rio in 1992, making plans and projections for the future—only to discover, as one did in Kyoto in 1997 and Buenos Aires the year after, that big business is stronger than pious declarations. I shall argue later that, while capitalism can invent profitable green operations, it is intrinsically unable to ensure our ecological survival, because of its need to expand relying on exchange value, not use value. But let us deal here with another limitation.

Today everybody knows that the biosphere just could not bear the extension of the levels and patterns of consumption prevailing in the rich Western countries to the world at large. The very thought of two-car families in India or China is enough to give nightmares to an environmentalist. This, incidentally, is why all the talk about spreading the American way of life around the globe is just that: talk. What the talkers really have in mind, if they do think that far ahead, is the inclusion of a small section of outsiders into the rich man's world, and the exclusion from that world of a good part of the Western population. In any case, ecological survival can be temporarily assured and the habits of the privileged preserved at the same time only by preventing the bulk of the world's population from even approaching those living standards. The only way out of this dilemma is through new forms of cooperation with developing countries—giving that term a real meaning—and the combined elaboration of a new mode of production and new patterns of consumption, again raising the imperative to think internationally. This is something that a progressive movement, by definition, must act upon. After all, it cannot pretend to eliminate inequality and injustice at home, while tolerating inequality in foreign relations.

10.

A Society Of Equals

*. . . for buying and selling is the great cheat that robs and steals
the Earth from one another: it is that which makes some Lords,
others Beggers, some Rulers, others to be ruled; and makes
great Murderers and Theeves to be imprisoners and hangers of
little ones, or of sincere-hearted men. . . .*

> Gerrard Winstanley, *A Declaration
> from the Poor Oppressed People of
> England*

*We must not play with the phrase about equality. This is playing
with fire.*

> Joseph Stalin at the 14th Party
> Congress, 1925

ALL HUMAN BEINGS ARE BORN, or created, equal and spend the
rest of their lives finding out that this splendid proclamation is pure fiction
in our "really existing" society. And yet the belief in this principle, or rather
in its desirability, lives on despite striking proofs to the contrary and
remains a popular source of inspiration. Indeed, egalitarianism—not in any
watered-down, charitable version, but one striking at the very roots of
inequality—must figure at the very heart of any progressive project today
more than ever before, as we have entered the age of growing social
injustice and polarization.

Our establishment has problems handling the concept. Its propagandists
are bound to pay lip service to the idea, which figures prominently in so
many constitutional documents, starting with the American Declaration of
Independence and the French Declaration of the Rights of Man. All they

can do is reduce equality to the vague concept of equity or to the undefined and rather meaningless equality of opportunity. They can also stick to a purely formal definition, in which "one person, one vote" is taken to suffice for political equality, whereas equality before the law is ensured by the fact that neither Bill Gates nor the bag ladies have the right to sleep in the New York subway (to bring up to date Anatole France's celebrated dictum about the Rothschilds, the clochards, and the bridges of Paris).

Official attitude towards equality varies with the social climate. During the years of postwar prosperity, it was one of benign neglect. Egalitarianism, in the abstract, was treated as well-meaning though not very relevant. With the pie growing fast, everybody was going to get a larger slice and over time, it was argued, slices were actually being cut more fairly. Highly debatable even at the time, the argument can no longer be sustained, and the search for genuine equality is now branded as a dangerous, bloodthirsty utopia, which can only lead, whatever the original intentions, to Stalin or Pol Pot, to the Soviet gulag or the Cambodian extermination.

This new hostility is dictated by the change in both the mood and the circumstances. In the earlier period, the general assumption was that "the tendency towards income narrowing is a common or universal feature of advanced industrialization."[1] John Kenneth Galbraith could maintain that "production has eliminated the more acute tensions associated with inequality" and "increasing aggregate output is an alternative to distribution or even to the reduction of inequality."[2] Since money is the main yardstick of our society, such theories were based on the apparent reduction of the gap between high salaries and low wages after the Second World War and, to a lesser extent, by a certain redistribution, with the very rich on both sides of the ocean owning a lesser proportion of total wealth. On closer scrutiny, the progress proved to be less impressive. The high fortunes after the war were underestimated, because they did not include capital appreciation and fringe benefits. The drop in the share of total net capital owned by the richest 1 percent (from 56 percent in 1936 to 43 percent in 1954 in Britain and from 36 percent in 1929 to 24 percent in 1954 in the United

---

1. Assumption reported in Frank Parkin, *Class Inequality and Political Order* (London: Paladin, 1971), 116.

2. *The Affluent Society* (London: Penguin, 1962), 87-88.

States) was partly due to transfers carried out to avoid inheritance taxes. The decline was less steep if one looked at the richest 10 percent (in the British case, at the same dates, from 88 percent to 79 percent). Other studies showed that the levelling trend did not last, that in Britain, for instance, the number of the very poor started rising again in the 1950s.[3] The very nature of this debate altered with the reversal of the economic situation. As the pace of production slackened dramatically, the argument about the irrelevance of redistribution weakened. It lost its significance altogether when, with America leading the way, the gap between the rich and the poor, instead of narrowing, conspicuously widened. Inequality had to be faced in all its nakedness.

It was and is obviously at its worst in the contrast between the have and have-not nations. The obscene equivalence between the wealth of the world's top few hundred billionaires and the income of nearly three billion wretched of the earth illustrates this point. If not all the money moguls come from the advanced capitalist West, the overwhelming bulk of the poor live in Asia, Africa, and Latin America.[4] The same is true of the other disgusting contrast. In the thirty years after 1960, the share of the richest fifth in the world's income climbed from 70 percent to 85 percent and is still rising. During the same period, the share of the lowest fifth dropped from 2.3 percent to 1.4 percent and by 1994 it was down to 1.1 percent. The ratio of the income of the top 20 percent to that of the bottom 20 percent thus rose from 30 to 1 to an astonishing 78 to 1.[5]

Admittedly, the very report including this scathing statistical indictment talks also about the important progress made in the developing countries during the last half century, notably in reducing illiteracy and infant mortality. This achievement, however, is spread unevenly. Incidentally, the countries which did best in terms of income, meaning those which went

3. For the figures and their discussion, see A. B. Atkinson, ed., *Wealth, Income and Inequality: A Reader* (London: Penguin, 1973).

4. The OECD accounts for 143 of the 225 super-rich (United States, 60; Germany, 21; Japan, 14), Asia for 43, Latin America for 22, the Arab states for 11, and Africa for 2 (both South Africans). See *Human Development Report 1998* (UN Development Program: Oxford University Press), 30.

5. *Human Development Report 1997* (UN Development Program: Oxford University Press). See also same report for 1996.

furthest on the road of capitalist development, like South Korea, Malaysia, and Thailand, are the very ones hit worst by Asia's financial crisis in 1997-1998. They are discovering our woes, such as mass unemployment, without the instruments of defense, of protection, that working people in the West had conquered over years of struggle.[6] Besides, poverty in the third world has changed nature by changing location, moving to some extent from country to town. It is among the uprooted peasants seeking salvation in the huge, polluted, unhealthy, overcrowded agglomerations, the "parachutists," as these mass migrants are called in Mexico City, who may be found in the *favelas* and *ranchitos* of Latin America, or in the slums of Cairo or Karachi, that you find a good number of the 800 million people reported to be half-starving, the 800 million who lack sanitation, or the 1.2 billion without access to clean water. These are the statistics, rough and written in blood. The epidemic of AIDS, spreading like the plague through Africa and Asia, is just the latest reminder of human inequality in the face of death.[7]

The gap between North and South, between East and West, between the ex-colonials and the colonizers in new clothing was no news. Inequality, however, only reappeared as an item on the agenda when its relevance in the West was no longer possible to conceal. This resurrection of social inequality destroyed the fashionable myth that, since we were all now on the capitalist road and capitalism was bringing everybody into the middle class, then, ultimately, we would all be equal. Of course, the West, too, has always had its fantastic differences of income as well as wealth. I do recall that when, in 1987, Michael Milken, the king of junk bonds, declared officially to the tax authorities an annual income of $550 million, I divided the amount through the yearly earnings of an American on the minimum

6. Even in relatively "privileged" South Korea, a member of the OECD, according to figures approved by the minister of labor, only half of the regular workers were entitled to unemployment benefits lasting from two to six months. The official number of unemployed reached 1.65 million or 7.6 percent of the workforce in July 1998. If those working less than eighteen hours are included, the figure climbs to 3 million or 13.8 percent of the workforce. *International Herald Tribune*, 26 August 1998.

7. Of the sixteen thousand people who become infected with HIV each day, 90 percent are in developing countries. The problem is not essentially African. India has the largest number of people with HIV, between 3 and 5 million. Thailand has 750,000, or 2.3 percent of its adult population. *Human Development Report 1998*, 34-35.

wage and reached the staggering conclusion that it would take the latter roughly seventy-five thousand years to earn that amount. The beneficiary having been put in jail—where he was not confined for as long as a typical minor black offender would be, and did not completely lose his fortune—I stopped quoting him as an example. Then, in 1992, George Soros was reported to have made more than a billion dollars in the brief battle over the devaluation of the English pound. Since this financier was domiciled in the United States, where the minimum wage had not budged in the meantime, it was easy to draw the contrast between the reward for a few weeks of speculation and for one hundred and fifty thousand years of labor.

These figures are, naturally, exceptional, though with the stock options distributed by Disney and other corporations to their presidents, they no longer sound extraordinary. What matters, however, are comparisons and trends. In 1996, for instance, the average salary and bonus for a chief executive officer in the United States rose by 39 percent and his total compensation, including stock options, by 54 percent. The average wage of a factory employee went up by 3 percent. No wonder that the CEO's full pay, which had been 44 times the average worker's wage in 1965, was by then 209 times higher.[8] Indeed, between 1973 and 1995, the average weekly earnings of "production and non-supervisory workers," those below the managerial and technical grades, dropped in real terms by 18 percent. During a shorter spell, between 1979 and 1989, the pay of CEOs rose by 19 percent and, if tax concessions are taken into account, by 66 percent. It is natural in the circumstances that the number of Americans earning more than $200,000 grew more than fifteenfold—to 993,326—between 1977 and 1993.[9] Finally, switching to property, the share of U.S. wealth owned by the richest 1 percent climbed back between 1975 and 1990 from 20 percent to 36 percent.[10] This, you may recall, was exactly the proportion

8. *Business Week,* 21 April 1997.

9. This last figure from the *New York Times,* 18 April 1997. All previous data from Simon Head, "The New Ruthless Economy," *New York Review of Books,* 29 February 1996. Barry Bluestone and Stephen Rose, "Overworked and Underemployed," *American Prospect,* March-April 1997, suggest that hourly wages have declined by 13 percent since 1973.

10. *Human Development Report 1996,* 20. According to *The Economist,* 30 May 1998, "the United States already boasts 170 billionaires, 250,000 deca-millionaires and 4.8 million millionaires."

back in 1929. As the figures do not come from the same source, the comparison may not be perfectly precise; it nevertheless gives an idea of where we are heading. Nor is the United States, while the pacesetter, the only one moving in that direction. It was even overtaken at one stage by conservative Britain, since Maggie Thatcher had even more room than Reagan for slashing taxes on the rich. The resistance was stronger in continental Europe, particularly in Scandinavia, though even there it weakened. The complete removal of controls over the movements of capital inevitably encouraged tax concessions at the top and social dumping at the bottom. It is difficult to see how this trend can be reversed without a major political counteroffensive of the labor movement.

In any case, it soon became impossible to pretend that inequality was vanishing or that it was unperturbing. The servants of the establishment began the ideological shift with the usual twaddle about human nature and the nature of things, the selfishness of the former and the cruelty of the latter. It was rapidly realized that the growing discrepancies required more positive backing. People were getting their worth, it was then said, because of their performance. They earned high incomes because they deserved them. Nobody quite argued that Michael Milken or Michael Eisner of Disney were worth several thousand hardworking nurses, though the assumption was implicit: those at the bottom of the income ladder also "deserved" to be where they were. Neither bright nor brave nor meritorious, they had only themselves to blame. In this new climate, theories about genetic racial differences and inherited IQ were magically revived. Fortunately, not everybody was ready to descend to the pseudoscientific gutter in order to defend the established order, though even among decent people the gradual substitution of charity for equality was a sign of the road travelled in the last quarter of a century, of the almost unbelievable ideological shift to the right. But this general shift has also a message for the left. If, in the new context, it remains committed to equality—in a full-blooded version—as its aim, this has very radical implications for its conduct.

Let us take the example of North-South relations. It has always been taken for granted that a genuinely progressive government, or a socialist one if you choose, cannot eliminate the exploitation within its frontiers and practice it without.[11] Ideally, it should seek progressive partners in the developing countries with whom to invent a different kind of collaboration. In the meantime, it should be able to use its scientific knowledge, its experience, its resources to help, in direct consultation with local communities, to sow lasting and productive seeds, irrigate land, make clean water available, and develop indispensable health services. Even all this does not tackle the real issue that must be faced. Most of Europe and North America have reached the advanced stage of capitalist development, with declining employment in manufacturing and the bulk of the labor force in the services; they also happen to use a disproportionate share of the world's resources. The developing countries are still at various stages of the industrial revolution. We who live in Europe and America fear, rightly, that if they follow in our footsteps, they will pollute the planet, dilapidate its resources, and, through emissions of carbon dioxide and sulphur dioxide, threaten its very future. Yet, even if we managed to somehow reduce our distorted consumption, we would hardly be in a position to tell poorer countries to do what we preach, not what we did. We could not keep on consuming as we do, while advising countries with much lower living standards not to expand. The only way in which we could recommend another method of development, less wasteful of natural resources and more conscious of human needs, would be if we plainly converted to it ourselves. Then we could find a common model together while helping the developing countries in the process of transition. On reflection, what the principle of equality compels us to do at home is exactly what we should be doing in any case: seeking a radically different way of development.

Women's equality, another key issue, carries the left even further in a radical direction. Feminism and ecology are the two subjects on which our culture is less reactionary than it was, say, thirty years ago. On social and economic topics, within a short span of time, we have gone back to the dark ages, travelling even faster in Europe than in the United States. Compared with a dignitary of New Labour, a liberal Tory of yesterday sounds like a

11. Here is an example from *The Communist Manifesto:* "In proportion as the exploitation of one individual by another is put an end to, the exploitation of one nation by another will also be put an end to. In proportion as the antagonism between classes within the nation vanishes, the hostility of one nation to another will come to an end." Karl Marx and Frederick Engels, *The Communist Manifesto* (New York: Monthly Review Press, 1998), 36.

fiery radical. Set against the leaders of the ex-Communist Left Democrats (DS), Italy's progressive Christian Democrats of yesteryear look like dangerous reds. The same cannot be said of problems connected with women. Here the feminists, by words and by deeds, have managed to alter the language and the agenda. They have changed something in many men's minds, broken some professional barriers, and weakened a few biases. Yet there is a tremendous contrast between the progress made so far and the immense task still lying ahead, and not merely in the lands of the exploited, where women are the victims of the victims.

In the advanced capitalist world, women working outside the home will soon account for close to half of total employment, but everywhere their wages and salaries lag behind men's. The gap may be bigger in southern countries than in the Scandinavian ones, but there are no exceptions. In public service, even where equal pay for equal work is the official rule, women's average remuneration is substantially lower, because you find them plentiful at the bottom of the pyramid and diminishing as you climb up. The same is true of the academic world and even truer of the professions, where the limelight thrown on a few token star performers should not be allowed to confuse the picture. The promotion of women in political parties and labor unions is a valuable phenomenon which should not conceal the fact that their power has still no genuine connection with their numbers. With so much still to be done, the battle against these open forms of discrimination, the political and social even more than the legal struggle, is undoubtedly important. It is, however, far from sufficient.

We must ask ourselves why the open biases and the hidden handicaps persist. Following the interesting studies, conducted mainly by women, we must realize that, even if in a couple both are employed outside, it is still the woman who has more work and more responsibility at home. We must ponder over the role models, over the values with which we are impregnated from childhood. We men in particular must proceed with a deep self-examination to discover the prejudices inherited for generations, their unsuspected weight, the extent to which they condition our behavior, often combining bad conduct with good conscience. Such a collective and lasting introspection is indispensable for the left. The massive presence of women is vital for a progressive movement not only because numerically they represent more than half of humankind, but also because their struggle, by its very nature, clashes fundamentally with the surrounding stratification. There can be no emancipation of women within a hierarchical society.

At this point, I can already hear the outcry: "You wretched levellers, harbingers of drab uniformity, with your political correctness—you are destroying the precious variation that gives life its color." The effrontery! We who are trying to bring about individual fulfillment in a collective context, who in keeping with the *Manifesto* of Marx and Engels are thinking of "an association in which the free development of each is the condition of the free development of all" are continually accused of stifling personality—by people for whom the expression of individualism is to be able to say: "To hell with you; I'm all right, Jack." Yet funnier still is the sight of the apologists of capitalism parading as arch-enemies of uniformity, simply forgetting what their cherished system has accomplished. Just visit Britain, the birthplace of the Industrial Revolution. You don't even have to go to where it all began. London will do, with its interminable rows of terrace houses, undistinguishable except for an occasional door painted a different color. The drab monotony of the surroundings and the dreary standardized life it implied was the basis for the one about a man who came home drunk one night, landing in the house next door; he only discovers his mistake in the morning when, together with the milk, he picks up the wrong paper, the *Daily Mirror* instead of the *Sun*.

But such conformity is not quite enough. At the threshold of the new millennium, the latter-day capitalists have much greater ambitions than their ancestors. They want to spread uniformity across the globe. Not just the eating of Big Macs and the drinking of Coca-Cola. With canned mass culture and information highways, they hope to do one better than Big Brother and control our dreams, not just our thoughts. Yet the apologists for this system dare to accuse anybody who questions its legitimacy, and particularly the new egalitarians, of trying to deprive the world of its diversity, its fantasy, its color. In fact, the last thing we want is to turn women into men, blacks into whites, or, in the name of family values, homosexuals into heterosexuals. Our aim is to create the material and social conditions that not only give meaning to people's work, but which enable them, by the same token, to seek the fulfillment of their desires and their dreams. There is only one thing that we want to eliminate: social injustice, the possibility of oppression or domination based on class, race, or gender. This we want to do thoroughly: not to diminish, reduce, or alleviate oppression, but to uproot it in the literal sense of the term.

Such a conception of equality and of a potential society of equals dictates a political conduct. It must also be clearly distinguished from versions that sound similar but are fundamentally different. Let us look once again, for instance, at the concept concealing much confusion, the oft-quoted slogan, "equality of opportunity." Depending on the interpretation, it can be simply meaningless, or it can imply a major social upheaval, "the world upside down." It is empty if it only suggests, say, that a student reaching university entrance examination should be judged fairly, like any other, or that young people starting work in a factory or an office should get the same treatment as their colleagues. Such non-discrimination on the grounds of class, sex, or color sounds fine. But considering the weight of the heritage in the full sense of the term—the influence of the environment, of which neighborhood you were born in, what school you attended, what sort of culture you absorbed at home, of your connections, of your ability to extend your studies or to wait for the right job—considering all that, to describe formal non-discrimination as equal opportunity requires either blindness or hypocrisy. For the opportunities to be really equal, all the handicaps, the biases, would have had to be eradicated. Those who speak of equality of opportunity in the present tense are thus implying that equality can exist through good intentions today, whereas we, the most eager advocates of the society of equals, know full well that in the best of cases it is very distant on the horizon.

Distant but not unattainable: this is why we must reject all the projects based on the opposite assumption. We cannot, for instance, take as a categorical imperative the precept provided by the philosopher John Rawls that inequality above the median is acceptable insofar as it helps to reduce inequality below the median.[12] Nor can we be satisfied with equity, a theme based on the premise, whether plainly stated or implicit, that inequality is the eternal rule and the most that can be done is to temper its effects. Of course, there is nothing wrong with reducing the effects of social injustice.

12. John Rawls, *A Theory of Justice* (Cambridge, MA: Harvard University Press, 1971).

It would be better if more children from working-class homes, more blacks, and more immigrants were admitted to the Ivy League colleges, to Oxbridge, or to France's *grandes écoles*. It would be better if more women got equal pay and fewer stayed at the bottom of their respective professions. Yet the "chosen" remain the exception to the rule. Even now, without any equality of opportunity, the kids from poor homes who are very good at passing exams do get a chance to compete. The ruling class absorbs some of the brightest . . . and some of the pushiest and the most servile. But their absorption in no way undermines the structure of inequality or prevents its reproduction.

Let there be no mistake. Even with a radical change of power and institutions, it would take a historical period to supersede the existing social division of labor on which inequality rests. In the meantime, especially as there is no radical change on the horizon, anything that can counter the injustices inherent in the system is welcome, and we are, therefore, firmly in favor of affirmative action. The have-nots have so many handicaps, the downtrodden so many drawbacks, that anything done to help them, to equalize their chances is, in the best of cases, partial compensation. The equality here lies, it goes without saying, not in the means employed but in the less unequal result. Our reservation is of a different nature: affirmative action is, or rather should be, only a provisional measure. In the long run we must deal with the causes, not the symptoms, of the disease. We must strike at the roots of inequality. The ultimate aim is a society of equals.

This conception of the future has immediate practical consequences, particularly in relation to social benefits. During the attack on the welfare state, launched in the 1980s and intensified in the 1990s, the argument was developed that, since the funds are limited, one should reserve them for the really needy. This should not be confused with affirmative action. It is one thing, say, to provide places in the university to students who, because of adverse circumstances, would not be able to get there otherwise; an attempt is thus being made to open up institutions to the socially disadvantaged. It is quite another to single people out, by some form of means-testing, as objects of assistance. Politically, it is much wiser to distribute, say, family allowances to everybody, rich and poor, and then get that money (and much more) back from the wealthy through progressive taxation. In general, social services have a chance to survive at a certain level if they are not limited to the needy.

If equality were the objective, social services such as health, education, housing, and pensions should be provided socially by national and local institutions. The best medical treatment, involving if necessary costly equipment, should be reserved to the most complicated cases requiring it, not to the patients with fat wallets. Similarly, the best teachers, or a greater number of educators, should be sent to deprived areas. This, evidently, is abstract theory. In practice, you have the public, the private, and the money that tends to turn everything into a two-tier system.

Actually, comprehensive social service on a national scale is a rather recent idea. While there were church and state schools before, it is only in the second half of the nineteenth century that you have, both in Western Europe and in America, a real drive for free public elementary education which, in some countries, would soon become compulsory. For free secondary schools you had to wait a little longer. The beginning of social services is usually traced back to the introduction of national insurance against sickness, disability, and old age in Germany in the 1880s by an Otto von Bismarck trying to counter the rise of Social Democracy. Though social insurance then spread to other countries and continued to expand in the interwar period—notably during the Popular Front in France and Roosevelt's New Deal in the United States—the idea of a social state ensuring its citizens against the risks and vicissitudes of life and enabling them to advance through education is really the product of the years of expansion and prosperity after the end of the last war. People emerged from that horrible conflict determined not to go back to the old ways, to the mass unemployment, the misery and the uncertainty of the 1930s. Everywhere it was being said that liberty, however valuable, was empty without social content, that the social compact must include the right to work and freedom from fear of social insecurity. The potential attraction of the Soviet model was an inducement for the Western establishment to make concessions. The long stretch of expansion and prosperity created a climate in which the labor unions were able to widen their claims. Working people got not only higher wages but also a greater degree of social protection, with insurance against sickness or injury and some guarantee against poverty in old age. In the United States, we saw, many of these social benefits were won by at the level of a company or an industry, whereas in Western Europe these conquests of the labor movement were translated by parliamentary assemblies into the law of the land.

If one adds to the general progress in living standards and social protection the extension of secondary and higher education, one understands better the mood described earlier, the prevailing impression that inequality mattered less, because somehow equality was becoming a fact of life. Radical critics picked holes in this presentation, insisting that, just because people entering production have a secondary instead of a primary education, it does not prevent them from being exploited; pointing out that the real differences in health, housing, and education remained huge; stressing, above all, that power relations in the workplace were fundamentally unchanged. Whatever the echo and impact of such criticism, the dominant feeling at the time was that we were moving inexorably towards a more equal society. This was the conviction that was first shaken and then shattered by the structural crisis that opened in the mid-1970s.

Not that social spending was immediately reduced. In fact, for quite a time, it had to keep on rising. Partly as a result of the progress of medicine, because of both its higher cost and the price of its success, which brought about the survival of a much larger elderly population. Partly because of the fast escalating number of the jobless, which had the double effect of increasing costs and reducing tax or insurance contributions. What altered rapidly was the attitude: the propaganda machine ceased seriously to pretend that the society aspired to be egalitarian. Since resources are scarce, it was now argued, social services should be confined, if possible, to the poverty-stricken, and more important still, they should be limited to the strict minimum. Naturally, such a strategy is restricted by political constraints. To deprive America's senior citizens at one blow of their social security, for instance, would be electorally suicidal. In Europe, to attack the welfare services boldly, as Juppé discovered, is dangerous. But it can be done gradually, surreptitiously, keeping in mind the new basic principle: that the public should always be cut and the private expanded. We have already gone quite a way in that direction. In the United States, for instance, "unemployment insurance provided a weaker safety net in the 1990s than in the 1970s."[13]

13. L. Mischel, J. Bernstein, and J. Schmitt, *The State of Working America 1996-97* (Armonk, N.Y.: M. E. Sharpe, 1997).

In Britain, the national health plan, with its long waiting lists for operations due to the lack of funds, is a mockery of what once looked like a bold social experiment. In most continental countries, the conditions of the long-term unemployed have worsened. One of the symbolic signs of this Americanization—in the worst sense of that term—is the strong pressure throughout continental Europe to encourage, notably through tax concessions, the development of private pension funds, prelude to a reduction (first relative and then absolute) of state pensions. The trend is unmistakable. Social protection, once presented as a solution, as a golden brick in capitalism's widening road toward a just society, is now being dismissed as an unbearable burden that all countries must rapidly and drastically unload to recover their dynamism.

Ideology, too, was refashioned. The right to work or to be insured against the vagaries of life ceased to be basic human rights to be enshrined in a constitution and, above all, to be expanded. Charity supplanted social protection. Stripped of its halo, welfare appeared as a latter-day version of the Poor Laws, a means to control and contain the "dangerous classes." And the mild reformers of yesteryear, who welcomed steps taken against social injustice, underwent a transformation. They were once ready to favor measures leading to a reduction of inequality, especially if these consolidated the consensus and, therefore, propped up the prevailing social order. Their attitude shifted altogether when the establishment began to argue that the expansion of the social services came into conflict with the system, threatening the profit motive and the very process of accumulation. Social rights suddenly lost their sanctity. They had to be subordinated to the superior interests of existing society.

What do real egalitarians say when told that social expenditure has to be reduced because the society just can't afford it? They answer plainly that in that case there is something fundamentally wrong with the system itself, and that what has to be changed is not the emphasis on human needs and rights but the very structure of society. This is the new dividing line which will not only reveal the true nature of the defenders of privilege, hitherto parading in pseudo-egalitarian clothing. It will force less hypocritical actors to make a choice, notably those advocates of a "non-profit sector" who are demanding a drastic reduction of working hours or a decent "social wage" not directly linked to a job, and who do so without raising their eyes beyond the capitalist horizon. Very rapidly they will have to realize that, while in periods of prosperity this society can make all sorts of concessions, their demands, if they are developed consistently, clash with the present logic of the system. Therefore, they must decide whether to lower their ambitions, or, on the contrary, drop their illusions about existing society. This is the sense in which the Western left, if it puts equality at the heart of its project, is making a crucial choice. To opt for full-fledged equality—naturally, not as an instant possibility but as a long term target, a real objective—implies a radical break with capitalism.

The incompatibility between equality and the private ownership of the instruments of production was obvious and well-known in the past. It is impossible to put a sign of parity between the employee and the employer, between the person who sells her or his labor and the person who buys it. This is the relationship between servant and master, even if it is concealed by the abstract screen of shareholding in a joint-stock company. What is new or, to be more accurate, what is now plain to see is that the elimination of private ownership of the means of production does not, on its own, get rid of inequality, does not give working people a mastery over their fate. This was shown in the rather superficial postwar nationalizations in Western Europe as well as in the much deeper expropriations carried out by the Russian Revolution and then exported throughout the Soviet bloc. The failure of social democracy and Stalinism, despite their rhetorical claims to foster equality, has undoubtedly helped the capitalist establishment to revive the cult of the private.

Seen from a distance of historical perspective, the fairly extensive nationalizations enacted after the last war in Britain, France, and Italy, and the second wave initiated by the left in France in 1981, look like attempts to save private enterprise by increasing its profitability. Entirely forgotten by now is the once-fashionable slogan about the conquest of the "commanding heights of the economy," which some people interpreted seriously as a way to dominate and gradually take over capitalist society. Naturally, nothing of the kind was ever attempted. Publicly owned basic industries, like coal and steel, and financial institutions were used to revive and relaunch the economy. It may be argued that, particularly in the second French attempt—which, coming late, went against the trend and did not last—efforts were made to build big national firms in, say, electronics, aircraft, or chemicals, capable of standing up to foreign competition. But nowhere were the nationalized industries used to challenge the capitalist mode of production or the role played within it by working people. Once the firms had been refinanced by public money into a profitable position, they were handed over to private enterprise. If necessary, the state kept the unprofitable side, like the distribution of mail, passing on the juicy side, like telecommunications, to private investors. With hindsight, it is more obvious that the whole operation fits well into the established rule that public debt should be the source of private profit.

The failure to turn the public sector into a genuine alternative undoubtedly weakened the opposition to the privatization drive, launched in Britain in the 1980s and then extended throughout Western Europe. Not that the campaign met no resistance. There was a great deal of talk about the sale of "family silver" at bargain-basement prices for the simple purpose of covering current expenses. There was, and there still is, in many parts of Western Europe, a feeling that whatever its defects, the public system—say, for the railways or telecommunications—is preferable, less committed to the imperative of serving the rich, than its actual or potential private successors. For the employees, in addition to this conviction, there is the job security provided by public service. Yet this is merely a material advantage which can be balanced by a bribe, the offer of some shares at a reduced price in their privatized company. There is no doubt that resistance would have been much stronger if employees had the impression they were defending a different way of life and the people in general had the feeling that the public sector presented the outline of another society. The propaganda machine of the various West European governments embarking on privatization was helped in its task by the low esteem of nationalization at the time, not unconnected with the collapse of the Soviet model.

In the Soviet Union, after all, no one could suspect that the whole operation had been designed to come to the rescue of capitalist enterprise. In 1917, the opposite had obviously been true. To understand what went wrong, we must rely once again on the crucial distinction stressed by István Mészáros between the rule of capitalism and the reign of capital. Capitalism in its classical form, which admittedly did not have as strong roots in Russia as it did in the West, was eradicated completely by the Revolution. The factory owners and bankers were expropriated without any compensation.

But the reign of capital, that of dead over living labor, of the machine over the human being, survived. While the method of extracting surplus labor changed altogether—from one dictated by economic mechanisms to a political one imposed by the machinery of the party and the police—the working people did not gain any control over the determination and the distribution of that surplus. The vertical, hierarchical division of labor went on, if anything, strengthened by the new mechanism of command from above. With no labor market and no fear of unemployment, other methods were used to maintain discipline on the shop floor and to impose it on peasants come to town. The workers were the masters of their factories only in official speeches, in the writings of teachers of "Marxism-Leninism," today converted to the Chicago School, and in the illusions of a dwindling band of foreign admirers. This system, based on a political extraction of the surplus which had nothing to do with socialist democracy, ran into increasing trouble as the economy grew. The last attempt to repair it by combining it with a capitalist market, Gorbachev's perestroika, was bound to fail, not only because of its inner contradiction. Those in positions of power and privilege, whom Gorbachev represented, wanted to go whole hog and consolidate their position by making the power and privilege transferable to their children. The workers were not going to fight to defend a system that was alien, that was not their own. They were not stupid enough to believe the weakening incantation about their being the ruling class of the Soviet Union.

The ideology of private property is triumphant today neither because people are especially fond of it nor even because the propaganda in its favor is so overwhelming. The campaign is successful because of a void, because of the Soviet bankruptcy and the social-democratic failure. Why fight for something else when it turns out that it is either roughly the same thing with another label or a different, though no lesser, form of exploitation? For social property to be attractive once again, it will have to be perceived as the means to an end, as an instrument enabling the "associated producers" to gain mastery over their work, over their social environment, and thus, in a sense, over their fate.

Honesty requires us to make it plain that this end will not be reached at once, that the society of equals will not be built overnight, if only for the simple reason that the old hierarchical division of labor cannot be eliminated by the stroke of a pen. The transition will have to take time, even if the progressive movement does not repeat its errors and does not abdicate its power to a party and its central committee, even if the working people try from the very start to gain a certain control over the way their factories or offices are run, even if they look beyond their factory gates to find out what is the social purpose of their output. This alone puts an enormous strain on the democratic imagination, because it will be necessary to invent methods of self-management not only in the unit of production, but also links at all levels, so as to extend *autogestion* to the country as a whole. And this is not all. For quite a period it will be indispensable to have some sort of national organization, a form of government, to prevent the threatening collapse of production, to speed up the end of class rule, to bring about equality between regions and races, branches and professions.

The abolition of the existing hierarchical division of labor will take time because it must involve a complete restructuring both of production and of its organization. To switch from an economy geared to exchange value, which does not care whether the product is needed as long as it can be sold, to one whose targets must be determined by social needs, will require a profound reappraisal of our own behavior. We shall not only have to dismantle an essential part of the present economy, the huge empire of commercial advertising and hidden or open persuasion, but also liberate ourselves from its impact, get rid of our conditioned reflexes. After years of distorted growth and artificial need creation, it will not be easy to discover what our individual tastes and preferences are or our collective values and priorities. It will be all the more difficult since we will not be seeking some lost spartan purity from the days of acute scarcity. We will be trying to discover, or even forge, our personality for the present, extricating it from the distortions of modern capitalist development.

This search will also involve a complete overhaul of production, both of its instruments and its organization, to fit an entirely new purpose, since the aim will no longer be to expand output, extract more surplus labor, and gain more profits, but to adapt production to human needs. The toolmakers, the writers of programs, will have to switch to a new mentality since their task will now be to subordinate the machinery to the human being and no longer to submit the human being to the machine. They will have to think how to render work less exhausting, more comfortable, and more interesting. They will have to think of the quality of the product, of its durability and not of built-in obsolescence. They will have to calculate in terms of cooperation, instead of competition, between various enterprises. All this, in turn, implies a new role for science in society—obviously not a rejection of scientific method but an important change in the field of research—and, inevitably, a wholesale reconfiguration of existing technology. It also implies a fundamental modification of the system of education. One could go on. Yet the most complicated part in this attack on the division of labor belongs to working people themselves, who are to be at once subjects and objects of this movement. They are to initiate the move, to be transformed by its operation, and, so transformed, to re-enter the process to take new initiatives. No wonder that the elimination of the hierarchical division of labor, like the "withering away" of the state, are changes that cannot be carried quickly by order from above. They actually go hand in hand, feed one another, and are together a crucial part of the transition to a different society.

Even if you do not think all this is a figment of my imagination, even if you accept that such a road exists and may be traveled successfully, you may still remain unconvinced. You may argue that in the society of equals, which the gradual suppression of the existing division of labor would foreshadow, there would be no room for genius, for talent, for distinction, and therefore no scope for poetry, for beauty, for the artistic creation. My answer would start like the one against accusations of uniformity. Since at each stage in the transition efforts will be made not only to render labor more varied and interesting but also to increase the time available for other activities, it will not be necessary to wait till Marx's communist society "to do one thing today and another tomorrow, to hunt in the morning, fish in the afternoon, rear cattle in the evening, criticise after dinner. . . ."[14] In less bucolic terms, it is possible much sooner to imagine people combining their activity as draftsmen, nurses, or accountants with that of sportsmen and singers, gardeners and painters, writers and critics for their own pleasure and society's satisfaction. With social time properly husbanded and reorganized, everybody should also get longer periods, sabbaticals, for distant travel, special study, or completion of some independent work.

14. See *The German Ideology* in Karl Marx and Frederick Engels, *Collected Works*, vol. 5 (London: Lawrence & Wishart, 1976), 47.

If in such a society, the general level of intellectual or artistic creativity would inevitably be much higher, this does not mean that the exceptional would vanish or cease to be appreciated. The genius for mathematics and abstraction, the extraordinary gift to make words jump off the page, the ability to draw images that grip our imagination, or a talent for composing music lifting us to a different world would flourish and be loved more than ever. The only thing that would change is the reward for such achievement. In our degrading conception, reducing everything to money as the lowest common denominator, the latter-day Shakespeares and Michelangelos, the Beethovens and Einsteins can only be "produced" or inspired by financial incentives. The assumption would be very different in a society with labor as we know it disappearing, with the socially necessary work carried out as a natural contribution. In that society, brilliant, successful performance would be a reward in itself. After all, by then we would be living in a society governed no longer by the maxim "unto whom that hath shall be given" but by the rule by which Marx summed up all the past aspirations of the egalitarians: "From each according to his ability, to each according to his needs."[15]

I hear the voice again: "It may all look splendid in your imagination at the end of the road, but on the way you can do plenty of damage. In your fervent quest for equality you will not only bring down the monument raised for Mammon which dominates our horizon, you may destroy the Statue of Liberty in the process." To this accusation, echoed in many versions, the obvious reply is that our purpose, on the contrary, is to put an end to the divorce between equality and freedom, a separation that has lasted for much too long, leading to the triumph of liberty with a hideous face. Indeed, only this reconciliation between the two can restore the image of freedom.

Of the three symbols put by the French Revolution on its banner during its ascending period, the third, fraternity, was a superb moral and international link, its essence expressed in the saying "all men are brothers" (which today should be translated as "all women and men are sisters and brothers"). The two other symbols, liberty and equality, though conceived at the same time, did not stay together for long. As soon as the revolution fully revealed its bourgeois nature, they clashed, liberty assuming as its main function the protection of private property: increasingly, the freedom

15. Marx, *Critique of the Gotha Program,* in ibid., vol. 2, 23.

to own and the freedom to exploit. Equality, during that time, preserved an official presence only on the etchings above the entranceways to French town halls, together with its two verbal companions. Otherwise, across Europe, egalitarianism became the rallying cry of those opposed to the established social order.

In a sense, it had been that from the start. Marx's famous slogan about ability and needs is very much an echo, a succinct reproduction of the ideas of Gracchus Babeuf and his companions who, in 1795-1796, argued that "equality must be measured by the capacity of the worker and the need of the consumer, not by the intensity of the labor and the quantity of things consumed."[16] The difference is that in the years they fought, the infancy of the bourgeois republic, they were too few and, therefore, too weak to matter; their struggle was known as the Conspiracy of Equals. Even eighty years later, when Marx coined his formula, the number of urban wage-earners in Europe was still too small to carry the day. By now, however, we, the would-be shapers of a radically different system, are no longer a conspiracy. We are the overwhelming majority, a vast potential movement which could start to build a society of equals from Naples to Newcastle today and from Seoul to Seattle soon after.

It should be clear by now that there can be no liberty without equality. It is idle to pretend that any Jane, Hans, Pierre, or Gianni are really free, when their fate is dependent on the financial moves of a Soros, or the production decisions of a Gates, when they are collectively brainwashed by the televisions and publications of Newhouse or Murdoch, of Bertelsmann or Berlusconi. The question is whether we can reconcile the two, whether we can move towards equality without trampling liberty in the process, whether we can invent organizations and institutions that will take us there and then ensure the freedom of the individual in a self-managing society. Thus, last but not least, we should confront the issue the left must face if it wants to regain mass popular support: how, after terrible experiences and bitter lessons, to reinvent democracy.

16. Philippe Buonarotti, *Conspiration de l'Egalité dite de Babeuf*, vol. 1 (Paris: Editions Sociales, 1957), 213.

11.

Reinventing Democracy

We have always revealed the hard kernel of social inequality and lack of freedom hidden under the sweet shell of formal equality and freedom—not in order to reject the latter but to spur the working class into not being satisfied with the shell, but rather, by conquering political power, to create socialist democracy to replace bourgeois democracy—not to eliminate democracy altogether.

Rosa Luxemburg,
The Russian Revolution

You delude yourself, dear angel, if you believe that King Louis-Philippe really reigns and he does not share your delusion. He knows, as we all do, that above the Charter stands the saint, the venerated, the solid, the lovable, the beautiful, the noble. the young, the all-powerful five franc piece.

Balzac, *Cousin Bette*

SOCIALIST DEMOCRACY can no longer be taken for granted. The horror of Soviet camps, the corpses of Kolyma and Vorkuta, have seen to that. While it is important to dissociate the two, it is also natural for people now to ask what kind of institutions will be provided and what freedoms guaranteed in the post-capitalist society. Thus, Soviet crimes cannot be ignored and in examining them we realize how the "liberty to know, to utter and to argue freely according to conscience," how all the freedoms we called "formal"—freedom of expression, assembly, organization—are precious and never more appreciated than when you are deprived of them.[1]

1. The phrase is from John Milton's *Aeropagitica* (1644).

235

And yet, however valuable, without social content, they are also empty, hollow, formal. We cannot be content with Western democracy as it is practiced, if we want the working people, once they have seized power, to keep it. They are bound to forge new instruments of democracy, both to keep that power and to carry out their own transformation in what will not be a "leap" but a long march, a long period of transition from the "realm of necessity" to the "realm of freedom."

Provided it is made in its historical context, our judgment on the crimes committed in the name of socialism must be ruthless. The trouble is that this story is being used by right-wingers for obvious political purposes—to frighten people, to warn them that any radical resistance, any serious search for change, is bound to end in a bloodbath. Take the latest blockbuster on the subject, *The Black Book of Communism,* which was a great success in France and Italy.[2] It may be doubted whether the very many people who bought this book as a result of a well-orchestrated campaign read all of its 846 pages. Yet what they and the general public certainly did get was the message: this was the greatest slaughter in history. One hundred million dead, claimed Stephane Courtois in his introductory chapter. "Eighty-five million victims" said the wrapper on my copy of the book. Then, after some criticism of the exaggeration, the figure on the wrapper went down, I think, to seventy million. No matter. Even a much lower figure, a fraction, would have been a horror. The purpose, however, was to strike the imagination and the significance was plain: capitalism, like it or not, provides you with a quiet place to live; communism, or any other attempt to radically alter this society, leads inexorably to mass murder.

Such obvious propaganda invites a reply, and not just about the scientific seriousness of adding or subtracting 30 million dead with the stroke of a pen. It prompts one to compile a black book of capitalism with its own list of victims. Without even going back to its origins, to the ruthless uprooting of peasants and the inhuman imposition of industrial discipline in the factories, just sticking to our terrible century with the slaughter of two world wars, the Holocaust, colonial oppression, mass massacres like those of

2. S. Courtois, N. Werth, and others, *Le Livre noir du communisme* (Paris: Robert Laffont, 1997). This is not the place to assess this very uneven piece of research, but the purpose of its chief editor, Stephane Courtois, and the political operation surrounding the book, was unmistakable.

Indonesia or more recently of Rwanda, you get a frightening number of dead. This piling up of corpses on the other side of the balance is, in a sense, necessary to convince people that, contrary to insidious and persistent suggestions, by sticking reluctantly to the capitalist regime they are not buying an insurance policy guaranteeing them peace and quiet.

Yet, if we were to leave it at that, we would be stooping to the silly level of Stalinist propaganda, as illustrated by the old joke about the American team of specialists visiting Ukrainian railways. When they dared to venture that, though the tracks looked fine, they had not seen any trains running on their five-day visit, they got the inevitable and damning reply: and what about the oppression of blacks in America? Actually, with such a balancing act we would be stooping lower still, since it has always been our belief that "capitalism was sweating blood and filth with every pore from head to toe," and not only at birth, whereas socialism—after an initial violence, whose necessity and degree really depended on the nature of capitalist resistance—was supposed to usher an entirely new era. This is why, while dissociating socialism from Stalin's crimes and stressing Soviet specificity, we must nevertheless draw lessons from that bitter experience. We must remember that if people are deprived of their liberties, for whatever seemingly valid reasons and for however allegedly short a period, it is terribly difficult for them to recover those freedoms. More generally, we must ask ourselves: what went wrong, why, and what sort of rules must be respected to prevent a repetition?

To this last part of the question, the most fashionable answer is Winston Churchill's famous quip: "Nobody pretends that democracy is perfect or full wise. Indeed, it has been said that democracy is the worst form of government except all those other forms that have been tried from time to time." But which democracy? The Athenian, with the direct participation of citizens and the exclusion not just of women and aliens but of the principal labor force, the slaves? Or the system prevailing in most Western countries, and which until this century was based on the ballot restricted to property owners? Or the democracy for males only, as it was practiced in the United States until 1920 and in France and Italy until after the Second World War? Or for whites only, as it was in fact limited in the southern states of the United States until the 1960s? The very extension of what is known as universal suffrage shows that democracy, too, can be filled with

new content. Indeed, Churchill modestly dropped an adjective in front of the name, though it is quite clear that what he was extolling above all other forms of government was bourgeois democracy, a system based on the strange premise that economic differences have no political relevance, and thus a system plainly designed to perpetuate the established economic order.

The trouble is that money does matter. Could one seriously imagine that social inequalities have no political consequences, that Messrs. Gates, Murdoch, or Soros have no more clout, are no more equal than their fellow citizens, that the mighty advertisers can sway customers but have no influence on the electorate? Money actually matters more than ever. If the Nazis had not degraded the term, we could describe our system as the government of the wealthy, as a plutocracy, but, since they have, we must call it plainly the reign of money. The rule, as Balzac reminds us, is not new nor is it specifically American, though it has been brought to perfection in the United States, where at least half the population does not take part in the electoral game, convinced that its vote does not count or, even if it did, that the result would in no way alter its fate.

The phenomenon is best perceived in the United States because there the reign of money is unashamed and unconcealed. If the business of America, as Calvin Coolidge put it, is business, its organs are openly discussing which party they should subsidize more because it better defends their interests, whether they should, for instance, switch some money from the Republicans to the Democrats, because the former, in wooing the religious right, show signs of disobedience, forgetting that profits from exports are more important than a ban on abortion. And what is true of party finances is also true of the campaign funds of individual candidates for the House or the Senate.[3] To object that industrialists and financiers are not the only ones to back politicians who further their cause, as labor unions do exactly the same, is to admit that we are functioning under a modern version of the property-qualified democracy, since one employer, industrial or financial, is equal here to umpteen employees.

3. Naturally, it is more complicated to find out who gets what, from whom, and for what reason. An excellent guide to this financial labyrinth of American politics is Thomas Ferguson, *The Golden Rule* (Chicago: University of Chicago Press, 1995).

What makes the American case so revealing is the decisive role that money clearly plays in the whole setup. In the way electoral campaigns are now run, TV advertising is paramount, and there is no ceiling on total expenses nor on the amount spent on television advertising. Thus, not only do people with a big private fortune, like a Steve Forbes or a Ross Perot, have an initial advantage in emerging as candidates, but in the later stages of the actual campaign, superior funds, whether party or private, can sway the verdict. The Americans may not be bribed as the Neapolitans were in the proverbial story by the candidate who handed out one shoe before the vote and the second after, once he got elected. But they are to a large extent conditioned by a costly TV campaign, notably by the better-funded candidate demolishing the character of the poorer opponent. Money talks in America, literally, and it has a constitutional right to do so, since the Supreme Court decided that to put a limit on what a rich person can spend on paid advertising would be interfering with his freedom of expression.[4]

True, western Europe has not traveled so far. In most countries, political advertising on television is forbidden. During electoral campaigns, parties are given TV time for political broadcasts according to standards varying from place to place. In many countries there are strict limits on political spending by the parties and in some the state helps their activity with subsidies, usually based on the proportion of the total vote they gathered in the previous election. And yet Europe, too, seems to be moving the American way. Because of the major role now played by television, electoral campaigns are not what they used to be. Gone are the gatherings in schoolyards or small halls, forgotten the propaganda carried from door to door, replaced by a few jamborees and the performances on the little screen. The parties, particularly the left-wing parties, are no longer what they used to be, either. The activists, who canvassed, distributed leaflets and papers, and glued posters are being gradually replaced by professional pollsters and specialists in public relations; the party of militants is purposely turned into an electoral machine. And all this costs money, if not to pay for TV advertising, then to organize glittery meetings, with celebrities and bands, to attract the attention of the media. Indeed, one of the

---

4. In *Buckley v Valeo* (1976), the Supreme Court decided that limits, notably on individuals' contributions to their own campaigns, were unconstitutional violations of the First Amendment's guarantee of free speech.

reasons given for the corruption scandals in the 1990s which decimated Italy's political establishment and then spread to France was the Americanization of European politics—its rising cost in the last fifteen years or so.[5] Admittedly, the novelty of corruption should not be exaggerated. In the early 1890s, for instance, France was deeply shaken by what came to be known as the Panama Canal scandal, in which an impressive number of politicians was involved. The difference is that money has now invaded all walks of life, penetrated all the pores of our society more than it had a century ago, and the domination of political life by financial power is, therefore, more intrusive, more profound, more absolute than it was.

In the circumstances, it is only natural that we should turn away from the model of government presented by Churchill, with false modesty, as less bad than any other, and opt for Rosa Luxemburg's more ambitious project: to transform the existing forms of democracy by filling them with economic substance and social content. There can probably be no better guide than this great internationalist, a woman born Jewish in Poland, having fought most of her political battles in Germany and treating socialism as her real home. Her fame as a revolutionary is undisputed. She gained it not only with her writings and her speeches. She paid for it with her life: on January 15, 1919, she had her skull smashed and was shot at point blank by thugs in uniform in the service of a Social-Democratic government. Her revolutionary activity, however, had always been coupled with a passion for democracy. This feature is well known to the general public because of the publicity given to her criticism of the Bolshevik leaders on this subject. Usually that is taken out of context. Luxemburg was not opposed to the Russian Revolution. On the contrary, she condemned Western Social Democrats, notably the Germans, for betraying their principles, and praised the Bolsheviks for saving the honor of socialism. She also knew under what terrible handicaps the latter were laboring. Nevertheless, she pleaded with

5. *Tangentopoli*—Bribesville, or City of Kickbacks—is the name given to the huge anti-corruption campaign launched in 1992 by the public prosecutors of Milan, which subsequently involved hundreds and hundreds of businessmen as well as politicians throughout the country; it brought about the collapse of the ruling Christian Democratic Party and its ally, the Socialist Party of Bettino Craxi. Seeing how little the economic and political balance of power in the country was affected by this tremendous scandal and purge, one is tempted to echo the words of Tomasi di Lampedusa in the Leopard: "If we want things to stay as they are, things will have to change."

Lenin and Trotsky that, if there was a way out, it led through more, not less, democracy. Nor was she using that term in the phony sense it was later to acquire in Stalinist propaganda. She was calling a spade a spade and saying plainly that "freedom is always and exclusively freedom for the one who thinks differently." She insisted that "without general elections, without unrestricted freedom of press and assembly, without a free struggle of opinion . . . only the bureaucracy remains as the active element."[6]

This, in fact, was not an entirely new conflict. Back in 1904, Luxemburg had already gone through a controversy with Lenin over the nature of party organization and the discipline within its ranks. Then already she had argued against a strict line imposed from above on an obedient party by an omniscient leadership and concluded that "historically, the errors committed by a truly revolutionary movement are infinitely more fruitful than the infallibility of the cleverest Central Committee."[7] Indeed, her attitude sprang from her general conception of the construction of socialism, a conception which, incidentally, the modern movement would do well to study. She saw the building of a socialist society as a long, drawn-out process based on the development of the political consciousness of the mass of the working people, a growing awareness they could only gain through their active participation in that transformation. Hence, her rejection, in both texts, of ready-made plans or formulae, of socialism conceived as a gift handed down to the rank and file marching to orders, and hence her oft-repeated preference for the "active, untrammeled, energetic political life of the broadest masses of the people" over "His Excellency the Central Committee."[8]

Her differences with Lenin should not allow anyone to push her to the other side of the fence. The way in which the social-democratic heirs of Friedrich Ebert and Gustav Noske—if not her direct executioners, the inspirers of her murderers—tried to appropriate her, very selectively, for the sake of anticommunist propaganda was, to put it mildly, indecent. To try to get her converted to Churchill's brand of democracy would be just

6. Rosa Luxemburg, *The Russian Revolution and Leninism or Marxism?* (Ann Arbor: University of Michigan Press, 1961), 69, 71.

7. The 1904 polemic with Lenin is included as the second essay in book mentioned in ibid.

8. Luxemburg, *Russian Revolution,* 62, 107.

absurd. If Luxemburg was in favor of free debate and assembly, she never believed in the parliamentary road to socialism. How could she, since she was convinced of the extra-legal nature of the bourgeois domination? Socialists could do useful work in parliament, in her opinion, if they were backed by a mighty extra-parliamentary movement. After all, at the turn of the century, Rosa Luxemburg had been the most active defender of the revolutionary orthodoxy of the German Social Democracy against the reformist "revisionism" of Eduard Bernstein. (How strange that sounds knowing the subsequent course of that party's history.) For her, democracy was a weapon in the vital struggle between labor and capital and also an instrument necessary for the construction of a socialist society. She was sure that hers was a superior form of democracy because it represented the interests of the vast majority of the working people against the vested interests of a minority of property owners and their subordinates. Indeed, to destroy the ridiculous idea of Rosa Luxemburg as a mild socialist reformer, it is enough to recall that for her, with all her emphasis on the spontaneous movement from below, socialist democracy was but another name given to the dictatorship of the proletariat. It is important to add that in the very paragraph in which she made that equation, she also stressed that socialist democracy is not something to be put off until doomsday, until "the promised land," until the economic foundations of socialism have been built, but that it must start "simultaneously with the beginnings of the destruction of class rule."[9]

Having clearly chosen Luxemburg's conception of democracy, whereas the average reader is probably more familiar, more at ease, with Churchill's vision, I owe that reader an explanation of my preference. When we come down to fundamentals in our discussion of democracy, beyond the freedoms and the guarantees, the idea that is probably central and that you certainly find highly attractive is the equality, however abstract, between individuals, as illustrated by the formula of one person, one vote. I am not trying to score points here once again, recalling that it was, in the past, one slaveowner or one white *man* of property, one vote. I am taking universal suffrage in its fullest version, which enables you and me every four or five years to elect a president, a parliamentary representative, and a local

9. Ibid., 77.

administration. I am not even questioning the weight of our vote or the influence of this whole exercise. I am simply suggesting that if you tried to apply the same democratic principle to where it matters to you most, that is to say to your workplace, you would be treated as crazy or subversive, a crank or a crypto-pinko. To say that the workplace is different because there the problem of competence arises is no reply, since nobody proposes a vote weighted in favor of the skilled and the learned. The much simpler reason is that beneath the surface of Churchillian democracy lies the real rule of our society: one share, one vote (to which may be added the corollary that small shareholders count for peanuts).

Despite persistent proclamations that any alternative is unthinkable, it is quite easy to imagine a radically different socialist society emerging after a long and problematical period of transition. It is the road that presents the real difficulties. Assuming the obstacles cleared on the way, the main features of the alternative are obvious. The epochal conflict between capital and labor having ended with the victory of the latter, the two protagonists have left the stage—capital, because it was defeated; labor, because it can only win by destroying all classes, including itself. In a classless society, where the division of work has become purely functional, the superfluous state has withered away. People having plenty of time at their disposal, all the instruments of production and communication having been converted from the reign of competition to that of cooperation, the organization of output and consumption is carried out with only human needs and respect for the environment in mind. In the circumstances, complexity of operations, once used as a bogey, has ceased to be a serious obstacle to democratic social control. On an international scale? Indeed, only at the world level can a full socialist society can be envisaged. Incidentally, it will not be as boring a world as you may think. Having got rid of ours, the citizens of that society will have their own contradictions and their own passionate debates, the subjects of which we can hardly imagine. All I would venture is that, while Freud might be still relevant, Marx will be relegated to the department of history or, rather, pre-history.

Come back to earth. Even allowing for the acceleration of that history, we are a huge distance away. Obviously, the real problem is not how that society will look but how we can get there, and do so by democratic means,

it goes without saying, since the advance in that direction is dependent on a movement from below growing in awareness as it proceeds. Let us imagine that the working people take over—hopefully without undue violence, though not by vote alone, because of the predictable resistance and, therefore, the need for extra-parliamentary pressure—say, in France or in Italy, and that the contagious movement then spreads to the bulk of western Europe, providing a sufficiently solid base for this experiment to last. What can be done to guarantee that it will not go the Soviet way and turn what was supposed to be socialist democracy into a dictatorship *over* the proletariat? True, in a sense, the experiment would start under incomparably more favorable auspices, in a country neither devastated by a world conflict nor, under our optimistic assumption, bled white by a civil war. Far from being dominated by semiliterate muzhiks, western Europe has a fairly sophisticated and educated working population so that, if some managerial or scientific staff decided to boycott or emigrate, there would be plenty of people to take their place. The advantage, however, should not be overstated. What is at stake is a passage from one integrated, coherent system, the capitalist one, to another with a completely different logic and coherence, a transition involving by its very nature the uprooting, the upheaval, the superseding of institutions, links and habits much more solidly ingrained in the advanced capitalism of Western Europe than they were in backward Russia.

Something has to be done from the start at the very bottom, where forms of direct democracy can be applied and particularly in the places where people work. In the factories and offices that will be socialized (I prefer that term, which implies the involvement of society, to nationalization, standing for the takeover by the state in the name of the nation), even if the principle of single command survives for quite a time, not only will the manager have to be elected or approved by the staff, but the latter must have an important say in the debates and decisions over such matters as the organization of production, the pace of work, its distribution, the pattern of pay; the working people should exercise control over production projects as well as the accounts. Only in this way will they feel from the very beginning that something is being done to destroy the despotism dominating the enterprise, that a new era has begun which should ultimately lead to a society in which expansion for the sake of extracting labor surplus is

no longer the rule and in which the human being, therefore, is no longer subordinated to the machine. The second part of their emancipation, the switch to a production entirely geared to human needs, will take more time. Even if they try at once to understand the purpose of their work, its social utility, and its insertion in a wider project, the conversion takes us beyond the gates of a single factory and beyond the confines of direct democracy.

Before we ponder the necessary instruments of such representation, we must ask why a society trying to change completely its regime does require a central authority, some form of a state? The usual answer is: to defend itself against the capitalist counteroffensive from without and from within. There is no doubt that any country attempting to break with the system would be subjected to a terrible attack, including flight of capital, trade restrictions, boycotts, and, possibly, more violent means. To stand up to such aggression, a newly socialist country would probably need, even more than central state power, a capacity to explain the situation, to mobilize the support of its own citizens, and, to speak across frontiers, above the head of government, to attract the population of its adversary. A second, related, and equally valid reply is: a central authority is required to preserve the coherence of production on a national scale, to prevent a collapse, a crisis, or economic disarray which would be seized to discredit or even bring down the new regime.

But there are other and more lasting imperatives imposing some central-ized structure of power. A state is needed to prepare the ground for its own dissolution, to reduce and then progressively eliminate the contradictions and antagonisms which rendered its existence indispensable. In other words, it would have to tackle private property, the differences between rich and poor regions, and the gaps in wages and salaries on a national scale. It would also have to overhaul entirely the institutions, the equipment, the millions of jobs connected with the preservation of the existing regime. The task looks immense, and its very importance raises the suspicion that the state, far from vanishing, might gain ground once again and, backed by a bloated bureaucracy, overshadow society. This danger can be averted only by the permanent vigilance of organs of popular power. On top of a vibrant base of direct democracy at the lowest level, that of the factory or the office, the commune or any other small local unit, one must build a system of

representation guaranteeing that, ultimately, power will always flow from below.

Naturally, there are no absolute rules prescribing what shape the institutions should take, what guarantees they should contain, and what electoral laws should apply. These will inevitably vary from continent to continent and from country to country, in keeping with different historical traditions, including the traditions of the labor movement. They will also depend on the manner in which the power was taken over. While nobody now really believes in instant revolution, a seizure of the Winter Palace after which everything moves in the right direction, the transfer of power can take more or less mild forms, varying with the degree of obstruction and resistance. In cases of relative continuity, the problem will be to put new wine into old bottles. Where there is a real break, it will be easier to innovate. In all cases, the newcomers will have to adapt institutions to fit their task: the reshaping of society.

Let us take, just as an example, the idea that one of the two organs of popular power, or if you prefer one of the two houses, should represent on the national scale the delegates from the workers' councils set up in all the places where people work throughout the country. This would have some advantages. The state is not really fit to run production directly. The working people, acting as "associated producers," are. But, for quite a time, they will require the services of a central planning institution to coordinate their cooperative efforts, to distribute supplies, and also to make calculated projections into the future. As production switches to the satisfaction of social needs, the role of the planning center may progressively change, but for a long period its targets will be at once debatable and imperative. The workers' councils should feel more at ease if this planning body is an integral part or a subordinate instrument of the assembly representing their interests. Naturally, there would be another house, elected on a territorial basis, dealing essentially with such matters as education, health, housing, and culture, as well as justice, order, defense and foreign affairs. The decisions agreed by the two houses would be carried out by an executive chosen from their ranks and responsible to both.

Some may object to one part of the electorate getting a double vote. Others will argue that it is better to have a single assembly, acting as the lawmaker and providing the executive, while using other means to ensure

the interests of the workers' councils. Whatever the choice—this is simply an example—the problem remains of preventing the elected assembly from being a parody of genuine representation, as most Western parliaments are, with a ballot every four or five years and no control in the interval over your so-called representative or deputy. The classical remedies against this distance and, therefore, the impotence of the electorate are well-known. They include the "imperative mandate" (party memberships instructing their delegates' votes) and the right of recall. The usual objection is that a representative should be a woman or man of conscience, not the slave of a party. This is not really the point. Say the woman in question was elected on a platform; if she changes her mind or if a new issue arises on which she disagrees with the party that has put her up, there should be a possibility of dissolution and by-election, giving the electorate the last word. Another method is the rotation of representatives; it would necessitate in most countries a change in the electoral law, allowing one to vote for a list and not a single candidate. For some, this method has the disadvantage of not allowing the representative enough time to learn his trade properly. For others, this is actually an asset, since the delegate does not become a specialist divorced from the people. Another way of narrowing the gap is to keep his or her salary to the level prevailing in their constituencies. A regime in transition to socialism should be doing this in any case, as part of its general leveling of remuneration.

A government guiding such a transition should use all these means and others, too, to keep the representation as close to the people as possible. In its panoply it could include a new method, known as subsidiarity, a neologism invented in European negotiations. The dictionary defines it as "the principle that a central authority should have a subsidiary function, performing only those tasks which cannot be performed effectively at a more immediate or local level." In eurojargon this is just a gimmick enabling euroskeptics to oppose the transfer of powers to Brussels. In a society in transition, trying to reshape its institutions and its habits by a vast movement from below and fearing to be overwhelmed by too mighty a state, it could be a most useful principle. With cooperative production being organized to satisfy human needs, quite a lot could be done at the local or regional level, reducing bureaucracy and avoiding the costs of transportation. This is even more so for welfare and other social services, a field in

which the national institutions are often perceived as distant and inhuman. In cultural activity, too, there is plenty of scope for regional initiative.

Quite a lot can be done, though clearly not everything, which brings us back to the need for some form of state power during the period of transition. The most obvious examples were already mentioned. Planning for the economy as a whole must, by definition, be done on the national scale, and it is idle to expect—except in spells of enthusiasm that do not last—regional assemblies to vote for the shift of their resources to less favored areas. But the transition to a radically different society is a much deeper change, involving a total transformation of innumerable jobs, of the organization of production as well as of its instruments, and, as a result, a modification of mentalities. Let us start with the simplest example, the production of arms. A transitional regime may have to preserve it for a time because of the danger of encirclement and intervention, but it should opt out of the international arms trade at once and not prevaricate, hiding behind arguments about the loss of jobs.[10] Much more complex and all-embracing is the problem of advertising. The new society will need some people to inform the general public of the qualities and defects, the advantages and the drawbacks, of various products. It will have no use for the services of the army of persuaders now busy convincing us that we love one and not the other of two identical toothpastes; that only this magic cream will give us eternal youth; and that life will be infinitely more fulfilling with this latest model of a car or that brand of computer. Yet, if you take advertising out, you subtract much more than its share in the national income. The whole pattern of production and consumption would be upset and would then have to be reshaped beyond recognition. Besides, the present structure of such key branches as the media, sports, and entertainment would simply collapse.

Take the example, say, of pharmaceutical research. It would be good in the new society, too, to have many teams of scientists working, occasionally covering an identical field. The big difference—profit no longer being the driving force—is that their competition would turn into cooperation. Once the discovery was made, the result would be passed on. No need for lawyers

---

10. A left-wing government using such an argument invites the obvious reply that Colombian peasants growing coca must also earn a living and they are in an incomparably more miserable position than Westerners working in arms manufacture.

fighting over patents, no need for secrecy and industrial equivalents of James Bond. Actually, the whole of research would change its nature—basic research gradually, as a result of the shift in objectives and funds, and applied research immediately, because of an entirely new purpose. At present, the aim is the production of commodities with a brand name, a short life cycle coupled with a rapid rate of innovation. Waste is built into the system. In the new society, the objective will be the output of useful and lasting products based on human needs, not profit. The emphasis will be on quality and on the careful, economical use of both human and natural resources.

If research will undergo a conversion rather than a reduction of employment—the number of scientists should actually increase—the world of finance, on the other hand, which has been in the forefront of expansion in recent years, would see its ranks dwindle. As the transition proceeds, there will be a rapidly declining need for hedge or mutual funds, for merchant or investment banks, for commodity or stock exchanges, for the now growing number of people involved in the collection of small savings and the distribution of large profits, for the big army in the service of speculation. Not that all their minds should be wasted. Those who used their wits and their gift for juggling numbers to invent all sorts of derivatives and to help speculators dealing across the globe could also use their talents, say, to assist producer cooperatives in their relations with one another and with the central authority, thus contributing to the improvement of democratic planning.

More generally, the specialists in electronics and information—and not just the wizards among them—could, by inventing the appropriate robots and by producing the necessary programs, help to eliminate a great deal of monotonous work and to subordinate the machine to the human being. For that, however, they would have to take sides and decide that their role was not to make the rich get richer, but to enable the ordinary people, including themselves, to become masters of their fate. Thus, though millions of jobs would disappear in the early years of the transition, the atmosphere would not be one of gloom, like the one surrounding our own downsizing. Indeed, it would probably be the nearest thing to a joyful "creative destruction." The gradual disappearance of jobs connected with the old society would give scope for the provision of others linked with the new, in an

increasingly lifelong education system, in the reformed and decentralized social services, in urban planning going well beyond the elimination of slums, in the reinvention and spread of popular culture, in environmental reclamation. All this, and a significant increase in the free time at people's disposal. What is the purpose of changing society, if not to change people's lives?

This very brief survey of some of the transformations this transition of society would imply confirms what might have been expected, namely that you cannot carry out a genuine perestroika, a real restructuring, without a profound upheaval and a re-evaluation bound to raise apprehension, which will inevitably be exploited by those with vested interests to defend. The lesson to draw is that such a transition can only be carried out by an effective government resting on solid democratic institutions. Why should it be more dependent on democratic backing than our governments are? Because in all Western countries today the institutions fit neatly into a system they are designed to perpetuate. They are linked, to use the fashionable word, with a civil society resting on the principle of private property. The big property owners, a shorthand here for the main beneficiaries of the system, stay in power even when the parties they back lose office. This does not mean that elections do not matter. They are important, marginally. They do not alter the rules of the game or the nature of the regime. The economic mechanism has a life of its own. This, incidentally, is the great political advantage the Western regimes had over the Soviet one. Unlike Stalin and his successors, the American president, the British or French prime minister, did not have to drive the people to the factories and impose the pace of work. The capitalist economy performs that task ruthlessly on its own, asking simply for a favorable legal framework. This automatic economic compulsion provides scope for a great deal of political freedom, especially since any measures clashing with the logic of the capitalist economy naturally provoke a strong resistance and reaction of the system. It is only in a situation of deep crisis, with people refusing to play according to the established rules and clamoring for a change of regime that we shall see whether our system, when rejected, is willing to leave the stage in democratic fashion.

A government of transition to a different society, which can only be born in such circumstances, will have to function against much tougher odds. By definition, it will not be able to fit into existing institutions and run

things as they are, since its appointed role is to alter them radically. It will have to struggle not only against the resistance of capitalists, but also against the logic of the existing system, the force of habit, the power of inertia. It has been said, wisely, that it is easier to "expropriate the expropriators" than to get rid of their heritage, easier, that is, to take over the factories than to abolish the old methods of work and the solidly entrenched hierarchical command structures.[11] In a nutshell, the job of the movement and of its government is to seize state power, change its institutions so as to be able to get on with the work, and then start at once the dismantling of the foundations on which its power as a state would rest. This task of "permanent revolution"—if such a dramatic term may be applied to a lengthy process including retreats as well as advances and periods of consolidation in between—can only be carried out with the sustained support of a popular movement, which raises the complicated and difficult question of the political consciousness of such a mass movement.

To consider it properly, we must spell out some of the unwritten assumptions of our argument. The first is that the progressive forces, using that loose term purposely, which have gained power through the vote, strikes, and mass demonstrations, a combination indispensable to break the resistance—that these forces represent at the time the majority in their country. In other words, that the extent of discontent with unemployment, with social injustice, with the absense of perspective and the absurdity of life, is such that the majority of the people find the whole system intolerable and decide to get rid of it. The second and closely connected assumption is that this victory is achieved by a wide coalition. At its heart is the working class in the very broad definition we have given to it—a heterogenous formation stretching from frustrated professionals to the growing mass of the precarious. Together with this working class, you have the "movements," whose members are often themselves working people, but who have their own agenda they consider crucial, like women, people of color, and environmentalists.

The problem is not only that the various groups may react differently as the transition proceeds. It is that the political awareness within each group will alter, and not always at the same rhythm. The industrial workers, for

11. See István Mészáros, *Beyond Capital* (New York: Monthly Review Press, 1995), 792.

instance, will not enter this process with perfect awareness of where they are heading. It is only as they run their factories and meet new difficulties that they may gradually grasp which kind of society they have to forge. But will the evolution of mentalities be coherent, and will it keep pace with the change in conditions? This matters because of the third unwritten assumption, namely, that if some brand of socialism is to emerge at the end of the transition, it can only be achieved by people consciously and rationally gaining control over their society. With such a conception in mind, it is simply useless to cheat or bribe yourself into office.

How will the unity of the coalition be preserved and the political consciousness developed to match the pace of events? Who will help the movement to make projects for the future while also acting as the guardian of its memory? Who will keep up with it when it suddenly leaps forward, but also help it resist the urge to pack up and run when it has to retreat? Clearly we cannot avoid the issue of organization—call it party or movement—that the social forces need to assist them in this process of transition.

However awkward, the discussion on organization has two advantages. Since nobody now envisages the revolution as a neat, sudden break between two worlds, the organization needed for the period of transition does not have to be very different from the one required to conquer power or, to put it otherwise, the instrument of the present should somehow prefigure, foreshadow the future. Hence, the second advantage: relative realism. Though we had good reason to examine problems connected with the transition to a different society, readers may be forgiven if they think that such speculation is a pure flight of fancy. Reflection on the kind of party that could win power may also be dismissed as a case of highly wishful thinking, but at least it is one belonging to the real world.

The only certainty is that none of the established parties can serve as a model, not even the big left-wing formations of Western Europe, which by now tend to look more and more like the American Democratic Party. Loosening their organic links with the trade unions, opting for passive supporters rather than political activists, they, too, are being turned into smooth, efficient machines for winning elections, preferably parliamentary or presidential. Since the reign of capitalism will not be ended by parliamentary battles alone and the shape of society changed with the exclusive help of faithful, obedient voters, such parties are not of much use if the aim

is to alter the human condition. On reflection, the big social-democratic parties ceased to be the instruments of real change long ago, when the interests of the labor movement channelled through the trade unions were subordinated to those of the parliamentary party. At first it was not obvious. Now we are dealing with a caricature, parties whose practice flaunts residual rhetoric about defending the interests of the working people or being active agents of social change. In most cases, like Britain's New Labour, they have even stopped pretending.

The electoral party discarded, the potential social forces might be fitted into a vast coalition of social movements, with at its center the largest of them all, the labor movement. It would figure at the core not only because of its size or its crucial role in the process of production. It would do so also as a potential driving force toward a classless society. Individually, workers may now have much more to lose than their chains, but as a class of people deprived of the means of production they have fundamentally the same interest as ever in the uprooting of the system. To use Marx's image, in the historical struggle between labor and capital, the former, which is to say living labor, can only defeat the latter, its dead embodiment, by destroying all classes, including itself. It can only win by putting an end to the reign of capital.

There is a long way from that abstraction to the concrete conduct of the really existing trade unions. They are numerically less representative than ever, probably more corporatist than they were, and certainly more reluctant to indulge in any political activity likely to threaten existing institutions. And yet, if they do not wish the downward curve to become fatal, they will have to become more political. Not in the sense of making deals and backing electoral candidates, but in the broader one of having a vision of the role labor can and must play within a fast-changing society. When faced with transnational corporations, with global capital, the unions cannot fight back only factory by factory, or even sector by sector; they must have a national and international strategy.[12] Similarly, if a good part of your would-be members are the unemployed, as in Europe, or the working poor, as in America, or if they are in precarious jobs with limited social benefits, you cannot even assume that you will be the representative of a "labor aristocracy," since the latter's privileges, too, are potentially threatened. An

12. For problems facing the labor unions and their limited action, see Kim Moody, *Workers in a Lean World* (London: Verso, 1997).

organization must have some unity even if it defends varying interests. Besides, some of the expanding groups—technicians, researchers, programmers—may actually be less interested in money than in control over their work. Altogether, unions launching an ambitious platform, egalitarian but also insisting on new powers on the shop floor and in the office, are likely to gain much more among the mass of the working people than they would lose amid some sections of more privileged members.

I called the role for labor *central,* not unequal. Labor should not just impose its views and its strategy on other social movements within the coalition. It is tempting to imagine what would have happened if in the last hundred years the Western left, the socialist movement, the trade unions had had a different policy, if they had from the start put women's equality near the top of their agenda, if they had fought tooth and nail against any example of racial discrimination, if they had thought, not a century ago but much earlier than they have, about the consequences of uncontrolled growth for life on this planet. Probably we would still have had feminism, some form of black power, and an ecological movement, but they would have originated and developed within the labor movement. The Western left, however, has failed to fulfill its task and the labor movement must now deal with women, ecology, gay liberation, and other social movements as outsiders. Thus, it is important that it should henceforth treat them as equals. It is together that they must elaborate their projects and see how they can be combined, how the struggle for the emancipation of labor can be linked with that of women's liberation, how discrimination should not only be uprooted but compensated for, how all development must take into account the impact on the environment. Or, to put it in more general terms, they must see how the struggle against inequality, social injustice, and hierarchical structures can unite them in action around a common project. If the social movements thus manage to cooperate in democratic fashion within the coalition, it should not only help them to win power. It should be a good omen for the future, for that phase of the transition when the working people will take over the factories and offices.

It looks splendid on paper, it will be objected, but in real life things seem to be going the opposite way: the power of the unions is dwindling, there is little collaboration between the various social movements, and a common

project for reshaping society is to be seen nowhere on the horizon. This undeniable contrast between the desirable and the actual leads us to a third solution, which we may call the stopgap organization or the provisional party, performing on a smaller scale what the broad coalition is still unable to do on the wide stage. It should regroup the most militant and politically most conscious activists from the labor unions and all other social movements. Deeply immersed in their own constituencies, they should know their moods and be able to judge how far they can be carried at a given stage. Within this provisional party, they should take up the tasks that we have put on the agenda of the ideal coalition. They should compare their experiences, integrate their activities, and elaborate common projects. They should show how popular aspirations clash with existing institutions, suggest that the citadels of power are not as solid as they look and thus lead the broad movement out of the prison bearing on its gates the paralyzing slogan: "there is no alternative."

But are we not smuggling here through the back door our old friend, the "vanguard party"? Not at all. First, this is not to be a close-knit organization of professional revolutionaries who, driven to fight underground, accept an iron discipline. On the contrary, its attraction should lie in the openness of its debate in the search for new solutions. The second difference follows: it would not have blueprints, ready-made plans to be imposed from above on orders from "His Excellency the Central Committee." Its ambition would be to help the social forces find their own voice, to encourage the development of the political consciousness of the broad mass of the people. Indeed, a party might not be the most accurate name for such an organization. But if it is not a battalion of disciplined revolutionaries, will it not go the way of all social-democratic flesh and succumb to the attractions of electoralism? In principle, it should not. Even if it puts up candidates for elections—either directly or because some of its members represent their own constituencies—the primary purpose would be to use the electoral campaign as a good occasion for mass propaganda, which it still is in the bulk of Western Europe, and then to use parliament as a permanent platform, though that pulpit, in this age of television, is no longer what it used to be. Yet what lends specificity to this concept of a provisional party is this very function of filling a gap. It does not want to absorb the social movement, as some parties clearly do; it hopes to be absorbed by it. As

soon as the masses really enter into motion, it wants to be overtaken, though, naturally, not swallowed, by the movement. It is eager to cede its place to a broader coalition by then ready to fulfill its historical task.

Party or movement, whatever the form of organization, they must still cope with one issue, the dilemma that has faced all socialist parties and, really, all movements not resigned to run the world as it is. The problem is that they must struggle within the rugged reality of existing society and provide solutions that, sooner or later, lead beyond the confines of that society. If they limit themselves to the questions connected with the future, as we have done in the bulk of this chapter, they will find themselves miles ahead of the movement in splendid sectarian isolation. Yet, if they become bogged down in daily battles and ignore the future, they will forget that their original purpose was to reshape society in order to alter the fate of working people. Judging by precedents, they will thus gradually move through three stages—first as critics, then as reformers, and finally as pillars of the established order. The real question, which we shall examine in the concluding chapter, is how to reconcile the two, how to defend the interests of working people within the existing society and build up this struggle into a general offensive challenging the very foundations of the system.

At this point our still-skeptical reader may again raise objections. Is it at all realistic to talk about the search for a radically different society, considering the balance of forces and the political climate prevailing in the Western world? In the United States, as the saying goes, there is one party in two reincarnations and everything is being done, by law and otherwise, to prevent a third one from disturbing the consensus. The labor unions, while somewhat less subservient than they were in the recent past, are not even dreaming of challenging the established order. Yet, even if you take France, the Western country where the prospects look least gloomy, what do you get? A government of the so-called plural left, headed by Lionel Jospin, dominated by the Socialists, including also Communists and Greens. True, it is less enthusiastic than its British or Italian counterparts in carrying out the Americanization of Europe. In its struggle against unemployment, it even ventures some nonconformist policies like the legally imposed thirty-five-hour working week. But none of its plans,

projects, policies, or actions look beyond the capitalist horizon. This applies equally to the proposals of the Socialists' junior partners.

Actually, the French situation is more complex than this summary suggests. Since the winter of discontent of 1995, the mood of the country has changed. The *pensée unique*, we saw, is no longer so dominant. More intellectuals dare to question its rule. Books criticizing the reign of money and that of the establishment, notably in the media, have a great success. The "left of the left," that is, the left not satisfied with the moderate policies of the ruling coalition, is showing progress, even electorally—which poses problems for the Communist Party particularly.[13] If these dissenting ideas crystallize and develop, they will find an echo within trade unions, old and new, among Communists or Greens, and even among the Socialist rank and file. Indeed, France could provide scope for the "provisional party" of radical change.

And yet what a huge gap exists between these early stirrings and a real challenge. Thus, we must still deal with a final question: is it really utopian to think in terms of a radically different society, to treat capitalism not as an eternity, but as a historical phase with a distant beginning and a possibly proximate end?

13. In local elections of March 1998, Trotskyist candidates suddenly got nearly 5 percent of the vote. The reason for Communist difficulties is obvious. In a counter-reformist period the question is whether there is really room for one moderately reformist party. But for two—Socialist and Communist?

12.

Realistic Utopia

Be realistic, demand the impossible.

French slogan, May 1968

THIS SURREALIST-SOUNDING SLOGAN could serve once again as the message for the confrontations at this turn of the millennium. For the rebel students and the striking workers of 1968, it was not interpreted as a form of escapism—like "take your dreams for reality," its companion on the walls of Paris—or of tilting at windmills, but as a call to action against the established order. Actually, the watchword is more topical today, because in the intervening years the establishment has managed to convince many people that there is nothing beyond the capitalist horizon and, therefore, that you can do no more than tinker with the system. To the successful sermons that to change society is unthinkable, inconceivable, and unattainable, the only realistic reply is to demand what they describe as impossible. But that will, in turn, invite damnation with what is by now apparently the worst condemnation: *utopian,* a word pronounced as if it were soaked with all the blood of the gulag.

Of course, associating utopia with totalitarianism is itself a distortion. Whatever the crimes of the Soviet leaders, let us repeat, they were not inspired by utopia. Stalin did not dream of an egalitarian society, of the abolition of the hierarchical division of labor or of the withering away of the state. Neither Brezhnev nor Chernenko aspired to spread the self-government of "associated producers" across the planet. The obvious absurdity of such suggestions reveals the crooked purpose behind the slander. If utopianism is to be sentenced, it should not be by such artificial tricks of guilt through association.

Realistic Utopia

Utopia, says the Oxford dictionary, means *nowhere,* from the Greek *ou,* not, and *topos,* place. The term originated with a book describing an imaginary island with a perfect political and social system. Naturally, the habit of contrasting our wretched condition with an imaginary ideal was not born in 1516, the date of publication of Sir Thomas More's *Utopia.* The genre can be traced back to Plato's *Republic.* It was practiced by celebrated authors like Francis Bacon, Tommaso Campanella, Edward Bellamy, and William Morris. In the nineteenth century it included such socialist visionaries as Fourier, Leroux, and Owen, and in the twentieth, stretching somewhat the definition, the dystopias, like Aldous Huxley's *Brave New World* and George Orwell's *1984.* A vast and fascinating literature emerged that we have neither the space nor the need to study here, any more than we need to feel obliged to revisit all of the Marxist criticism of utopianism on the grounds that it is based on the projections of an imaginary ideal and not on real-life struggles and contradictions.[1] We have no need to do so, because utopia is taken here in the very limited sense mentioned above: if any attempt to change society, and not just mend it, is branded angrily and contemptuously as utopian, then, turning the insult into a badge of honor, we must proudly proclaim that we are all utopians.

We must do so because the double lesson we can can draw from this last part of the book is that in the struggle for human emancipation all the elements are closely connected and that, once combined, they take us inevitably beyond the confines of the existing order. The attempt to gain control over the labor process leads inescapably to the question of the internationalization of production and finance. The search for equality, which cannot proceed without attacking the hierarchical division of labor, in turn puts the invention of new forms of democracy on the agenda. All the struggles are linked. Each one has its importance, yet it is as parts of a bigger whole that they acquire a new meaning, their fully subversive significance. Indeed, if the establishment now looks so solid, despite the circumstances, and if the labor movement or the broader left are so crippled, so paralyzed, it is because of the failure to offer a radical alternative.

1. See the well-known books of Karl Mannheim, *Ideology and Utopia* (London: Routledge and Kegan Paul, 1936) and Herbert Marcuse, *Five Lectures: Psychoanalysis, Politics, and Utopia* (Boston: Beacon, 1970). Among the interesting recent French work on the subject, there are the writings of Miguel Abensour, Bronislaw Baczko, Michael Löwy, and Henri Maler.

Whose Millennium?

In the absense of such a vision, the different protests, the various movements, however dynamic, soon meet their limit. This makes sense. If you accept, as almost every political party now seems to do, that the only form of development is through the profitable expansion of private enterprise, at some point your demands for higher wages, shorter hours, and a different form of organization of labor, or for sustainability, or for genuine equality for women, will clash with the logic of the established order. You then have to oppose the system (which you are politically unprepared to do) or yield. Today's political and social battles, if one may use so strong a term, can be compared to an exercise in formal logic. Everything seems perfectly coherent as long as you do not bother about the premises. Indeed, the basic principle of the game is that you question neither the fundamentals of the argument nor the foundations of society. Only a global alternative, breaking with these rules of resignation and surrender, can give the movement of emancipation genuine scope.

So as not to give an appearance that the choice is the apocalyptic one between all or nothing, this statement requires several qualifications. One springs naturally from the adjective *realistic*. For the utopia to be realistic, the political project, far from promising the moon, must be based on the potentialities of the existing society. Not that the potential would become reality without a radical break. But the ingredients for the new must already exist in the old society. Another way of saying the same thing is that the project must be rooted in current struggles. The ideal clearly would be for industrial workers and technicians, for women and ecologists, having discovered through their activity that their objectives cannot be attained within existing society, to be compelled to look beyond its frontiers.

The second qualification is to reject the idea of "instant revolution" and to keep in mind the impressive distance between the ultimate goal and the present position. The hope that one day the frontier between labor and leisure may vanish does not mean that we can already now reduce dramatically the amount of socially necessary labor. The idea that socialism is by its very nature universal does not imply that all revolutions will take place simultaneously, any more than the aim of determining production and consumption by social needs should be interpreted as meaning that the market can be dispensed with overnight. Nonetheless, we should never lose

sight of the distant objective in the daily struggles, with their compromises and concessions. The third qualification concerns unity. The radical alternative can only be effective if it is global and comprehensive. But the individual struggles and movements must preserve their autonomy. Their unity is not to be imposed from above. It must be achieved from below through the recognition of common interests and the elaboration of a joint strategy.

All these reservations are signs of a problem, and there is no denying that there are at least apparent contradictions in our attitude. On the one hand, we are arguing that, because of painful precedents, people will no longer buy pie in the sky. They may rebel, explode, and break out in anger, but quite understandably they will not join a long-term movement of social transformation, one that used to be called hegemonic, unless they know where it is heading and how it is proposed to get there. They may even require guarantees about the democratic nature of the journey. On the other hand, we are pleading against detailed blueprints, against full-fledged models imposed from above. To say that the movement simply needs a vision of a different society and a few signposts along the road, however, is not quite sufficient. The "negation of the negation," the projected elimination of the fundamental features of the capitalist system, is not enough. The movement may very well have to produce a fairly complex set of proposals, provided they are elaborated in democratic fashion and not treated as a sacred text, but as a draft, a provisional guide, which will be amended, improved, and broadened as the movement advances, drawing lessons from its struggles and gaining in political consciousness.

All these difficulties and apparent contradictions spring from the dilemma facing any movement that struggles within a social framework and provides solutions that cannot be contained within that framework. How do you preserve continuity between the vision and the daily routine without embarking on quixotic ventures or betraying your basic principles? Back in the 1960s, when Europe admittedly knew almost no unemployment and grew at an average rate of 5 percent, a strategy was evolved to deal with this dilemma. In Italy, where it originated, it was known as the strategy of "structural reforms." In France it got the ambiguous title "revolutionary reformism," and it is under this new name that it then traveled around the

world.[2] The strategy was, in a sense, already then an adaptation to a fast-changing world. The labor movement could not stand still and simply wait for the day of the great confrontation. It had to make counter-proposals. Each one of them was to act as the thin edge of the wedge so that one series of demands should lead inexorably to the next. For the most radical exponents, each position conquered was merely a place for recruitment and a base for new offensives. In this way, they hoped to carry the movement to the frontiers of capitalism and beyond.

As its ambiguous name suggests, the strategy was also open to much more moderate interpretations, which finally prevailed. Some of its theoreticians who at the time were thinking about how to get rid of capitalism now cannot even contemplate the idea of questioning capital's reign. Rather than criticizing individuals, it is preferable to attack an institution. Take the CFDT, the ex-Catholic labor union which we saw, under the leadership of Nicole Notat, as a pillar of the establishment during the French winter of discontent of 1995. The position of that union had been very different during the great upheaval of 1968. At that time it was the French Communist Party and the labor union it dominated, the CGT, which revealed the emptiness of their revolutionary proclamations. When the big social movement was really set into motion, rather than helping it to go as far as it could, they desperately put on the brakes. The CFDT, then toying with the ideas of "revolutionary reformism," got on much better with the radical students and those striking workers who saw in the exceptional circumstances an opportunity to gain more than a hefty rise in wages. In fairness to Notat, it must be added that she is not responsible for the conversion. The Western structural crisis that culminated in the mid-1970s rendered the ambiguous position untenable.[3] Forced to choose, the leadership of the CFDT opted for plain reformism and then, as the scope for concessions dwindled, for the counterreformist management of capitalist society.

And yet there is something in this strategy of radical counterproposals, designed to promote action and develop consciousness stage by stage until

2. The book of André Gorz, *Le Socialisme difficile* (Paris: Seuil, 1967) introduced this term and the subject to a wider public.

3. On the ambiguity of the CFDT and the doubts about its conduct already in 1968, see Daniel Singer, *Prelude to Revolution* (New York: Hill & Wang, 1970), 99-101.

the movement is driven to confront the logic of the system, that is worth considering. Despite the depth of popular discontent and anxiety today, the number of people convinced that their own vital problems can be solved by reshaping society is very limited. Indeed, it is smaller than it was, say, thirty years ago. People will not be remobilized simply by being shown the bright image of a different society and by being showered with arguments, however convincing. They must learn in action, through bitter experience, that their hopes and aspirations cannot be fulfilled within the framework of our society.

Obviously, the platform planks cannot be the same as in the 1960s. Though the questions raised at the time—notably about the nature and purpose of growth—are now more relevant than ever, our context is very different. At the time, women's liberation was in its infancy, ecology had not yet made its impact on the progressive movement, and the economic situation was not at all the same: mass unemployment, precariousness, and the attack on the welfare state were not the main issues the movement had to face. And in Western Europe there was not the same need then to invent policies for the region as a whole. European counterplans today would have to articulate ideas for how to ensure full employment; to reduce the workday sharply; to equalize incomes through a substantial increase of wages and an increase in the taxes on the rich; to reform democratically, not cut down, the health service and other institutions of social benefit. If such and similar plans were produced, and if attempts were then made to implement them, both the drafters and the movement as a whole would find out fairly rapidly that their conflict was not just with neoliberalism or any other version, but with the capitalist system as such. Because of precedents, this would still leave one unanswered question: what forms of organization, of control from below, are needed to prevent the leaders from misguiding the movement once again, from shifting it from "revolutionary reformism" to submission and surrender?

We have already perceived a lot of obstacles on our way to a realistic utopia, though we have not yet gone very far. In particular, we have not crossed the crucial ideological front. Here, we shall see, our task is tremendous, and so is the inevitable resistance, because of the dominant ideological position of the ruling class. There are moments when its power looks irresistible.

Faced with such odds, it will be argued, we cannot afford to disperse our forces and should present a united front in what is the real *kulturkampf* of our times, the conflict over the very nature of our society, which is now made to seem outside of history, immutable, and unchangeable.

The ideological task is indeed immense, because we have gone so far backwards that sometimes one has the impression of starting all over from scratch. It took the workers quite a time after the Industrial Revolution to grasp that their fellows in the factory were allies, not rivals, and that their employer was no benefactor. It took longer to realize that they had common interests with workers in other factories or trades and common conflicts with the employers. It took longer still to extend this elementary class consciousness to the national, let alone international, level. Now that solidarity has suffered a setback, as it is hammered home all the time that their condition, their job, and their survival are dependent on the profitability of their firm (however dubious that proposition, since the firms doing best on the stock market are those that ruthlessly downsize), and as efforts are made to eliminate industry-wide or national contracts and to tie gains, whenever possible, to individual performance. It has become difficult to unite people working in the public sector with those in the private sector, those still enjoying relative job security and decent fringe benefits with those in precarious employment or simply out of a job.

The kind of solidarity linked to the conviction that through joint action you can not only defend but also improve your paycheck, your working conditions, or your benefits was once fairly prevalent throughout the Western world. But there was also a higher form of consciousness—rare in Anglo-Saxon countries and more frequent in, say, France or Italy— which rested on the belief that you can go even further, that through collective action you can alter the very circumstances of your life by changing society. It is this second version of solidarity that must now be revived and spread, because that is the one that could help in the unification of the working class and simultaneously prepare the ground for its alliance with other social movements. That kind of consciousness is also necessary to resist the current offensive against working people based on the unquestioned assumption that private property, capitalist accumulation, the extraction of labor surplus, and the search for profits are natural facts of life, and that the triumph of the market, national or global, is beneficial, or at least

inescapable. The last thing the establishment wants is to have these unwritten premises critically examined, especially in broad daylight in front of a vast public.

In assessing the power of the establishment and the sway of its ideology, the material incentives at its disposal should not be neglected. Jobs, grants, careers, and promotions are obviously much easier to get if you are a defender of the established order, or somebody who takes it for granted, than if you are its open critic. The reluctance to tolerate dissidents increases with the size of the audience or readership. It does not do too much harm to discuss certain matters in a small magazine with a restricted public. When *The Economist* in the 1960s had a circulation of less than one hundred thousand, it was the bourgeoisie talking to itself and it could talk quite frankly. Now that it sells more than six hundred thousand copies, its ideology has not changed, but it has to be an instrument of propaganda to a greater degree than it once was. Likewise, there must be more control, say, in mass television than in the academic world. Yet, even in the universities, particularly in the social sciences, it is easier to get an appointment, tenure, or a research grant if you are studying how to make the system work rather than critically examining the workings of the system—contrary to neoconservative laments about the "adversarial culture" promulgated by academics.

The problem is not, however, merely one of bribing and crass ambition. It would be much simpler if it were. The difficulty is that the ruling ideology is like the air we breathe, and most of the time we are unaware of its existence. Take my favorite example. In Paris, where I live, it is customary for newscasters on television to talk about a meeting "between social partners." They mean negotiations between representatives of the employers and the labor unions, and everybody finds the phrase perfectly normal. Now, imagine for a second that the newscaster were to speak about a meeting "between class adversaries." There would be an outcry: violent accusations of ideological bias. Now, both definitions are ideological. The first assumes that the relationship between labor and capital is a partnership, the second that it is a conflict. But the former is part of the ruling ideology and, therefore, does not raise an eyebrow; the latter, as it questions that ideology, is shocking—and would no doubt be the one *tagged* as ideological.

Whose Millennium?

As a rule, it is easier to fit in than opt out, to accept the established than to dissent, especially when everything is done to make the existing order look natural and any attempt to escape it unthinkable or harmful. We are living in a society where production is dictated by monetary power, not by social need. Many enticements encourage an inventor to produce, say, a mechanism allowing the simultaneous price quotation on all the stock exchanges, facilitating the purchase of shares across the globe; or a commodity that combines novelty with a short life span; or a piece of equipment, for factory or office, that forces its user to maintain high productivity despite permanent stress. The inventor will find less encouragement to create a program helping cooperatives to collaborate as part of democratic planning; or a product whose main quality is that it can last a long time and is adaptable; or a machine designed to treat its user as a human being and not a provider of profit. Today inventors are not even supposed to think in such terms, and it is the role of the social sciences to explain that this is none of their business.

Actually, there is nothing fundamentally original in this domination or in the refusal of a regime to admit that it might not be eternal. What is new is the size of the ideological machinery and its impact across the world. Profitability has now penetrated all the pores of our society. Television, with its twin commands of ratings and advertising, has invaded our lives more than did press and radio before it. The same commercial culture is now to be found all over the globe. Even when new potentially liberating spaces are invented, like the Internet, they are rapidly harnessed by the magnates of communications for profitable purposes. How can one resist the pressure of such a juggernaut? To some extent, the question is rhetorical. To criticize the system in the Western world, while it may involve sacrifices, does not require the heroism it took to be an oppositionist in the Soviet Union under Stalin, or even the courage needed to be a dissident under his successors. And, after all, there is plenty of room for action.

Two contrasting pitfalls, however, must be avoided. One is the illusion that, because a radical managed to appear on the little screen or be heard on the radio, because critical articles found their way into the mainstream press, because a progressive publication increased its circulation, or because nonconformist professors gained a foothold in some universities, the reign of the ruling ideology is seriously threatened. Our regimes have quite

a lot of room for manoeuver and it will take much more to undermine their effective control. But the opposite and much greater danger is the prospect of inaction resulting from a feeling of impotence. Since capitalism can put up with quite a lot and the establishment would not allow dissent to become *really* disruptive, what's the use? Matters are not so simple. Once the situation gets out of hand, it is not so easy to regain control. Besides, the real threat to the system comes from its own contradictions. The task of dissenting intellectuals is, to the best of their capacities, to help the discontented people discover the real cause of their discontent and the reasons why they cannot find satisfaction within existing institutions. Every occasion and opportunity must be seized, every available platform, newspaper column, and Website must be used to disturb the routine and counter the relentless propaganda chorus of the establishment—without illusion, but with persistence and determination.

It is a great pity that some potential forces of protest are, sometimes unwittingly, giving a hand to the other side. It is in this context that we must look at what is loosely called postmodernism, so fashionable in the United States. For some people on the left, it is a dangerous French flu that has beset American campuses. Actually, the phenomenon is much more complicated than that. In its subversive activity of deconstruction, it often does harm to the establishment. After all, if you will permit me a bit of license, deconstruction is what socialism did best in its heyday—revealing the real interests beneath the deceptive surface. Marx could be presented as the most ambitious of all deconstructionists, since he spent his life trying to show the real workings of our capitalist system hidden by the appearances described by vulgar economy and idealist philosophy, while Gramsci's dictum that "truth is revolutionary" could figure at the top of many an essay in deconstruction. But the question is not one of the order of precedence. In disclosing racial or gender biases (they are clearly less concerned with class), deconstructionists undermine the dominant ideology and, hence, the rule of the establishment. I see no harm, either, if "metanarratives," including the socialist one, are submitted to close scrutiny. Any Marxism worthy of the name will test views against changing reality and frequently examine its most basic premises.

The snag is that in their attacks against the "grand narratives," the postmodernists do not limit themselves to the content. It is the very idea of a coherent and comprehensive alternative that they reject. They do not lament that the various social movements are divided and fragmented. They make a virtue of fragmentation. They accept as their own the thesis, so precious for the establishment, that *total* is *totalitarian,* that to try to unify the different discontents, to rally them together around a project of social transformation, is not only absurd but dangerous. Thus, having weakened the system through deconstruction, they prop it up and the rescue operation is, alas, incomparably more important than the demolition job, because capitalism has proved time and again that it can absorb, or at least cope with, all sorts of sporadic, separate, divided protest movements, however solid, serious, and powerful they be. Those who today, while under the ideological influence of postmodernity, are doing useful work will ultimately have to choose which side they are on, particularly when the movement gathers momentum again on the campuses and beyond.

For the real cultural conflict of our time is between those who believe that you can change our society and those who think that, at best, you can only hope to make changes within that society. Or, to be more accurate, that is the cultural war to come, since the dividing line will only emerge clearly as the struggle proceeds. For some time to come, the radicals and the mild reformers will find themselves on the same side of the divide against not so much the upholders of the status quo as the champions of social regression. After all, even in countries with the most radical traditions, like Italy or France, the number of people who think in terms of a radical transformation of society is today very limited. It is only in specific battles—over employment, wages, and workplace power, over ecological disasters provoked by uncontrolled growth, against racism and for the protection of immigrant labor, over abortion and the rights of gays and lesbians, in the defense of social benefits against the global offensive—that the real cleavages will appear between those for whom capitalism is a product of history to be discarded, as was feudalism its predecessor, and others who, when it comes to a choice, will cling to the established order.

Intellectuals can help in this process of clarification as the movement tries to forge its project, to glimpse the vision of an alternative society. Obviously, not as the keepers or prophets of some revealed truth but, within their capacities, as providers of historical memory, of foreign comparisons, of technical or scientific knowledge, and, importantly, as active participants in a democratic construction. The French strikes and demonstrations of 1995 as well as the subtle modification of the intellectual climate that followed those events were a reminder that when social forces are set into motion, the intellectuals stir. Thus awakened, they can in turn help the social movement and, in the ascending phase, the two can, hopefully, educate one another.

Finally, we must still deal with the argument the ideologists for the establishment use, when all else has failed, to prove that our project to reshape society is foolishly and bloodily utopian, not realistically so: namely, that it rests on an overoptimistic assessment of human nature, on a Rousseau-inspired conception of the "noble savage" spoiled by civilization. The paradox is that the concept of human nature as such does not figure in our reasoning, but it is at the heart of the ideas of our fiercest critics. From the undoubted fact that our commercial soil is not particularly propitious for the proliferation of saints, they have drawn the extreme conclusion that greed is the mainspring of human action. For your private conscience or consolation, you can have religion, charity, and other solutions, but money is the only mechanism for social relations, and greed is its human engine. Forget that and you will bring the economy, and with it social life, to a standstill. Our social scientists, if you strip their discourse of its mathematical models and its verbiage, have raised the logic of capitalism to the metaphysical stature of human nature.

We, on the contrary, look at people and society in a historical perspective. They are neither saints nor sinners, neither noble savages nor greedy monsters. They are the product of circumstances, but also, within the limits set by their physical and social conditions, products of their own action. The "associated producers," on whom we rely to forge a different kind of society, will not be proletarian heroes, red knights in shining armor, with a purity and political consciousness out of hagiographic tales. They will be ordinary people, like you and me, with all our quirks and imperfections, our habits conditioned by the world we live in, our tastes distorted by television and advertising. As these ordinary people search to gain control over their work and their fate, they will begin to reshape society, they will be affected in the process, and, so transformed, will resume their task. In this mutual reaction, in this advance of step by step and stage by stage, lies both the difficulty and the grandeur of the project.

It is hardly necessary at this stage to restate the reasons people have to wish to change this world radically. Each day brings some new ones, particularly if you bother to look below the surface. As I am writing these lines, France is just emerging from a bout of collective euphoria. Millions of people celebrated in Paris and the provinces as if they had just stormed the Bastille. The reason for this extraordinary rejoicing was the victory of the French soccer team in the World Cup. The media, which had helped greatly to whip up this mood, then hailed the celebration—even more than the victory—as a sign of national unity, nay, as a symbol of resurrection. There was one good thing about this rather crazy inference. The French team was very multiracial, and the triumphant tricolor, on this occasion, was white, black, and *beur* (the slang term for children born to North Africans in France). The team's tremendous popularity silenced the xeno-phobic Le Pen for a spell and did strengthen the conception of France as a multiethnic nation.

But there was another side to this story. Sports now serve as a distraction for millions and are, therefore, very big business. You learn on such an occasion that ten-year-old Pakistani girls get thirty cents for stitching a soccer ball. The Pakistani kids, if they work long hours, make $1.50 a day at best, while quality balls sell in London retail shops for $95.[4] The transnational corporations selling sportswear and equipment make billions, and this jamboree of the world's most popular game, with its huge televi-sion audience, was for them a golden opportunity.[5] Unkind souls even suggest that the final was not really between the French and the Brazilians, who had forgotten how to samba, but between their respective sponsors— Adidas, the German-controlled transnational, and America's even mightier Nike—for a bigger share of the sports market, for the right to exploit more kids and adults in Pakistan, Indonesia, and beyond. One cannot help wondering how lonely people are, how they are yearning for a common

4. Rob Hughes, *International Herald Tribune,* 11-12 July 1998.

5. The final round was watched by 20.6 million French people. The world audience for the whole tournament is put at the staggering figure of nearly forty billion people. *Le Monde,* TV supplement, 19-20 July 1998.

rejoicing, that a commercial operation succeeds in sending them into such a frenzy. True, *panem et circenses*, bread and circuses, is no modern invention. Yet this is just another example of our extraordinary capacity to commercialize and debase anything: sport, dance, art, literature, private relations, love, and passion. We are one better than King Midas, who could turn into gold anything he touched. We can turn sentiments into money, feelings into finance. No wonder that one is often ready to echo Baudelaire's anguished cry, "anywhere out of this world."[6]

But we do not want to escape anywhere, into fiction, into some *paradis artificiels*. We want to change the world and, therefore, we must ponder why people now have less confidence in the possibility of moving beyond the reign of capital than their ancestors did more than 150 years ago, when Marx and Engels wrote *The Communist Manifesto,* or simply at the beginning of this century, before the Bolshevik Revolution. Two connected webs of explanation have been suggested in this book, woven around the declining popular belief in the inevitability of socialism and the unexpected resilience of capitalism.

We quite rightly deny that socialism ever existed in Eastern Europe and refuse to accept Stalin's crimes as part of an alleged socialist record. But 1917 is a date in our heritage and we must draw lessons from what happened after. Things that used to be taken for granted must now be scrutinized and often rejected. It was vaguely assumed—though, admittedly, never said plainly—that once the revolution occurred, there would be a more or less smooth, more or less inexorable advance towards a socialist future. We now know that even if forces seeking a socialist solution were to take power in the advanced countries of Western Europe, the transition would be a lengthy period, far from smooth, full of difficulties and of risks, including not just reversals but possible restorations.

The surprising longevity of capitalism has two causes. One is that it has taken much longer than Marx thought for the reign of capital to stretch across the world and to eliminate precapitalist forms in the conquered territory; passages in *The Communist Manifesto* about foreign expansion read as if they were written today about globalization. Naturally, capitalism

---

6. The title, in English in the original, says "Anywhere out of the world," but the ending, in French, says *this* world, *ce monde.* Baudelaire, *Oeuvres,* vol. I (Paris: Pleiade-NRF, 1935), 487-89.

does not have to invade the whole planet and mop up every nook and cranny before it makes its exit from the historical stage. It can and should be removed long before. Nevertheless, this room for expansion did help, and still does to some extent, in the process of survival. The second cause lies in the system's underestimated capacity for what we called distorted growth, spurred by the creation of artificial needs and the declining rate of utilization. Advertising and obsolescence, as somebody has remarked, are more sophisticated ways of destroying value than was coffee burning.

One of the great attractions of Marxism was its subtle association of economic necessity and political will: the capitalist system seemed historically condemned, the objective development of the productive forces was aggravating its contradictions, but it would only fall under the subjective pressure and the blows of the revolutionary labor movement. This could take the form of a very fatalistic version which may be summed up in terms closer to Calvin than Marx: you are predestined for paradise, but you will get there only if you deserve it through your own action or obedience. Before the First World War, under the Second International, the theory was reduced to a very mechanistic interpretation, the productive forces more or less doing it on their own, with the help of an expectant but passive movement. Then, under the Soviet Union and particularly in Stalin's hands, the whole combination was broken into pieces. There was no need for democratic pressure from below, because economic development was going to bring the stage of communism to Russia. At the same time, all sorts of shortcuts were possible, since in 1936, at the height of the purges, it was proclaimed that the Soviet Union had achieved the penultimate phase, that it was already a socialist society, with communism on the horizon. To top it all, iron discipline was required from Soviet citizens and from the obedient foreign faithful so that the USSR could reach its historical destination. We know what happened to this unholy mixture of religious belief and barrack-room discipline.

If we want to recover the dialectical link between the movement and its objective, we must draw clear distinctions between actuality, necessity, and inevitability. Socialism may be a historical *possibility,* or even *necessary* to eliminate the evils of capitalism, but this does not mean that it will *inevitably* take its place. This departure from the fatalistic conception is, in a sense, a return to the more distant past, when socialism was not considered as bound to happen, since there was always the possibility, to quote the terms of Rosa Luxemburg, that barbarism would win out. Above all, uncertainty as to the ultimate result should not imply passivity, obedience, or resignation. On the contrary, it dictates greater participation, more activity, and more militancy since, within the limits of objective conditions, the future will be what we shall make it. And this renewed conviction and activism would be particularly welcome today, because the power of the ruling class and the arrogance of its ideologues is largely due to our weakness, to our surrender, to our acceptance of the established rules of the game.

There is nothing discouraging in shedding illusions and dropping certainties which paralyzed the critical spirit and, by the same token, the capacity for independent action. And indeed, if it were not for the time factor, which we shall see darkens the horizon, I would not be unduly pessimistic about the future. In this book I have concentrated on the Western world and particularly on Western Europe, anticipating that it may be the place where the next opportunity will arise. But this is guesswork, not a scientific forecast. The world is full of surprises and, as the rising of the Zapatistas in the Chiapas or the first strikes in South Korea show, not all surprises are unpleasant ones. Above all, everything now has to be seen in its international context and the times clearly are a-changing once more. Without reverting to catastrophic predictions of capitalism's impending doom, it is legitimate to notice the growing gravity of the economic crisis and its implications.

Within a year, the famous Asian tigers have disappeared as an economic species. In Thailand, Indonesia, South Korea, and elsewhere unemployment has risen dramatically, living standards have tumbled, and poverty has spread, as a growing number of factories and banks faced bankruptcy. Japan, at the heart of the regional upheaval, keeps on exercising a downward pressure and China, its foreign trade deeply affected, will sooner or later have to react. The crisis can no longer be described as purely Asian, which it never really was. The Russian default on August 17, 1998, the ensuing fall of the ruble, and the repercussions in Latin America underscored its international nature. The Western powers, particularly the United States, were using this occasion, with the help of the IMF, to remove obstacles and strengthen their position in Asia. But at the same time, they seemed to be losing control over what looked like a classical capitalist crisis of overproduction aggravated by uncontrolled movements of capital. The immediate effects on the labor movement were on the surface paradoxical. The militant South Korean unions, while showing their fighting spirit, were thrown on the defensive, and their budding Indonesian counterparts may have difficulty harnessing the rage of the jobless and nearly starving millions into an organized assault on the regime propped up by the army after the departure of Suharto. But declining economic stability will have political consequences both in Asia and throughout the world. The assertive self-confidence of the establishment's propagandists has foundations as solid as the shares rising to unprecedented heights on Western stock markets did.

The other cause for cautious optimism is that the world now has the material and intellectual means to cope with the issues that must be solved. Not that we can take over the modern infrastructure and all, put another label on it, and proclaim that we are living in a different society. A slogan describing socialism as, say, "information highways plus soviets" would be a crude misinterpretation. The organization of work, the tools, and, ultimately, the people themselves will have to be altered throughout a long period of transformation. Nor are we hankering after a paradise lost or ascetic purity. While the romantic reaction against the horrors of capitalism has inspired very valuable criticism, we cannot seek solutions looking backwards. Not all contemporary needs, even those artificially created, are superfluous. To go back to the poverty and the scarcity of the past would be to return to another ghastly society that should not be idealized in retrospect. We have the level of education, the potential knowledge, to cope with a transition to a new society, without reversion to scarcity or uncritical reliance on existing instruments.

At the stage of development we have reached, the world is crying out for some kind of an international governance. We need it to rethink the purpose of growth, exercise control over development, and decide rationally and carefully what chemicals can be used or biological changes tolerated, if we want to avoid ecological disasters. We require coordination to deal with international crimes, but also to fight disease effectively on a global scale. If planned international cooperation were to replace our present combination of overproduction and underconsumption, we could fairly rapidly cut unemployment, eliminate starvation, and reduce poverty worldwide. Indeed, with the knowledge at our disposal, work for all and a basic decent living standard could be an obtainable goal. The maddening thing is that it is both so near and so far. While we could start working on this objective at once, we will never get there if we stick to the established order. The gap between the existing and the possible, the contrast between our fantastic technological ability and the absurdity of our social organization—though there is capitalist logic to this madness—are such that one is inclined to hope that in the not too distant future we shall be forced to change course.

Sooner, or later? We need time. Time to get rid of the clever lessons distilled from the Soviet tragedy by the establishment and to revive the basic belief in the possibility and value of collective action. Time to re-establish closer links across frontiers, not in order to set up a new International with commanding headquarters and obedient members, but to exchange information and experiences, and then gradually coordinate tactics and strategy. Time also for labor and other social movements to get together, here again not to describe in every detail the future utopia, but to agree on the broad features of the world towards which they are striving—a society not clashing with its ecological limits, not driven by capitalist accumulation, putting use value above exchange value, free from racial and gender discrimination, democratic and organized from below. We can argue over its shape and even its name, though I personally would call it socialist. It goes without saying that disagreement over details would not rule out common quests and joint action, quite the contrary.

Time indispensable, alas, runs up against time available. Ecologists tell us that we are already doing things that in the long run will affect the whole planet and the species itself. But they are not speaking of geological time. They give us stern warnings about our society's difficulties with nature in the near future. If we do not exercise control over an economic expansion driven inexorably by the search for profit, or if we limit that control to measures tolerated by the system (such as the purchase of pollution quotas by the rich countries from the poor), we shall pay a price already in the first century of the new millennium. Depletion of natural resources is not the most serious risk. The greatest danger is the impact of expanding production and waste on ecosystems. The massive introduction of all sorts of chemicals, untested for their long-term effects, threatens our soil, our atmosphere, and our health. The virtual disappearance of certain other species should be a sign it is time to worry about human fate and study more carefully, say, the increase of carbon dioxide in the atmosphere or the possible effects of global warming. True, views vary as to the size of the danger and its timing. However, considering the impact of development on the environment in the last fifty years, qualitatively different from the past, it is perturbing to think of the consequences were it allowed to proceed in roughly the same way for another century. If we do not get rid of a social system which can only deal with the symptoms but not the cause of the problem, the expansion imposed by capital accumulation, we are preparing for ourselves and our children unenviable tomorrows.

Yet there is an even more immediate danger, which is political. Like nature, politics abhors the void. If the left fails to provide rational, progressive solutions to the growing economic and social traumas, the extreme right will come up with reactionary and irrational ones, playing on the fears aroused by globalization and on prejudices reinforced by apprehension. Hatred of the other, the different, and the alien, spurred by racism, jingoism, or religious fanaticism can lead to major tragedies. The genocide of the Tutsis in Rwanda was an extreme example. The dismantlement of Yugoslavia revealed what a combination of exacerbated nationalism and religious bigotry can still achieve today in the heart of "civilized" Europe: you start with kith and kin, or symbols of faith, you move on to the historical recollection of battles between Christians and Moslems, and you end with the slaughter of neighbors, the rape of women, and buckets and buckets of blood.

The ghosts of Europe's terrible past are embodied in Jean-Marie Le Pen. He and his xenophobic National Front took off in the early 1980s thanks to the economic crisis and the popular disenchantment with the French left, which came into office "to change life" and rapidly took on the conservative policies of its predecessors. Le Pen consolidated his position as unemployment rose and as deflationary policy made European integration seem to many people not an opportunity but a threat to their way of life. The political consensus on economic policy enabled Le Pen to appear as the only outsider, offering scapegoats instead of solutions: immigrant workers, sinister Moslems, invading aliens. And this foreigner-bashing has gained him fellow travelers elsewhere in Europe, particularly in Belgium and Austria. Naturally, the immediate threat should not be exaggerated. Short of economic catastrophe, the extreme right is unlikely to take over anywhere in western Europe. Still, that nearly one French voter out of six is now ready to cast his or her ballot for a leader for whom—and he stresses the point—the Holocaust is no more than a "detail" in the history of the Second World War: this fact is a sign that the evil ghosts of the past have not yet been laid to rest.

It is this sense of urgency combined with potential promise, of time running out, which may have set the tone of this book, admittedly conceived from the start as a call to action. It may be easy to dismiss accusations that those who refuse to be the prisoners of the existing society are dangerous and unrealistic utopians, but there is no use denying that this book, in addition to providing objective analysis, contains its share of the subjective—of political commitment, and even a form of Pascalian wager.

Put at its crudest, that bet is the assumption that when there is a need there is a way, or, to say the same thing in more elaborate fashion, history both sets problems and provides at the same time the elements of possible solutions. This should not be reduced to caricature, to the clumsy proclamation that capitalism, together with its contradictions, will automatically generate a proletariat fully armed with political consciousness, which will take us triumphantly to a joyful future. There is no promise that a social transformation will happen in the near future, no guarantee for that matter that it will happen at all. Historical maturity, political awareness, and plenty of other factors affect the forecast and its realization. Still, our society contains the elements of its *potential* transformation, and in this interaction of the existing and the possible—a possibility perceived realistically, but lying beyond the confines of our society—lies the burden of our responsibility and the mainspring of political action.[7]

Another bet is the unwritten postulate that people prefer to shape fate than to be its playthings. Here, risking the accusation of bringing through the back door the just-discarded "human nature," we should compare our

7. Naturally, one can also, with honor, fight losing battles, like the Communards did in 1871 or Luxemburg and Liebknecht in 1919, but they are usually seen as part of a bigger conflict, as defeats leading to ultimate victory.

views with those of our opponents. Our accusers, the defenders of the established order, do not only argue that human beings are driven by narrow self-interest. Echoing the words of the Grand Inquisitor in Dostoyevsky's *Brothers Karamazov,* they claim that people are frightened of freedom, that they want to be led like a herd, to obey and not to challenge. Our premise, on the contrary, is that human beings want to shape their lives, that they want to be actors in their own drama. One could argue that history itself, with a different class playing the crucial role in different periods, is really the story of humankind's struggle for mastery over its own fate. I would not go so far as to describe history as linear progress. Running through this book is the simpler idea that, within the existing structures and their class formations, burdened by their inheritance and conditioned reflexes, the people, women and men, make their own history and are, within those limits, responsible for their action.

I venture to add a personal thought, prompted by the contrast between historical time and the time of our lives. The rough half century that has elapsed since Stalin's death in 1953, or the close to a third of a century that has passed since those heady days of 1968, when young people from Berkeley to Tokyo prematurely proclaimed that imagination was seizing power, these are in the eyes of a true historian relatively short periods. In our own lives, however, they correspond to the passage of many of us from adolescence to old age, or to middle age. In moments of weariness and despondency, one tends to wonder what is the use of the struggle if one is not going to see the outcome. There is consolation in the thought that "revolution is the only form of 'war' in which ultimate victory can only be prepared by a series of 'defeats.'"[8] Still, to be frank, one would not mind an occasional success and a few more signs that events are quickening their pace. Yet let us not be too weighed down by ineluctable moments of discouragement. History clearly does not belong—even if superficial, immediate rewards may—to the contemptible turncoats who want everything here and now, and when there is no instant revolution promptly offer their services to the other side, in fact to the highest bidder. The only lasting effect of the contrast between historical and personal time scales is the tendency to look to a younger generation for hope.

8. Rosa Luxemburg, *Die Rote Fahne,* 14 January 1919.

Realistic Utopia

We are at a moment, to borrow Whitman's words, when society "is for a while between things ended and things begun," not because of some symbolic date on the calendar marking the turn of the millennium, but because the old order is a-dying, in so far as it can no longer provide answers corresponding to the social needs of our point of development, though it clings successfully to power, because there is no class, no social force ready to push it off the historical stage. This confrontation between the old and the new—the sooner it starts, the better—will now have to be global by its very nature. We have picked France, Italy, and Western Europe as the first probable battlefield, though skirmishes are already taking place from Chiapas to Jakarta and from Seoul to São Paulo. Tomorrow Moscow, Warsaw, and Prague may emerge from the utter confusion following their conversion to capitalism, while after tomorrow explosive struggles may even erupt in the heart of the capitalist fortress from New York to California.

On the ground littered with broken models and shattered expectations, a new generation will now have to take the lead. Chastened by our bitter experiences, they can advance with hope but without illusions, with convictions but without certitudes, and, rediscovering the attraction and power of collective action, they can resume the task, hardly begun, of the radical transformation of society. But they cannot do it on their own. We must follow their lead and, to the dismay of the preachers and propagandists shrieking that the task is impossible, utopian, or suicidal, and to the horror of their capitalist paymasters, proclaim all together: "We are not here to tinker with the world, we are here to change it!" Only in this way can we give a positive answer to the rhetorical question asked in this book: whose millennium, theirs or ours? It is also the only way in which we can prevent the future from being *theirs*—apocalyptic or, at best, barbarian.

Index

Index

and American hegemony, 200-201

and Bretton Woods, 189-90

and computers, 195

and corporate governance, 199-200

and east Asia, 201-3

and economics, 193

and financial deregulation, 194-95

and foreign investment, 185

history of, 186

and innovations in finance, 195-96

and internationalism, 209-13

and London eurocurrency market, 191-92

and manufacturing unemployment, 208-9

and mergers and acquisitions, 198, 205-6

and the nation-state, 206

and nineteenth-century British hegemony, 187-88

and pension funds, 196-97

and political decisions, 186-87

and privatization, 193-94

and profitability, 186

propaganda of, 184-85

and stagnation, 203-5

Gold-dollar exchange, 189, 191

Gold exchange standard, 188

Gold standard, 187

Gomulka, Wladyslaw, 107, 108

Gonzales, Felipe, 66

Gorbachev, Mikhail, 27, 28, 55

and collapse of Soviet Union, 49

decline of, 29-30

and perestroika, 2, 13, 230

regime of, 31-35

Gorz, André, 166, 173

Grachev, Pavel, 85

Gramsci, Antonio, 267

Great Britain, 60, 66

and Bretton Woods, 189

conformity in, 222

financial deregulation in, 194

and globalization, 186, 187-88

income inequality in, 215, 216

and independent workers, 181

labor force structure in, 160

and London eurocurrency market, 192

and manufacturing unemployment, 208

national health plan in, 227

nationalization in, 228

New Labour party in, 253

and pension funds, 197

privatization in, 229

and Thatcher's defeat of the miners, 161, 194

union membership in, 171

wealth redistribution in, 153, 219

Great Depression, 186, 188

Greece, 180

Green Party, 146, 256, 257

Grundrisse (Marx), 65, 173, 184

Guaranteed annual income, 173

Guldimann, Tim, 81, 82

Gulf War, 200

Gusinsky, 98

Hedge funds, 196, 197

Hilferding, Rudolf, 197

Hitler, Adolph, 47

Hockstader, Lee, 72

Hong Kong, 201, 202

Human nature, 269, 277-78

Hungary, 13, 22, 30, 45, 48, 70

Ideology, dominant, 263-67

41~ against